Cultural Strategies of Agenda Denial

STUDIES IN GOVERNMENT
AND PUBLIC POLICY

Cultural Strategies of Agenda Denial
Avoidance, Attack, and Redefinition

Edited by Roger W. Cobb
and Marc Howard Ross

 University Press of Kansas

Published by the University Press of Kansas (Lawrence, Kansas 66049), which was organized by the Kansas Board of Regents and is operated and funded by Emporia State University, Fort Hays State University, Kansas State University, Pittsburg State University, the University of Kansas, and Wichita State University

Library of Congress Cataloging-in-Publication Data

Cultural strategies of agenda denial : avoidance, attack, and
  redefinition / editied by Roger W. Cobb and Marc Howard Ross.
      p. cm. — (Studies in government and public policy)
    Includes bibliographical references.
    ISBN 0-7006-0855-9 (alk. paper). — ISBN 0-7006-0856-7 (pbk.: alk.
  paper)
    1. Political planning—United States—Case studies. 2. Policy
  sciences—Case studies. 3. Symbolism in politics. I. Cobb, Roger
  W. II. Ross, Marc Howard. III. Series
JK468.P64C85   1997
320′.6′0973—dc21   97-20359

British Library Cataloguing in Publication Data is available.

Printed in the United States of America

10 9 8 7 6 5 4 3 2 1

To Alexandra and Katherine

Contents

Preface

The roots of this volume can be traced to two books we read and talked about together as graduate students in the mid-1960s—E. E. Schattschneider's *The Semi-Sovereign People: A Realist's Guide to Democracy in America* (1960) and Murray Edelman's *The Symbolic Uses of Politics* (1964). Schattschneider placed a dynamic view of conflict squarely at the center of our understanding of U.S. politics. In 1960, his argument was radically different from previous conceptions of how the U.S. political system worked. Instead of focusing on individual actors such as a president or senator, on groups such as political parties, or on institutions such as Congress, he argued that the focus should be on the process of conflict. Most of politics revolves around the development and expansion of conflict surrounding evolving political issues. People with grievances need to gain the attention of additional individuals and do this by redefining their most intense concerns to draw others into the battle. A growing maelstrom of concern could catapult an issue to the top of the political heap.

The assumption that all political conflicts are dynamic was an important contribution to the work of both the coeditors, although we also came to the conclusion that Schattschneider had captured only one part of the political process. All conflicts have the potential to be inherently expansive. However, some are and some are not. Why? In addition to an expansive part of the conflict process, there is a restrictive part. Some groups do not want new issues on the political agenda because it will disadvantage them in some way. They use some or all of their resources to prevent the consideration of new issues. Schattschneider did not emphasize this process, although his analysis pointed to ways in which those who are winning when a conflict is defined along a particular dimension work to contain the conflict to maintain their power and control. In fact, one of the reasons the U.S. political agenda changes so little is the success of entrenched groups. Those in power often can effectively contain a conflict or keep it from expanding.

Edelman's focus on the cultural and symbolic dimensions of political life suggested answers to some of the puzzles Schattschneider left unanswered. He showed how cultural and symbolic processes affect the working of political institutions and motivate political action and inaction more subtly than do direct issue appeals. Material resources, Edelman's analysis made clear, matter, but so do symbolic resources that define problems and options around which political choice-making occurs. Along with Bachrach and Baratz's (1962) work on the two faces of power, the ideas of Schattschneider and Edelman suggested to us why certain issues receive serious attention from political decision makers and why others, which seem equally significant in objective terms, are virtually ignored. They did not, however, directly answer this question, which provides the core themes for this book.

Whereas Schattschneider pointed to strategic motives for losing groups to expand a conflict, Edelman suggested mechanisms by which expansion is sometimes achieved and at other times thwarted. He drew attention to ways in which organized groups and political officials provide symbolic benefits to the unorganized while securing tangible benefits for themselves. Politics, he told us, is a passing parade of symbols to which we respond with quiescence or arousal. Issues compete for attention, and the ability to define priorities and direct attention toward or away from particular issues through symbolic manipulation is now widely recognized but still not well understood.

Edelman's 1964 analysis and his later writings emphasized the role of language and the ability to connect particular policy concerns with deeply held cultural symbols. Strong political responses from the public are most likely when issue positions are linked to strongly felt culturally rooted values through political myths and rituals. Political conflict, it might be said, is cultural contestation. Certainly, recent political battles over social issues and cultural values associated with abortion, school prayer, family values, pornography, and welfare offer ample evidence for the core of Edelman's theory, which seemed much more problematic when it was first presented than it does today.

Our work in agenda setting over twenty years ago initially emphasized how groups such as old people or racial and ethnic minorities who are political outsiders can be successful in getting their concerns taken seriously (Cobb and Elder 1983). Next we broadened our understanding of agenda setting to account for ways in which political figures and other insiders also initiate consideration of new issues and then mobilize support from the public (Cobb, Ross, and Ross 1976). In thinking about agenda setting, it became clear that a full examination of its dynamics needed to focus on the opponents of new issues—those who sought to prevent their consideration by effectively containing the scope of the conflict. We even wrote an article in the late 1970s outlining what we saw as key questions and filled with charts, flow diagrams, and examples. After more than a dozen rejections (some more encouraging than others), we set the piece aside but remembered that one of the kinder reviewers had suggested that a book on the topic might be the right format. So here it is.

Our approach is to first develop a theoretical framework for the study of agenda setting and agenda denial that emphasizes symbolic processes and not just the role of material resources in explaining why some issues are denied agenda access. We then asked a group of experts in seven different policy areas to write cases that analyze agenda denial in terms of the issues we raise but also to feel free to point out where they think the scheme is wanting. Our first two chapters offer a revised and expanded version of our earlier article, first reviewing crucial questions about agenda denial—the political process by which issues that one would expect to get meaningful consideration from the political institutions in a society fail to get taken seriously. We then identify and delineate the various types of political strategies that opponents use to combat those seeking consideration of new issues. Issues fail to gain serious consideration for a variety of reasons, such as supporters' overestimation of the support their issue will generate from the general public or the ineptness of the proponents. But the major reason that issues are excluded from the political agenda—and the focus of this book—is the active effort of those whose interests would be ill served by the initiator's success.

We offer our ideas to encourage further discussion of this problem, recognizing that what we want to explain are events that one expects to occur but do not, such as consideration of national health insurance in the United States between 1948 and 1993. Unlike the earlier debate on nonevents and political power, we emphasize specific political actions and strategies that explain the nonconsideration of certain issues. Material resources of the opposing sides make a difference, but our analysis emphasizes the importance of symbolic and cultural strategies used to define issues and their proponents in particular ways that make active consideration of issues less likely.

How widely used are the strategies we posit? For the purposes of this volume, and given the expertise of the contributors, we focused on two domestic domains: federal regulatory practice involving business and drugs, and public health issues. In addition, we included one foreign case in which U.S. political actors played a significant role. Our conclusion demonstrates that such strategies are applicable across issues. We hope that this volume inspires others to elaborate on the model and apply it to other issues of public concern.

The book is organized into five parts. Part I consists of the first two chapters, which delineate the key actors and strategies. The next two parts deal with how federal regulatory agencies manage to keep some issues from appearing on their formal agendas. Part II involves the Securities and Exchange Commission (SEC) and Part III the Food and Drug Administration (FDA). In chapter 3, Billy Hall and Bryan Jones investigate how the SEC has been able to avoid dealing with critics who argue that its agenda is extremely limited and to evade issues dealing with regulation. In chapter 4, John Mahon and Richard McGowan show that the accounting profession has been able to dodge all federal regulation by the SEC, despite attempts by some to make it publicly accountable for its actions. In chapter 5, Christopher Plein argues that the FDA used a variety of strategies to keep challenges to a new bovine growth hormone off the regulatory agenda. In chapter 6, Jennifer Jackman studies how antiabortion forces kept the French abortion pill—RU 486—off the regulatory agenda of the FDA.

Part IV deals with public health issues. In chapter 7, Robert Hackey studies why national health insurance (with a few brief exceptions) has never made it onto the formal federal agenda over the past four decades. His analysis focuses on an early period in the conflict—during the Truman administration, when proposals were first introduced. In chapter 8, Cynthia Lopez and Michael Reich focus on how developers and the El Paso Public Service Board kept a large group of residents from attaining access to clean water.

Part V deals with agenda denial as a comparative political process. In chapter 9, John Bendix analyzes how Kurt Waldheim's service as an officer in the German army during World War II failed to become a decisive issue in his campaign for president of Austria, as politicians and party leaders of all stripes had reason to prevent consideration of the relevance of his (and the country's) Nazi past. In chapter 10, the major findings from the case studies are summarized. First we describe the characteristics of the issues, initiators, and opponents. Then we discuss the two principal strategies that dominate the case studies—attacks on the issue or the initiators, and symbolic placation—and briefly explore the implications of these findings. Finally, we conclude with a discussion of the importance of symbolic definitions of political life in general and, in particular, for U.S. political life. In a variation on Edelman's view that politics is about the distribution of both tangible and symbolic benefits, we suggest that agenda conflicts are about both the concrete decision whether government will or will not consider a particular issue and the competing interpretations of political issues to which people attach great emotional significance. Politics, from this point of view, not only determines who gets what, when, and how but also provides a forum for choosing among competing views concerning how we should live, what government ought to do, how we relate to the environment, and who our enemies are.

Over the years, we received a great deal of encouragement and many ideas as we pursued our interest in agenda denial. Charles Elder was involved in the initial conceptualization of the model. Remi Clignet read several drafts of our original article and encouraged us to continue writing about the problem, even in the face of many rejections. Our students at Brown University and Bryn Mawr College made many suggestions and, through their genuine excitement about the problems of agenda setting, convinced us that the matter was worth further study. Bryan Jones, now at the University of Washington, took some of our earlier work and developed ideas about government agendas in provocative ways, all the while suggesting that we pull together the partially developed ideas we had. Three reviewers for the University Press of Kansas provided important reactions, and our effort to address them has made our presentation more effective. Cynthia Lopez read a draft of chapters 1, 2, and 10 and made a number of helpful editorial suggestions. Michael Reich also read an early draft of chapters 1 and 2 and provided us with thoughtful comments. Aaron Ross prepared the figures and charts.

REFERENCES

Bachrach, P., and M. Baratz. 1962. Two faces of power. *American Political Science Review* 56: 947–52.

Cobb, R. W., and C. D. Elder. 1983. *Participation in American politics: The dynamics of agenda-building.* Baltimore: Johns Hopkins University Press.

Cobb, R., J.-K. Ross, and M. H. Ross. 1976. Agenda building as a comparative political process. *American Political Science Review* 71: 126–38.

Edelman, M. 1964. *The symbolic uses of politics.* Urbana: University of Illinois Press.

Schattschneider, E. E. 1960. *The semi-sovereign people: A realist's guide to democracy in America.* New York: Holt.

PART I
Theoretical Overview

1

Agenda Setting and the Denial of Agenda Access: Key Concepts

Roger W. Cobb and Marc Howard Ross

Agenda setting, the politics of selecting issues for active consideration, can be examined from a variety of perspectives. Most common are studies of how concerns such as illegal immigration, the environment, nuclear safety, or cigarette smoking, which at one time attracted little attention as political issues, become transformed into divisive policy questions that receive serious attention from decision makers. In these cases, while proponents are seeking consideration of new issues, others, for a variety of reasons, work to keep these items from getting serious attention. Having previously written about agenda setting from the perspective of those groups and individuals trying to get new issues on the agenda (Cobb and Elder 1983; Cobb, Ross, and Ross 1976), our main concern here is to understand the politics of agenda denial from the point of view of issue opponents.[1]

At the outset we want to address a commonly held, partially true, popular notion that explains agenda success and failure—that of resource differentials between proponents and opponents—although it is not our main focus of our attention here. We recognize that in many situations the material resource differentials of the two sides are strikingly uneven and that these differences often are the most important factor in accounting for why a particular issue does or does not receive serious consideration from the relevant government agency.[2] Quite often, however, such an explanation for success or failure in attaining agenda status is inadequate for several reasons: (1) there are a number of situations in which the party with far greater resources does not win an agenda conflict, (2) the resources of the opposing groups may be so different that making a clear decision about who possesses greater resources is far from straightforward, and (3) simple resource-based explanations avoid the question of how specific resources are converted into political outcomes in a given agenda conflict.

Agenda conflicts are not just about what issues government chooses to act on;

they are also about competing interpretations of political problems and the alternative worldviews that underlie them. These concern how people ought to lead their daily lives, how society ought to be organized, what should or should not be done by government, how we should treat the environment, and who threatens our security. We focus here on the strategic choices open to issue initiators and opponents and turn particular attention to cultural and symbolic forces that are crucial in determining opponents' ability to prevent the serious consideration of a new issue. Cultural processes, and especially the dynamics of identification and symbolization, matter when they invoke threats and deep fears and effectively link political grievances to existing worldviews and individuals to political groups. These connections often account for the high commitment to and intensity of involvement with matters that often seem trivial to outsiders.

Cultural dynamics are central, for example, in understanding the intense, long-term commitment of Japanese Americans and their allies to winning reparations for Japanese American citizens and their families interned in camps during World War II, the deep opposition to abortion that leads some activists to try to link this issue to all significant social and political debate, and the shape of the health care debate in the first two years of the Clinton administration. In each of these situations, significant (although not necessarily the same or equal) resources existed on all sides. What interests us about these agenda conflicts, and the individual cases that make up this volume, is that unless attention is paid to the political uses of culturally rooted resources, the analyst cannot understand why the outcomes of these conflicts took the particular forms they did.

This chapter offers an overview of the study of agenda setting, including a specification of key concepts and a review of existing approaches, updating and expanding our ideas about agenda setting as a political process (Cobb and Elder 1983; Cobb, Ross, and Ross 1976). We consider the sources of political issues and how private grievances become matters of public concern. We discuss the types of agendas as well as the kinds of actors involved in agenda disputes in the context of three models of agenda building. We examine the prospects for consideration of new issues in terms of the organization and distribution of power in national politics, the interplay between macro and micro political forces, and the role of the media. We emphasize how opponents in agenda disputes use cultural and symbolic forces to prevent consideration of new issues. Finally, we consider the question of issue containment, asking who is likely to oppose the consideration of new issues and examining the strategies and resources they are likely to use to do so.

WHERE DO ISSUES COME FROM?

The agenda-setting literature is rooted in the perspective that all conflicts are potentially expansive. As that expansion occurs, the nature of the conflict, the key actors, and the definitions of significant issues change, and new dimensions are added. The result is that the subsequent conflict may bear little resemblance to the initial dispute (Coleman 1957; Schattschneider 1960). Agenda-setting studies emphasize individuals and groups with new issues that are trying to gain access to decision makers and stress the importance of resources—scope (number of people involved), intensity (strength of commitment to a particular issue), and visibility (public awareness of the dispute)—to this process. A key dimension to the process is how issues are framed to appeal to a larger audience. From this perspective, if initiating groups are unable to expand interest in their grievances to more people or key groups, access to the political agenda is unlikely. Groups can be unsuccessful in reaching an agenda when other groups that believe that they will be adversely impacted actively pursue a set of strategies to prevent the new issues from attaining decision-maker attention.

The study of agenda setting has shown that issue creation is a complex political process (Rochefort and Cobb 1994). Problems need to be identified, organizations must be built or mobilized around particular issues and policies, and an issue has to be propelled through multiple layers of the policy process. Political problems are not just associated with objective conditions; rather, issue definition is associated with cultural dynamics related to proponents' ability to connect a problem to cultural assumptions about threats, risk, and humans' ability to control their physical and social environments (Douglas and Wildavsky 1982). For example, although the rates of death and injury caused by automobile accidents are far higher than those resulting from political terrorism, in most Western societies, the former are considered "acceptable" and are subject to modest restrictions that lower but do not end the threat. With terrorism, there is widespread support for far stronger policies, even though the number of persons affected is much smaller.

Grievance Transformation. Felstiner, Abel, and Sarat argue that the politics of transforming grievances into problems that engender public action consists of three separate steps: naming, blaming, and claiming (1980–1981, 631–7). The first step is to name a problem, but this name must be one that is accepted by the public at large. As Gusfield notes, "Human problems do not spring up, full-blown and announced, into the consciousness of bystanders" (1981, 3). For example, during the late 1950s and 1960s, increasing numbers of people were killed in automobile collisions. The automobile manufacturers had identified the problem as unsafe drivers and argued that reforms should focus on changing human behavior. However, in the late 1960s, Ralph Nader produced study results showing that the Chevrolet Corvair was structurally unsound and was the cause of many accidents. As a consequence, the problem was now named automobile safety, and it has been a concern ever since (Nadel 1971). Once the problem was named and accepted as being unsafe cars, legislation was formulated to regulate vehicles, not people.

Blaming is the second phase of transforming a grievance into a political issue. It involves identifying a culprit to blame for the unfair treatment that a target group—the victim—has received. In terms of issues such as job safety, pollution, and destruction of the wilderness, people who were made homeless, poor, sick, or despairing because of the actions of others can be portrayed as victims, and a natural enemy is business and its desire for maximum profits. Rochefort argues that social welfare populations tend to receive greater support if they are seen as victims of circumstances beyond their control, if they are people with a high degree of need, and if they are groups seen positively by society (1989, 132–5). Children and the elderly are excellent examples, particularly when they are seen as objects of any kind of abuse: sexual, physical, economic, or psychological (Nelson 1984). Schneider and Ingram developed a typology to identify different types of target groups. They focus on the strength of the group involved and whether it is seen positively by others. They argue that most support goes to those who are seen positively but also have power, such as the elderly. Those who have a negative image and are politically weak, such as drug addicts, receive far less attention from decision makers (1993, 334–6).

Claiming, the third step, involves making specific demands on government. Here, advocates of a new policy make arguments to attract support. Cobb and Elder (1983, 96–102) assert that how an issue is defined is crucial in attracting outsiders to the cause, and they identify five issue characteristics that groups can use to gain backers. *Ambiguity,* which is part of general arguments, allows people to read their own meaning into a message. An example would be portraying townspeople opposing a new chemical plant as being against "growth." Second, *social significance* shows that the problem will have a broad impact. A clean air problem affecting everyone in a geographical area would be an example of such an appeal. Third, *temporal relevance* or spillover adds a time dimension to a problem and suggests that if it is not checked it will affect additional groups in the future. "This problem will affect not only you and your children but your children's children as well" is a common refrain used by issue activists. Fourth, *nontechnical issue definition* helps the public understand a grievance. Here the initiator must avoid using complicated arguments to gain popular support (Best 1989). Finally, the absence of *categorical precedence* means that the issue is unique and officials cannot simply handle it as they did a past problem. For example, when activists are concerned with studying new diseases, the case must be made that new experimentation is required, that using old answers won't be sufficient. Activists had to stress that AIDS was different from previously known conditions to gain favorable public attention.

KEY CONCEPTS IN AGENDA SETTING

Types of Agendas. The term *agenda* is used here to describe both the set of concerns that the public has requiring governmental action and the policy options actively under consideration by governmental bodies. The former is called the *public agenda;* the latter, the *formal agenda* (Cobb and Elder 1983, 85–7; Kingdon 1994, 4). Every governmental unit—whether it is a legislative, judicial, or administrative body—has a docket for items that receive serious consideration. Our focus in this book is those items that are denied serious—not just symbolic—consideration on the formal agenda.[3]

For our purposes, problems on the formal agenda have three characteristics. First, there must be some objective evidence that a problem exists. Often this can be demonstrated through statistical evidence such as survey results, public health reports, government studies, crime statistics, or census data. Although such evidence can be debated, it shows that the problem has an objective element and is not just the shrill voices of a disaffected minority. As Stone notes, "the most common way to define a policy problem is to measure it" (1988, 127).[4] Second, many, but not all, items to be considered have already made the public agenda, and the public believes that there is a problem that might require some public action. Most commonly, such evidence is found in public opinion polls based on a ranking of serious problems or studies of specialized population groups focusing on certain issue domains.[5] A third consideration is a comparative one: is the issue already on the formal agendas of countries with similar social systems? If the answer is yes, then there is a case for asking why the question has not yet made it to the formal agenda.[6]

Relevant Actors in the Process. Cobb and Elder (1983, 104–8) define four kinds of groups that are active in conflict. The *identification group* consists of the people who raise the initial grievance; this group is often most impacted by the problem at hand and will benefit most if the problem is resolved in its favor. Members of this group typically have a great deal of knowledge about the issue and feel intense about it. However, they are often very small in number and cannot be successful by themselves.[7] The *attentive public* consists of those people— approximately 10 to 15 percent of the population—who follow current events and are conversant with most of the issues appearing in the media.[8] They often become easily interested and have strong views on new issues, which they express in a variety of settings. *Attention groups* are people particularly concerned with focal issues but lacking knowledge about or interest in most issue debates. They are often critical in the agenda-setting process, as their strong interest can be converted into political action. Converse (1964) calls them "issue publics." They provide the enthusiasm and numbers necessary for identification groups to expand the issue to more people.[9] The *mass public* is rarely involved in issues, and when widespread involvement occurs, issue commitment typically exists for only short periods. Most commonly, the mass public becomes involved following scandals, wars, natural disasters, or dramatic events such as political assassinations.[10]

In addition, there is a group of public officials who can be key participants. Bureaucrats, elected politicians, and staff aides to major political figures all figure in policy creation and avoidance. Loomis (1985) wrote that congresspeople, for example, are more predisposed than ever to be involved in policy innovation. Having entrepreneurial skills gains politicians a larger favorable audience for other aspirations they might have. Often bureaucrats push innovative policies for purposes of ego, good policy, or future career possibilities.[11]

Crucial Group Characteristics. Key characteristics of identification and attention groups and public officials constitute an important resource that affects their success in agenda conflicts. Of interest here is the *legitimacy* of the group and its visible leaders. The public at large—the ultimate audience for expansive politics—responds most favorably to someone or something that it already sees in a favorable light. The League of Women Voters has a certain aura of respect that is not found among most public groups. Groups of experts or scientists have a similar advantage. The Union of Concerned Scientists normally receives favorable coverage simply because its members have impressive credentials from major U.S. universities. The problem for many issue groups is that their legitimacy is low because the public has not heard of them and is unsure of who or what they represent. Acquiring legitimacy can take time. Martin Luther King gained respect in the view of many Americans not because of his background but because of the manner in which he pursued his objectives and the hardship he had to endure.

A second important component is *prior success.* If a group or a politician has been successful in the past, that group or individual will be taken seriously in the future. Prior success is often linked to strategic location in the political process (Cobb and Elder 1983, 90–1). For example, farmers have been enormously successful in pushing for governmental support for crops. In part, this is due to placing congresspeople from farming areas on the agriculture committees. Similarly, Senator Ted Kennedy has a successful record on social issues stemming in part from his seniority on the Labor Committee, which oversees many of the issues on the social agenda. The National Rifle Association can point to a number of legislative victories, but for most issue groups in their early stages, such victories are hard to find.

MODELS OF AGENDA SETTING

Early work on agenda setting developed the *outside initiative model,* which drew attention to nongovernmental sources of policy innovation, focusing on the efforts of a single person or group to transform its concerns into those of a larger movement (Cobb and Elder 1983; Cobb, Ross, and Ross 1976). Obvious examples are the civil rights movement in the 1950s and 1960s and the environmental movement of the late 1960s and early 1970s. Less well known examples include the efforts of Lois Gibbs to address toxic waste and Candy Lightner's activities to punish drunk drivers.

Issue initiation can come from two additional routes. In one, called *mobili-*

zation, public officials launch a campaign to gain public attention and support for an issue as a way to gain entry to the formal agenda and then to mobilize support once the issue is actively being considered. Examples include many education, health, and development programs that originate in government, such as the issue of hunger in America, which Senator George McGovern raised through Senate hearings. More recently, the efforts of Secretary of Energy O'Leary to publicize the negative effects of radiation testing in the 1940s and 1950s also fit this model.

A third model, called *inside access,* describes how an issue originates with a narrow group of actors and is placed on a formal agenda with little attention from the public. Fearful that public opinion will hamper their chances for success, proponents limit knowledge of the issue to bureaucrats, legislators, and affected groups. Obvious examples are many military weapons programs (Cobb, Ross, and Ross 1976). Sharp's (1994, 45) description of the Carter administration's drug policy fits the inside access model quite well. The policy had almost no public visibility and was controlled by inside experts, but when parts of it became known—especially the idea of legalizing marijuana—the policy collapsed.[12]

Issue Innovation and Power Configurations in the Federal Government

Studies of policy making and power configurations in Washington explain agenda setting in somewhat different ways. The most common, the subgovernment or iron triangle perspective, posits three sets of actors: pressure groups interested in a particular issue, legislators who sit on an interest committee (e.g., agriculture, armed services), and bureaucrats who oversee that particular policy (Kingdon 1994). These three act in concert in funding new projects and servicing the issue constituency. From this perspective, innovation is negligible. If a development occurs that can bring more money and personnel into that area, the iron triangle supporters move ahead. However, in most instances, the actors in the iron triangle maintain and advance an existing policy.

Some analysts have been perplexed by the rigidity of this particular model of policy making. Heclo (1978), for example, views the policy-making process as more fluid. Instead of a fixed set of actors, he emphasizes a series of networks in each issue area made up of individuals—whom he calls "technopols"—attached to the issue by their expertise. They share a concern about an issue but not a united perspective. In fact, substantive differences often divide them into competing groups. From this perspective, most legislators are moved from the role of active participants to observers when policy issue networks lobby them in front of congressional committees. The influence of the individual issue network in the policy area depends on which party is in power, or which faction within the party controls the presidency, and the prevailing political climate. In addition, there is a mobility of personnel and a fluidity of action—a dynamic feature lacking in the iron triangle formulation (Heclo 1978).

Kingdon (1994) developed this perspective further, studying two areas of domestic policy making at the national level: health and transportation. He combined two different ideas. From the issue network framework, he developed the idea of a policy community composed of legislators, bureaucrats, academics, and think-tank participants who debate current policy ramifications of a particular issue. From the "garbage can approach,"[13] he took the idea that fluidity is the overwhelming element impinging on the policy process. In fact, he notes that the process is so fluid that the actual sources of ideas are irrelevant for two reasons. First, the sources are too hard to locate. Second, it does not matter, because once an idea is dispersed, it becomes a bundle of information that is tossed around by participants subject to processes independent of the idea itself. Kingdon argues that ideas move in a world of competing problems and solutions within each issue area. There is no objective consideration of the merit of various ideas. Instead, there are series of individuals known as entrepreneurs who link problems and solutions and guide them through the policy process. Kingdon's metaphor for the entire process is the "policy window." He argues that there are short periods that are "ripe" for innovation in any policy area. If innovation does not occur within that time span, change will not take place. Each issue area has a few policy windows over time. Some of these windows are obvious: a change in administrations, for example. Others open unexpectedly when a crucial event occurs, a crisis develops, or an idea gains prominence—all of which can open the window for a short time (1994, 173–204).

Micro versus Macro Factors

Much of the work on agenda setting emphasizes micro-level factors at work in particular disputes. However, Kingdon's concept of the policy widow makes us consider the interaction between agenda-setting initiatives and macro-level political forces that affect the agenda-setting process. Macro forces provide broad parameters that shape the terms of political discussion and limit which issues can be considered and how they can be discussed. Among those at work are the following.

Climate of the Times. Most innovative ideas are successful within particular periods characterized by distinctive dominant ideological or social conditions. For example, during the New Deal of the 1930s and the Great Society of the 1960s, innovative social policy was occurring at a rapid rate. However, in the 1980s, when budgetary constraints and a national administration opposed to increased social spending dominated the U.S. political landscape, innovation was much more difficult.[14]

If a particular worldview or theme dominates the political climate, issue initiators would be wise to link their grievance to it. Kingdon shows this process occurring in both the transportation and the health fields in the 1970s. A key theme in Carter's social policy was deregulation, and those in the transportation area saw a window open in terms of reducing governmental controls on transportation carriers. By linking reforms to this theme, major changes occurred. Similarly, those health innovators who tied the idea of health maintenance organizations to deregulation in medicine also received a favorable hearing (Kingdon 1994, 6–13).[15]

The Life of an Issue.   Downs (1972) and others suggest the value of thinking about the life of an issue. Downs suggests that, as with the stages of the life cycle of living organisms, we can describe the stages through which issues pass. In the first phase, a problem exists, but few recognize it as a policy issue. Then an event occurs that brings about widespread attention and public concern. At this point, the problem is studied and is found to be complex and costly to solve. When the public realizes this, interest wanes. The problem then recedes into "issue limbo" and is replaced by other concerns, repeating the same cyclical pattern. Issues have little staying power, and the chance for significant innovation is present but quite constricted (1972, 38–50).

Episodic Disruption.   Baumgartner and Jones (1993) offer a view of policy innovation that contains both elements of stability, as reflected in the subgovernment approach, and agents of change, as reflected in the policy window approach. They argue that policy areas resemble a punctuated equilibrium, in that the political system often sees little change over a period of decades, and then the equilibrium is abruptly terminated by a short period of rapid change. They find that two crucial elements determine whether an issue resembles a policy monopoly dominated by a subgovernment or is open to penetration by new issue groups. The first is the public image of the issue. They argue that most policies that are dominated by triangles have a favorable public image. An example would be nuclear power. In the 1940s and 1950s, the dominant image of the energy source was as "efficient" and "safe." However, the image changed in the 1960s and 1970s and was replaced by more fear-provoking images emphasizing accidents and meltdown. The second factor is venue. Further developing Schattschneider's notion that the choice of battlefields is crucial in determining who will win a conflict (1960, 58), Baumgartner and Jones argue that the place in which the issue is debated is crucial. In the case of pesticides, the policy monopoly meant that questions about the danger of pesticides were considered by only favorably disposed committees in Congress (e.g., the agriculture committees). However, by the late 1960s and early 1970s, the issue of the health hazards of pesticides began to move to other committees, where legislators were much more critical. Moving to a larger venue beyond congressional committees can alter how an issue is considered. For example, Baumgartner and Jones show that when nuclear power moved from the halls of Congress to the courts in the late 1970s, judges were not as friendly to the nuclear power industry as some legislators had been in the earlier days (1993, 73–86, 203–7).

The Role of the Media. It is a truism to argue that the media play a crucial role in agenda setting in both the outside initiative and mobilization models described earlier. Creating issue visibility is critical to both models, and the media are the easiest way to provide it. As Iyengar notes, "The well-known 'agenda-setting' effect refers to the tendency of people to cite issues 'in the news' when asked to identify the significant problems facing the nation" (1991, 132). Baumgartner and Jones find a "lurching quality" in which the media's issue coverage gravitates back and forth between an all-positive image of an issue to an all-negative interpretation. They note that "there seem to be waves of enthusiasm or apprehension" (1993, 128). Few periods exist in which positive and negative elements of an issue are considered at the same time by the media.

Media coverage of issue disputes has a direct bearing on the outcome of the conflict. Like other parties to an issue dispute, the press and television bring certain, often unstated, assumptions to their coverage. These scripts, or implicit theories about politics, are then used in covering particular issues. Clearly recognizable are stories that have identifiable elements: conflict, celebrity, uniqueness, action (demonstrations, large crowds, fiery speeches), danger (particularly to animals, children, and large groups of people), death, destruction, and deviance. Proponents with a group of committed followers seeking to get a new issue on the agenda can often exploit these elements, as public demonstrations, conflict, fiery rhetoric, and the use of celebrity advocates have a certain appeal. However, there is one additional component of media coverage: boredom. The media rarely stay with any story for a long time. If an opponent can wait it out until the media find another story to cover, the initiator will have lost some of its advantage. However, the ingenuity of the initiator in using the media to present its grievance is important in determining the outcome of the issue conflict.

THE KEY ROLE OF CULTURAL SYMBOLIZATION

An important element in the discussion of policy innovation is what activates those who have grievances. Agenda conflicts answer this question at two levels. One is about whether government takes a particular grievance issue seriously. Analysis at this level often emphasizes how both proponents and opponents of policy innovation are motivated by rational self-interest, meaning that actors pursue objective interests to obtain concrete gains to maintain or improve their position in society. Economic grievances such as low wages or poor working conditions are certainly critical at times. Without disputing that self-interest plays a role, we argue that such a definition of motivation is too limited.

Therefore, we need to turn to a second level, which views agenda conflicts as about competing interpretations of political problems connected to competing worldviews. These interpretations address how people ought to lead their lives, how society ought to act, what should or should not be done by government, how we should treat the environment, and who threatens our security. Analysis of agenda conflicts at this level must pay attention to how issue initiators and opponents associate specific issues with these more general worldviews. From this perspective, initiators work to demonstrate that although the specific grievance they raise is new, acting on it is consistent with many long-standing values; opponents emphasize new issues as a threat to core elements of widely held worldviews. At this second level, cultural and symbolic factors come into play, drawing attention away from simple questions about whether the distribution of resources to different individuals and groups is equitable. The focus becomes how various groups perceive the fairness of resource distribution and how they interpret it in terms of group identity. When issues are tied to culturally salient ideas about identity, the structure of a conflict and the ways in which it develops go beyond simple self-interest, as individual and collective action become linked (Ross 1993a).

In objective terms, initiators are often disadvantaged when faced with powerful opponents. Yet their intense commitment, coupled with the belief that crucial elements of their core identity are at stake, motivates and sustains the group through hard times. Underlying their commitment are threats to identity and core values associated with powerful negative symbols (Ross 1995). For example, Gusfield (1963) describes prohibitionists faced with an entrenched industry, yet they ultimately created a moralistic tide that gained governmental prohibition of alcoholic products. He explained their intense motivation in an association between drinking and a threat to the lifestyle of rural Protestant Americans. The prohibitionists' status insecurity came into play when "the self-esteem of the group member is belied by the failure of others to grant him the respect, approval, admiration, and deference he feels that he justly deserves" (1963, 17–8). To defend their threatened cultural values and to seek their public validation through legislation, prohibitionists were willing to use legal and extralegal means and, for a time, gained the upper hand.

Symbolic processes are often essential in explaining the commitment and perceived threats that characterize bitter conflicts and puzzle outsiders, who see relatively little at stake. What such outsiders miss is how different protagonists tie their issue positions to a cultural identity that they feel is at risk in the conflict. The powerful cultural symbolization of core identities is seen in U.S. politics around such issues as homosexuality, abortion, sex education, school prayer, and other social issues in which each side believes that defeat is tantamount to a military humiliation (Hunter 1994).

Symbolic and ritual processes link politics to the social and cultural context in which it occurs. Connecting political claims to deeply rooted cultural concerns is one way in which all sides in agenda disputes (and other conflicts) try to gain and mobilize supporters (Edelman 1964; Cohen 1969). Sometimes these concerns can be explained in terms of individual self-interest. Often, however, we can make sense of such mobilization only in terms of group attachment and perceived threats to identity. Culture is politically relevant when it (1) frames the context in which politics occurs, (2) links individual and collective identities, (3) defines the boundaries between groups and organizes actions within and between them, (4) provides a framework for interpreting the actions and motives of others, and (5) provides resources for political organization and mobilization (Ross 1997, forthcoming).

Cultural and symbolic processes are seen in the competing definitions associated with alternative cultural images of an issue, such as pro-life versus pro-choice on the abortion conflict, or healthy children versus illegitimate teen pregnancy in the debate over welfare reform. Often, culturally linked issue definitions powerfully represent one side of an issue, and the strength of these images determines, in great part, whether an issue attains agenda status or not. For example, proponents of hand-gun control fared far better in getting their issue on the congressional agenda when they called it the Brady bill after former press secretary James Brady, who was paralyzed in the attempted assassination of President Reagan.

Symbolic versus Material Resources. In all agenda conflicts, we suggest, material interests are invariably linked to symbolic definitions, as each side seeks to widen support. Success can be viewed as the ability to do this effectively. For example, whether the children of illegal immigrants are seen as just as worthy as other American children or as outsiders taking advantage of U.S. wealth is likely to be associated with how one reacts to proposals to restrict social programs such as schooling or health care. At the same time, it is possible that the relative importance of material and symbolic resources for proponents and opponents varies across issue domains. It seems plausible to hypothesize that in issue areas that are relatively stable over time and defined in technical terms (such as labor versus management), material resources will be relatively more important; with newer issues involving less clearly defined opponents, symbolic definitions will play a relatively larger role.

When an issue conflict begins, there is always a discrepancy in the resources of the two contending parties. Most opponents have a considerable advantage in the standard resources available to groups in a political battle: number of people to draw on, money, experience, and political contacts. After all, most opponents were once initiators fighting to get their concerns on the formal agenda and then maneuvering through the decision-making phase to achieve some governmental attention that was favorable to their position. These groups include major pressure groups: labor unions; business organizations; occupational groups; interest groups formed around such principles as race, ethnicity, religion, gender, and age; and those asserting basic rights (e.g., gun owners). A major aim of these groups is to protect the gains they have already achieved. Any attempt to threaten them in economic, ideological, or cultural terms will be met with considerable opposition. This, combined with institutional obstacles in the way of outside groups, poses a potent deterrent to any new groups (Birnbaum and Murray 1987; Fritschler 1989; Spitzer 1995). As a result, Edelman (1964) argues that politics provides tangible benefits to the organized and symbolic reassurance to the unorganized.

However, focusing only on the material resources of each side ignores other tools in the arsenal of opponents. In fact, single strategies are almost never used in isolation. Money and political contacts help, but they do not tell the whole story. Some strategies involve a minimum of time and financial commitment, if they are used effectively. A key to a successful issue campaign, whether promoting or deflating a cause, is the use of words and images that summarize a point of view. Here is where the use of symbols and cultural strategies comes into play. These factors have not received sufficient attention in the battle between initiators and opponents. We contend that it is strategic skill that makes opponents so difficult to defeat. In fact, one of the problems for initiators is that they lack the skill to package an issue in cultural terms that will appeal to large numbers of people. Those that are successful are skilled in problem definition. In addition to money, access, and experience, there is a battle for the "hearts and minds" of the public, which occurs at a cultural level.

To see the interaction between the use of material and symbolic resources, consider the case of a group that was recently created to halt federal efforts to protect endangered fish species if they interfered with the development of industry along a river in the Northwest. It has a budget of $2.6 million. An adviser for the group produced the following memorandum: "while the public can and should be swayed by having the facts on the issue, the message must also appeal at a gut, emotional level. Too often, those who advocate a more rational approach to such issues fail because they compete against a well-orchestrated public relations campaign that tugs at the heart strings" (Fritsch 1996, A12).

ISSUE CONTAINMENT: THE SECOND FACE OF POWER

In the early 1960s, the pluralist paradigm dominated interpretations of U.S. politics. Essentially, the focus was on organized groups attempting to gain leverage in the political process through the use of a series of bargaining strategies. However, some observers argued that this perspective obfuscates the real power relationships in a community. Bachrach and Baratz contended that power is demonstrated in the creation of barriers that preclude the discussion of certain types of issues, as decision makers "limit decisions to relatively non-controversial matters, by influencing community values and political procedures and rituals" (1962, 949). Further, "defenders of the status quo . . . limit the scope of actual decision-making to 'safe' issues" (1962, 952). They called this process "non-decision-making," and although they did not specify the conditions under which this could take place, they drew attention to threats and sanctions against those who broached certain new ideas for consideration (1963, 633).

Later studies offer additional insights into the specific dynamics at work in non–decision making. Crenson studied decisional patterns involving "municipal neglect in the field of air pollution" in Gary and East Chicago and found that in both communities the political climate did not foster the consideration of certain types of political issues (1971, 3). After studying pollution policies in these cities, he concluded that power may be defined as the ability not only to resolve issues but also to avoid them. One of the most important resources possessed by the local leaders is the reputation for issue control. Issues are not randomly considered; they are linked in ways that make sense to local officials. He concluded by arguing that nondecisions are "instances of political enforced neglect" (1971, 184).

Gaventa (1980), in a study of coal mining communities in the Appalachian Valley, found that although coal miners had real grievances against the owners of the mines, these problems were not placed before the owners. He argued that a culture or ethos of powerlessness permeated the communities, and the workers did not feel empowered to raise their objections. When unionization was attempted in the 1920s and 1930s, it was met by violence from the owners. Physical intimidation and assaults were "everyday occurrences" (1980, 105). Further, the owners controlled the press, so the conflict was not widely reported. He found that low educational levels in the populace, combined with low participation levels in different types of political contexts, created an oppressive environment that made the active consideration of worker grievances extremely difficult.

At a more general level, there are always some groups that will oppose the efforts of those who want to "stir the pot" or raise new issues. Hirschman (1991, 7) argued that groups representing the status quo usually make three kinds of arguments to head off change advocates: (1) the perversity thesis—any attempt to change things will only make conditions worse; (2) the futility thesis—any effort to alter conditions will simply "fail to make a dent"; and (3) the jeopardy thesis—any action to alter conditions will only produce new problems worse than the current ones.

Opponents usually have more resources than advocates, but more significant is the fact that the two sides often have somewhat different resources. In addition to resource differences, political and cultural definitions of problems limit the consideration of new issues (Douglas and Wildavsky 1982). Culture reflects the set of beliefs that frames problems and defines what is permissible in dealing with them.[16] Cultural and symbolic strategies used by opponents can limit the serious consideration of certain political issues. From this perspective, the problem of agenda setting is not just one of what resources are available but also of how they are used to define problem approaches as reasonable or not in a given cultural context (Rochefort and Cobb 1994).

Types of Opposing Groups

Who are the actors most actively engaged in issue suppression? We first distinguish between actors inside and outside government. Sometimes they work in concert to thwart the efforts of initiators; other times, they work separately. Each can have considerable but different resources and motivations.

Public Officials. One group of potential opponents consists of public decision officials: bureaucrats, congresspeople, judges, and White House advisers. This is not to say that all officials are always opposed to raising new issues. Certainly after the election of a new president, there is a short time in which innovation is encouraged. But most of the time, officials are risk averse; issue avoidance is the norm. Why? The first reason has to do with ideology. The initiating group often represents an issue point of view that the officials do not share. A second is information—officials often feel that the outside group is ignorant and does not truly understand the complexities of the problem. For example, agricultural officials can be perplexed by consumers who do not understand some of the latest scientific studies showing that pesticides have acceptable risk levels. Third, officials believe that the plate is already full—that there are enough issues to be debated or dealt with without adding new concerns. The fourth reason is one of conflict avoidance. Decision makers try to duck potential battles because they believe that no matter what they do, some groups are going to be unhappy. Fifth is novelty. Newness brings uncertainty. Officials like to deal with given issues—ones for which they know the parameters. Uncertainty also raises costs. Officials will have to spend time learning about the issue, familiarizing themselves with the new actors, and determining what the consequences of the new issue will be. Thus uncertainty is to be avoided at all costs. Sixth is the political cycle. Election-year politics occurs at the national level every two years. Action is less likely in such years, when the parties turn all issues into matters of electioneering and are not predisposed to action. Action is more likely after an election than shortly before one (Light 1989). As noted by a Washington journalist, "It is a tenet of Capitol Hill that if cumbersome and controversial legislation is not enacted in the first year of a session, its chances are vastly reduced in the next year when the election cycle is in full swing and the legislation's opponents have far greater opportunity to derail it" (Lewis 1995, A1). Thus, for various reasons of ideology, information, conflict, comfort, and politics, officials have reason to avoid new concerns.

Affected Groups. A second group of potential opponents consists of those groups that will be adversely affected if the issue being raised is addressed. Most policy scenarios are understood as zero-sum contests in which some groups benefit and others lose. From this point of view, issue initiators are attempting to take something away from others. One of the most important characteristics of an effective opposing group is whether it "owns" an issue or not. Gusfield (1981) makes an analogy between issue control and property ownership, arguing that in some public policy areas, one group is so powerful that it is seen as the sole legitimate authority to act in the area. He writes, "there is a recognition that specific public issues are the legitimate province of specific persons, roles and offices that can command public attention, trust, and influence. They have credibility while others who attempt to capture public attention do not" (1981, 10). For most of the twentieth century, doctors owned nearly all medical issues. They had the credibility and the expertise to make decisions in this area. However, in recent years, medical care has become so expensive that other voices have been heard, and that ownership has been partially lost.

It is fair to suggest that many people enter the political process with the hope of attaining an economic redress of grievances, whereas potentially adversely affected groups seek to maintain their control over economic resources such as money and jobs. Threatened groups often do not meet a challenge head-on. Instead, most attempt to avoid dealing with a grievance, not wanting to risk the gains they have already achieved. Their assumption is that it will cost them less if they can dismiss the initiators by refusing to deal with the issue at all. This is demonstrated in many battles between developers and environmentalists, labor and management, and consumers and companies that provide services and products.

A second way in which groups are affected is not so readily apparent. It deals not with economics but with identity. This occurs when a group believes that an initiator threatens its core values or identity. If people feel that their way of life is threatened, they will fight to maintain their position. Those who oppose homosexual rights are battling not because of economic motives but because their values are being threatened and because of what gay people represent as accepted models of society. Government not only allocates economic benefits, it also confers legitimacy on various groups and individuals and endorses or sanctions their practices. Some of these endorsements can be quite controversial. Lifestyle battles associated with identity politics can be seen in controversies over school textbooks, abortion, the role of women in society, and the placement of a Confederate flag on a state office building. The intensity of the National Rifle Association's opposition to gun control comes not from economic sanctions but because owning and using guns are a way of life that its members value. Both types of negative impact—economic reallocation and symbolic threat—arouse the intensity of its membership. However, the latter can often arouse more passion than a mere pocketbook issue (Spitzer 1995).

Issue Containment and Agenda Denial: Synonyms or Overlapping Processes?

When a new grievance is raised, opponents want to defeat it at the lowest cost. Agenda denial concerns those tactics used to keep a grievance off the public or, more often, the formal agenda, although opponents can work to keep issue initiators from attaining success at any stage in the policy cycle from issue inception to implementation. For example, consider the rudimentary parts of the outside initiative approach shown in Figure 1.1: initiation, expansion through issue redefinition, attaining the public agenda (public awareness), moving to the formal agenda, decision making (deliberation in a legislative committee, floor discussion, and vote or a court hearing), and finally implementation (bureaucratic action concretizing a vague law or implementing a judicial mandate). Opponents need a victory at only one point in the policy process to prevail. If they fail to keep an issue off the formal agenda, they can continue to attack initiators and their issue at subsequent stages. Only when a grievance is transformed into a governmental decision that is implemented by the bureaucracy or a court have they lost. Many times, and for a variety of reasons, opponents do not fight against the consideration of an issue and prefer to attack it within the legislative or administrative setting, recognizing that many laws passed by Congress are modified as bureaucrats promulgate regulations from vague legislative mandates.

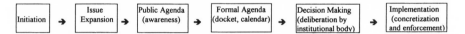

Figure 1.1. Outside Initiative Approach.

In discussing agenda denial, the concept of issue containment is often introduced, and it is helpful to present our view about the relationship between the two. Issue containment, sometimes called issue narrowing, refers to any tactic or set of tactics used by opponents of an issue to limit or restrict what is considered to the narrowest grounds possible. Containment in agenda denial, as we discuss it in the next chapter, redefines a broad-based grievance into much narrower, often technical, terms that diminish the number of people affected, the resources at stake, and its broader political relevance. Containment is part of agenda denial, and it is used when opponents recognize that they cannot either completely ignore or totally defeat an issue. This is illustrated by Hall and Jones in chapter 3, where they show how the SEC and its congressional allies use containment to restrict demands for securities regulation, thereby denying access to more broad-based grievances. In chapter 7, Hackey demonstrates how the opponents of national health insurance realized that the proposal would make the congressional agenda in 1993 but used the fear of "big government" to ultimately weaken its chance of passage.

Containment is a redefinition of an issue away from the concerns of its proponents, and it occurs at all stages of the issue cycle, frequently when outright agenda denial is not possible. Containment, although associated with many tactics used to achieve agenda denial, is not denial itself. Although most of the strategies examined in the next chapter—postponement, verbal attacks, the use of symbolic appeals, lawsuits, and even violence—are found in issue containment, containment is only one way that agenda denial can be achieved.

CONCLUSION

Agenda disputes, like conflicts more generally, are about both what government will and will not consider and how political problems are interpreted. Both competing interests and divergent interpretations are at stake (Ross 1993a, 1993b). Here we introduced key concepts in the study of agenda setting, asking where issues come from and defining types of agendas and relevant actors in the process. We discussed models of agenda setting in the context of policy innovation and drew attention to the interaction between micro and macro factors. Finally, we examined cultural and symbolic processes, especially as they are relevant to understanding the intensity of political conflicts generally and the dynamics of containment more specifically. In the next chapter, we examine the strategies that opponents employ in their quest for agenda denial.

NOTES

1. Although it should be obvious, we want to make it clear that neither proponents nor opponents of new issues are necessarily liberal or conservative. An examination of U.S. politics over the past thirty to forty years shows that liberals and conservatives have been in both positions a number of times.

2. Throughout our discussion, we talk about two sides in agenda conflicts, referring to proponents and opponents. However, we recognize that in most complex conflicts there are more than two sides, and even when it is possible to characterize a conflict in binary terms, there are usually factional differences within each side.

3. Most studies of agenda setting focus on the legislature at the national level. When compared with the bureaucracy, the White House staff, and the courts, Congress has been the focus of concern for several reasons: it is the only elected national body, it is the most open in terms of access, it is the center of media attention, and most people believe that new issues began in this arena. An obvious measure for the formal agenda would be bill introduction. However, less than 15 percent of all bills introduced in Congress are ever considered seriously. Much of bill introduction is symbolic, that is, no attention is intended by the sponsor; these items have been called "pseudo-agenda items" (Cobb and Elder 1983, 87). Therefore, serious consideration on the formal agenda means that a bill is introduced and debated within a committee or subcommittee. It does not have to be approved, but it

must be discussed in a deliberative context. This would eliminate most bills introduced in each session. Thus, a bill could be introduced for a number of years but never seriously discussed. Entrance on the formal agenda does not exist until serious deliberation occurs.

Another element that must be noted about the formal agenda is that it is already clogged. Lawmakers could debate the current items on an agenda with no consideration of new issues. There are certain items that must be discussed each year having to do with the budget. Then there are the recurrent issues that attain some attention on a regular basis: abortion, gun control, crime control and drug regulation (Cobb and Elder 1983, 88).

4. Of course, the numbers can always be debated, because "the choice of measures is part of strategic problem definition, and the results of measures take on their political character only with the costume of interpretive language" (Stone 1988, 146).

5. It is unclear how many people need to be concerned, other than "a significant portion of the populace." For one thing, the political significance of the number is always weighted by the intensity of feelings about the issue in real conflicts.

6. An obvious example for such comparative analysis would be the social welfare legislation underlying the welfare state that passed in most Western European countries by the turn of the nineteenth century but did not occur in the United States until the 1930s. Health insurance in the United States has lagged behind other countries as well. This gap provides evidence that opposition strategies were being pursued aggressively and effectively in the United States.

7. They may be the people affected by the construction of a proposed road or power plant or workers in a factory who are upset about working conditions. A more extreme example is that of Dave Foreman, who was concerned with aggressive logging policies in the Northwest that were rapidly depleting forested areas. He founded Earth First! a small group of individuals who were determined to stop lumber companies from logging and used tactics such as spiking trees, which threatened the safety of lumberjacks.

8. Typically, these people read an elite newspaper such as the *New York Times* or *Wall Street Journal,* regularly follow the news on television, and read newsmagazines. These people value information for its own sake but do not necessarily become active in issue politics. However, they do provide others with information on many issues, acting as opinion leaders.

9. For example, Dave Foreman would have to reach those who are "greens" or committed to environmental politics to have a chance for success. In large part, he has not, which means that it has been difficult for him to expand the issue as he defines it to other favorably disposed groups. Many attention groups are defined in demographic terms. The aged are concerned with elder-care issues, blacks with civil rights issues, veterans with war-related concerns, farmers with agricultural issues, and so forth. To be successful, every identification group member must think of strategies to reach attention groups.

10. Concern about gun control after the murder of a popular public official is one such outcome. Another would be concern about flood relief in a region. Ordinarily, the mass public is not a player in the expansive conflict game (Cobb and Elder 1983).

11. An example would be Reagan's secretary of the interior James Watt, who attempted to change land-use policies to reflect the concerns of the private sector rather than of Interior Department bureaucrats.

12. "Carter approached drug issues as a technical problem that could be ameliorated through quiet rational reassessment by experts in the drug policy field. Such a low visibility

approach might have been ideal if the agenda were restricted to narrow technical issues . . . but the call for decriminalization of marijuana was not a narrow, routine, or technical matter" (Sharp 1994, 45).

13. The garbage can approach to decision making describes a fluid process with four components: identifiable problems, generic solutions, changing participants, and random choice opportunities. Decisions are made without careful calculation, subject to the exigencies of the moment (Cohen, March, and Olsen 1978).

14. Sundquist argues that a climate-of-the-times thesis helps determine which party and ideology will dominate the U.S. political scene (1968, 499–505).

15. Climate of the times is not the same as public opinion, however, and Kingdon warns that overriding public concern or the nature of public opinion in general is a quixotic variable. In his investigation of health and transportation sectors, Kingdon noted that public opinion had some impact but was a minor variable. Its major role was as a deterrent, not as an aid to policy innovation. As he notes, "The negative public opinion effects . . . are probably more noticeable. Public opinion may sometimes lead government to do something, but it more often constrains government from doing something" (1994, 69).

16. For example, notions of atomistic individualism, materialism, and suspicion of political authorities have colored policy discussions (Cobb and Elder 1981, 402–8).

REFERENCES

Bachrach, P., and M. Baratz. 1962. Two faces of power. *American Political Science Review* 56: 947–52.
———. 1963. Decision and nondecisions: An analytical framework. *American Political Science Review* 57: 632–42.
Baumgartner, F. R., and B. D. Jones. 1993. *Agendas and instability in American politics.* Chicago: University of Chicago Press.
Best, J., ed. 1989. *Images of issues: Typifying contemporary social problems.* New York: Aldine de Gruyter.
Birnbaum, J. H., and A. S. Murray. 1987. *Showdown at Gucci Gulch: Lawmakers, lobbyists and the unlikely triumph of tax reform.* New York: Vintage.
Cobb, R. W., and C. D. Elder. 1981. Communication and public policy. In *Handbook of political communications,* edited by D. D. Nimmo and K. R. Sanders. Beverly Hills: Sage.
———. 1983. *Participation in American politics: The dynamics of agenda-building.* Baltimore: Johns Hopkins University Press.
Cobb, R. W., J.-K. Ross, and M. H. Ross. 1976. Agenda building as a comparative political process. *American Political Science Review* 71:126–38.
Cohen, A. 1969. *Custom and politics in urban Africa: A study of Hausa migrants in Yoruba towns.* Berkeley: University of California Press.
Cohen, M., J. March, and J. Olsen. 1978. A garbage can model of organizational choice. *Administrative Science Quarterly* 72:1–25.
Coleman, J. 1957. *Community conflict.* New York: Free Press.
Converse, P. 1964. The nature of belief systems in mass publics. In *Ideology and discontent,* edited by D. Apter. New York: Free Press.

Crenson, M. A. 1971. *The un-politics of air pollution: A study of non-decisionmaking in the cities.* Baltimore: Johns Hopkins University Press.

Douglas, M., and A. Wildavsky. 1982. *Risk and culture.* Berkeley and Los Angeles: University of California Press.

Downs, A. 1972. Up and down with ecology: The issue attention cycle. *Public Interest* 28:38–50.

Edelman, M. 1964. *The symbolic uses of politics.* Urbana: University of Illinois Press.

Felstiner, W. L. F., R. I. Abel, and A. Sarat. 1980–1981. The emergence and transformation of disputes: Naming, blaming, claiming. . . . *Law & Society Review* 15:631–53.

Fritsch, J. 1996. Nature groups say foes bear friendly names. *New York Times,* March 25, pp. A1, A12.

Fritschler, A. L. 1989. *Smoking and politics: Policy making and the federal bureaucracy.* Englewood Cliffs, NJ: Prentice-Hall.

Gaventa, J. 1980. *Power and powerlessness: Quiescence and rebellion in an Appalachian valley.* Urbana: University of Illinois Press.

Gusfield, J. 1963. *Symbolic crusade: Status politics and the American temperance movement.* Urbana: University of Illinois Press.

———. 1981. *The culture of public problems: Drinking-driving and the symbolic order.* Chicago: University of Chicago Press.

Heclo, H. 1978. Issue networks in the executive establishment. In *The new American political system,* edited by A. King. Washington, DC: American Enterprise Institute.

Hirschman, A. O. 1991. *The rhetoric of reaction.* Cambridge: Belknap Press of Harvard University Press.

Hunter, J. D. 1994. *Before the shooting begins.* New York: Free Press.

Iyengar, S. 1991. *Is anyone responsible? How television frames political issues.* Chicago: University of Chicago Press.

Kingdon, J. W. 1994. *Agendas, alternatives, and public policies.* New York: HarperCollins.

Lewis, N. 1995. Push for limits on lawsuits seems to have lost its way. *New York Times,* September 11, pp. A1, A11.

Light, P. 1989. *The president's agenda.* Baltimore: Johns Hopkins University Press.

Loomis, B. 1985. *The new American politician.* New York: Basic Books.

Nadel, M. V. 1971. *The politics of consumer protection.* Indianapolis: Bobbs-Merrill.

Nelson, B. 1984. *The politics of child abuse and neglect.* Chicago: University of Chicago Press.

Rochefort, D. W. 1989. *American social welfare policy.* Boulder, CO: Westview.

Rochefort, D. W., and R. W. Cobb, eds. 1994. *The politics of problem definition: Shaping the policy agenda.* Lawrence: University Press of Kansas.

Ross, M. H. 1993a. *The culture of conflict: Interpretations and interests in comparative perspective.* New Haven, CT, and London: Yale University Press.

———. 1993b. *The management of conflict: Interpretations and interests in comparative perspective.* New Haven, CT, and London: Yale University Press.

———. 1995. Psychocultural interpretation theory and peacemaking in ethnic conflicts. *Political Psychology* 16:523–44.

———. 1997. The relevance of culture for the study of political psychology and ethnic conflict. *Political Psychology* 18:299–326.

———. Forthcoming. Culture and identity in comparative politics. In *Comparative politics:*

Rationality, culture, and structure, edited by M. I. Lichbach and A. S. Zuckerman. New York: Cambridge University Press.

Schattschneider, E. E. 1960. *The semi-sovereign people: A realist's guide to democracy in America.* New York: Holt.

Schneider, A., and H. Ingram. 1993. Social construction of target populations: Implications for politics and policy. *American Political Science Review* 87:334–47.

Sharp, E. 1994. *Drug policy in the U.S.* New York: HarperCollins.

Spitzer, R. J. 1995. *The politics of gun control.* Chatham, NJ: Chatham House.

Stone, D. 1988. *Policy paradox and political reason.* Glenview, IL: Scott, Foresman.

Sundquist, J. W. 1968. *Politics and policy.* Washington, DC: Brookings.

2
Denying Agenda Access: Strategic Considerations

Roger W. Cobb and Marc Howard Ross

Agenda conflicts pit initiators seeking consideration of a new issue against opponents who want to keep that issue off the agenda. The discussion of agenda setting in the first chapter makes it clear that the burden lies with the initiators, for no action favors those who oppose putting the issue on the agenda in the first place. Although many discussions of issue creation take the point of view of proponents, here we consider the problem from the viewpoint of opponents. In a democracy, we presume that serious governmental consideration of issues involves the public. Yet sometimes this does not take place, and non–decision making comes to characterize a community. Although the concept of the nondecision is useful, it is also vague and fails to delineate a process that leads to the cultural and political construction of problems as central to the politics of policy making. Therefore, we need to spell out more completely key features of issue opposition.

As noted in chapter 1, opponents may be bureaucrats, politicians, or organized groups outside of government. Here we discuss the strategic choices they face in agenda conflicts. Our working assumption is that an opponent seeks to achieve its desired result at the lowest possible cost but will progressively turn to higher-cost strategies (or terminate its opposition) in the face of lack of success. Although the idea of a cost continuum is a useful way to represent strategic choices to disputants, we recognize that in practice the actual strategies that opponents use often represent a mix in terms of costs—in part because opponents (like proponents) are frequently part of a coalition in which different actors have different levels of resources and commitments.

This chapter focuses on the dynamics of agenda denial, spelling out in detail the low-, medium-, and high-cost strategic options that opponents use. The analysis gives a central role to cultural and symbolic strategies aimed at defining an issue in such a way that a group can win a specific agenda conflict and attain longer-run success. We focus particularly on four types of strategies used by opponents to defeat initiators: low-cost symbolic strategies such as nonrecognition; attack strategies aimed at undercutting the initiator; symbolic strategies that create the impression that a grievance is taken seriously but in fact do little to address the underlying problem; and high-cost strategies, including the use of violence.

In thinking about strategic choices in agenda disputes, it is useful to begin with a few general points that shape the use of material and symbolic resources in these conflicts:

- Opponents typically have the advantage. The agendas of legislatures, the executive branches of government, and the courts are already full. Elected and administrative officials are more than delighted to find reasons that they need (or should) not consider an issue. Opponents only have to convince the relevant decision makers that no action is needed, whereas proponents in agenda disputes must persuade officials that they need to act—and actually dispense scarce resources in the process.

- Time is usually an ally of opponents. The typical half-life of an issue is short, and frequently all opponents have to do is resist moving on a matter during the first flush of excitement, when proponents mobilize public attention on a grievance. In a short time, the mass public's interest wanes, and an issue that once seemed compelling becomes old and uninteresting (Downs 1974).

- Opponents often have more information about the political system and its workings, especially when they have been successful in blocking consideration of an issue in the past. This situation commonly occurs when proponents are mobilized around the moral dimensions of a dispute, such as human rights problems in a foreign land, but have little actual experience in dealing with governmental machinery.

- The media are important to each side in different ways. Proponents, even if they are well-placed officials, typically need to gain visibility and attract support for their issue to move it onto the agenda and displace other issues. They often go to great lengths to obtain coverage that brings attention to their cause. Opponents, in contrast, often seek to ignore an issue entirely. If the initiators succeed in gaining media coverage, opponents then focus on the issue's negative features (e.g., cost, creation of larger government) or the negative aspects of the proponents themselves (e.g., inexperience, questionable backgrounds). The media are particularly receptive to blaming and personalizing in their coverage, and to be effective, each side often seeks to shape news coverage in terms of these features.

- Short-run political trends—what might be called the proximate political climate—can have a great impact on what each side believes it can seek and how it characterizes the other side's position. An obvious example is the different ways in which the same social needs (e.g., education, health care) were presented—or opposed—during the expanding 1960s versus the contracting

1980s. There are many other situations in which particular issues, or opposition to them, are primed by political trends as well.

FOUR LEVELS OF STRATEGIC CHOICE

An opponent has different options to consider when facing a group that threatens its economic position or social identity. On the one hand, it does not want to expend resources that are unnecessary to fend off the initiating group. This would be costly, time-consuming, and counterproductive. On the other hand, it does not want to wait too long to give the initiating group an advantage. We describe opponents' strategies on a cost continuum that considers not only short-term resource expenditures to pursue a particular strategy but also possible future costs. Conceptually, we consider four choices that opponents face, while recognizing that in complex conflicts, several of these may be made simultaneously, especially when opponents themselves are part of a large coalition: (1) low-cost strategies that stress the nonrecognition of the initiator position; (2) medium-cost strategies aimed at attacking the proposed policy of the initiating group; (3) medium-cost strategies intended to symbolically placate the initiating group; and (4) high-cost strategies that are costly to both sides but more costly to the initiators than to the opponents, at least in the short run. Thus, opponents must know when and how to act toward an initiator over time. The assumption we make is that if initial low-cost strategies fail, the opposing group will deal with the issue in a more serious way. However, escalation is not sought and not undertaken until other avenues have been explored.

Low-cost Strategies

Although the history of an individual dispute may not follow this path, we suggest that opponents first consider, and often use, low-cost strategies involving little money, few people, and minimal time. From the point of view of opponents, it is more desirable to make sure that an issue is never considered than to defeat it once it is raised. As Stone notes, "keeping an alternative from explicit consideration is even better than defeating it. Just as a losing political candidate in an election can become the rallying point for new political efforts, an alternative that achieves a place on the decision maker's 'short list' of possibilities acquires a reality in people's minds simply by having been considered" (1988, 196). The reasoning is simple: if the public doesn't see a problem, eventually it will disappear. Consequently, to have its grievance heard, an initiating group must publicize it sufficiently so that strategies such as being unaware of a problem, denying that a problem exists, and not recognizing the initiating group are not viable.

Refusing to recognize that a problem exists is usually the first strategy used

by officials to deflect initiators. For years, decision makers "ignoranced" the problem of acid rain. While scientific evidence was accumulating that residues were
moved by weather patterns to different areas of the country, decision makers
acted as though there was no problem whatsoever (Radin 1994, 1). Similarly, in
Michigan, when improper chemicals were placed in animals' food pellets, the
State Department of Agriculture, the Farm Bureau Federation, and the chemical
companies simply refused to recognize the problem for a period of time. Reich
(1991) termed this the "non-issue" status of a public problem. A variant is for an
opponent to invoke procedural reasons that a particular issue is inappropriate for
consideration: it does not meet certain technical requirements, the problem has
been brought to the wrong person or office, or the demand for consideration has
been incorrectly filed.

Eventually, if the problem persists, "ignorancing" the problem is not sufficient, and opponents turn to outright denial that the problem exists. There is
minimal recognition of the grievance, but the reaction is that it is a nonproblem.
Tobacco manufacturers in the 1960s used this strategy when studies began to
emerge indicating the health problems caused by smoking. Private correspon-
dence, recently presented in Congress, now makes it clear that the manufacturers
were aware of these problems, although their public stance was one of denial. In
fact, denial is still being used by tobacco companies some thirty years later, although its effectiveness has largely disappeared (Hilts 1994a, 1). Lopez and Reich
offer another good example of problem denial in chapter 8, citing developers in
El Paso who argued that providing water to the colonia area was not a problem
because the residents could obtain water in other ways.

A variation of denial is what Ibarra and Kitsuse (1993) call "antipatterning."
The existence of a problem is admitted, but it is defined as an isolated incident
and not part of a larger pattern. Issue opponents then argue that "the incidence
of the phenomenon has been exaggerated or its nature misunderstood" (1993, 44).
At a minimum, this puts pressure on the initiators to demonstrate that their concern extends beyond a single occurrence and is weighty enough to merit serious
attention.

Parallel to denial is the refusal to recognize the existence of groups advocat-
ing that an issue be placed on the formal agenda. Here the opponent separates
the problem and the group, denying the political legitimacy of the initiators.
Southern officials used this strategy in the 1950s and 1960s when civil rights
groups demanded an end to racial segregation. Southern officials refused to grant
civil rights groups any role in the policy process, buying additional time to maintain segregation (Garrow 1978, 31–77).

Bendix, in chapter 9, shows this strategy at work in Austria in 1986, when
former UN Secretary General Kurt Waldheim ran for the mainly symbolic presidency. His service as an officer in the German armed forces during World War II
was not perceived by Austrian political parties or the Austrian public as politically relevant. Bendix argues that Waldheim's initial response was that his World

War II role was not a problem, because all such questions had been adequately dealt with in the past. It also was consistent with the views of Austrians, who were upset that a senior figure in the country was being attacked by outsiders.

The key element of low-cost opposition strategies is nonconfrontation. There is little or no direct communication between the two sides. In fact, stronger opponents use their refusal to recognize the initiator's issue position, the legitimacy of the initiating group, or the appropriateness of the presentation of the issue as a bargaining chip for which initiators will have to pay. This tactic can require the initiating group to gain additional information or to expend additional resources to gain outside publicity and allies to force the opponent into some minimal recognition of a grievance.

Medium-cost Strategies: Attack Posture

Medium-cost strategies combine two different types of issue avoidance. First, the attempt is made to discredit the issue stance of the group and the group itself. The target of the attack depends on the outside group's characteristics. A second strategy, often used if the first fails to derail the initiators, is to show symbolic concern in dealing with a problem. A variety of strategies accompanied with media coverage can create the impression that action is forthcoming. However, most of these strategies buy additional time for the opponent to keep the real grievances off the agenda.

The use of low-cost strategies can eliminate some of the "nuisance groups" that plague officials. However, if a group has some skill in expanding attention to additional participants and the media, low-cost strategies will eventually fail. The opponent then moves to a set of medium-cost strategies that require time, personnel, and other resources. Attack strategies raise the level of conflict, as verbal assaults against either the group and or its issue position raise the fervor of both sides. The opponent's goal is to link the initiating group or the proposed policy to negative characterizations that raise public doubt. The mobilization of further support by the initiating group is thus unlikely, and the issue fails to get on the formal agenda.

Here a basic decision must be made: does one attack the issue or the group? Each strategy has a different focus. A key element in making this initial choice is the legitimacy of the initiators. When the initiators have high legitimacy and are respected by the wider community, a group-based attack is foolish. Marginal individuals or groups that are behind a new issue may be easier targets for a direct attack. Let us consider both options.

First, in a conflict with a highly legitimate initiator, the opponents are likely to attack the substantive issue the initiator raises. One initial tactic is to argue that the issue is not a legitimate public concern and ought to be resolved privately. As Eyestone noted, "a non response particularly hard to counter is the claim that an issue is inappropriate for government action" (1978, 137). For example, although many education professionals are seen as legitimate decision makers, some conservative parents believe that sex education has no place in the curriculum of public schools and should be done only in homes or churches. Opponents of sex education often find it safer to define the issue as a "nonpublic concern" rather than to attack initiators directly.

This strategy has been particularly effective in cases dealing with the Securities and Exchange Commission (SEC). Hall and Jones show in chapter 3 how the SEC has used this strategy for several decades. Confronted with congressional criticisms of inactivity after periodic cases of business abuse, the SEC argued that it was not a public problem. Instead, the private sector had a self-correcting mechanism: the marketplace. Reliance on market factors would eliminate business malpractice. Similarly, Mahon and McGowan argue in chapter 4 that the accounting profession, when under attack by those demanding regulation, responded that the private sector was best able to handle this problem. Hackey in chapter 7 shows that one of the major arguments made by those who oppose national health insurance is that it is not a genuine governmental concern; the matter is best left to the private sector, and government should not interfere with the basic patient-doctor relationship.

The strategy of arguing that a certain grievance should not be dealt with through government action has also been used against groups with a moderate level of legitimacy. Consider the failure of the equal rights amendment (ERA). After the ratification of women's suffrage in 1923, decades followed before women's rights were taken seriously. For years, public officials dealt with the ERA by saying that its concerns fell outside the realm of governmental responsibility. As Eyestone notes, "on the prima facie evidence, then the denial of government responsibility for women's rights (except voting) reflects a grand sexist conspiracy" (1978, 139).

More commonly, opponents dispute initiators' facts, suggesting that they reasoned from faulty premises. For example, recreational boat safety has not made the agenda in most states, despite the large number of recreational boating accidents each year—including more than 300 deaths in the last decade alone. One side argues that boat owners need to be licensed and educated; the other side says that there is a minimal problem. Those who are concerned about the accidents and fatalities point to the need for licensing procedures that require training courses for all boat users. Those who do not want governmental intervention argue that the accident statistics are misleading. They believe that such deaths are caused primarily by drunk drivers and careless ones (e.g., those who don't wear life jackets). Their position is: you don't need to take a course to be told to wear a life jacket or not to drink. Both sides reason differently from the same statistics to reach different conclusions. Thus far, those opposed to regulation have been more successful, despite the evidence that many people are alarmed by the frequency of serious boating accidents ("Alabama Requires Boaters to Get License" 1994, A-14).

Opponents' attacks on issues can raise the fears of the general public. One way that this is commonly accomplished is by arguing that the proposed policy contains hidden costs that will make the situation worse. An excellent example of this has to do with the controversy over health insurance in 1993–1994. The official introduction of the Clinton health plan onto the formal agenda came in early 1994. However, just prior to the event, the insurance industry launched a series of advertising messages to discredit the president's plan. The Coalition for Health Insurance Choices designed one of the most effective campaigns, which involved a series of television ads showing a concerned couple—Harry and Louise—discussing their fears about the proposed health plan. Their discussions focused on pro-consumer terms and raised fears about pricing, limits on consumer choice, and the many confusing regulations. This campaign was quite effective in raising public doubts and undercutting the legitimacy of the president's health care experts (Kolbert 1993, A1).

In analyzing issue attack strategies, one way of understanding issue dynamics is to consider Cobb and Elder's five issue characteristics (1983, 112–24): ambiguity, social significance, temporal relevance, complexity, and no categorical precedence. Defining an issue in these terms can expand issue attention, whereas using the reverse of these issue characteristics can limit audience attention.[1] Hackey in chapter 7 shows how national health insurance opponents used these issue characteristics to avoid placing national health insurance on the congressional agenda. First, ambiguity raised fear of symbols such as "big government" and "socialized medicine." Second, in terms of social significance, they claimed that national health care would not meet the needs of many people as well as the current system did. Third, they painted an image of spillover to future generations with inferior health care over time. Fourth, complex images associated with complex bureaucracy and insurance-buying groups scared people who were afraid of losing their current coverage. Fifth, images of radical change challenged existing beliefs that, despite serious flaws, the existing medical system was successful and still the best in the world. Other chapters also illustrate the strategic use of these issue characteristics. For example, Mahon and McGowan show in chapter 4 that the accounting profession used complexity as a reason to resist regulation, saying that the issues involved were too difficult for nonaccountants to understand.

When initiators have low legitimacy, they become the objects of attack. This is most likely when they are relatively new and unknown actors. Attacking such groups is intended to destroy their credibility and that of those who support them. Identifying them with well-known unpopular groups is a common tactic. An attacked group is then put on the defensive and must prove that the charges are incorrect before it can resume its issue campaign.[2] For example, conservatives often linked weak liberal groups with the term "communist," putting them on the defensive. We see this dynamic in chapter 5, where Plein shows that supporters of bovine growth hormone (bST) attacked those who were opposed to its use by portraying them as the essence of the problem. The hormone's opponents were accused of being "latter-day luddites," opposed to technological change and progress and living in a romantic past. This view is often combined with an "us versus them" mentality in which two views of the problem appear: the correct view and the unacceptable view, which is that of the opponent.

Attacks on group credibility often focus on its leaders and their behavior. Questioning the patriotism, ethics, morality, and honesty of the leaders of a group may be sufficient to raise doubts in the minds of many. Raising doubts about the motives of leaders, or what Ibarra and Kitsuse (1993, 41–2) call the rhetorical strategy of insincerity, is an effort to separate leaders from their followers by suggesting that they are seeking personal power, status, or money. For years, racial conservatives used character assassination on Dr. Martin Luther King Jr. as they attempted to keep civil rights concerns off the formal agenda, charging that he was a communist, that he was engaging in immoral behavior, and that he was a liar. Many initiators are vulnerable to such attacks and seek public support from highly respected groups or individuals to thwart its impact. In King's case, the liberal community (politicians, academics, media) supported his effort and finally weakened the thrust of these charges (Cobb and Elder 1983, 125–6).

A common way of attacking the initiating group is to link it with negative stereotypes. For example, Lopez and Reich show in chapter 8 that one way that the political elite of El Paso avoided providing water to the colonias in the area was by fueling negative stereotypes of the people living there. The stereotyped colonia residents were seen as poor, low-income, undocumented, illegal Mexican immigrants, which made it hard to show the public why they were deserving of public aid. Although many of these specific images were incorrect, the widely accepted stereotype undercut the residents' attempts to obtain the water they needed.

Attacking the initiator became a clear strategy in Kurt Waldheim's defense when he was running for the Austrian presidency and details of his World War II past were revealed, as Bendix shows in chapter 9. To defend himself against charges that he was involved in possible human rights abuses during the war, Waldheim and his supporters attacked one of his main opponents, the World Jewish Congress, for conducting a "witchhunt," "defamation," and "mudslinging." Waldheim called it the "greatest slander campaign in the Austrian Republic since 1945," and an opposition political party that might have profited from the charges was accused of working with the World Jewish Congress in New York to undermine Waldheim.

One of the key elements in the attack strategy is the allocation of blame. When issue opponents can link a problem to the shortcomings of a particular group, the pressure for action diminishes. For example, Iyengar (1991) studied media coverage of four domestic issues: crime, unemployment, poverty, and racial inequality. He found that when media coverage was episodic, focusing on specific events or particular cases, the blame was much more likely to be allocated to the individuals involved in the problem. However, when the coverage was thematic or focused on political issues or events in some larger context, people were much more likely to blame the decision makers or those in charge. On most issues, episodic coverage predominated. This would aid opponents, who benefit when problems are presented in personalized terms. For example, blaming the poor for their plight makes the likelihood of ameliorative social programs to help the underclass much less likely (Iyengar 1991, 127–8).

A sometimes effective opposition strategy involves claiming the high ground on the victimization issue. One of the main appeals that issue initiators use is to claim that they have been victimized on economic, physical, sexual, ethnic, racial, age, or other grounds. Opponents need to neutralize this claim. One way of doing this is to reverse roles. An opponent claims that it has been victimized by the initiator. If successful, the force of the claim for action is weakened. An illustration of how this can work occurred in 1994, when President Clinton considered a casino tax to pay for part of his welfare reform plan. Negatively impacted casino interests reacted swiftly. Nevada's governor flew to Washington to lobby officials, and casinos hired lobbyists to make their pitch, arguing that casinos were being unfairly targeted to pay for the welfare plan. "What do casinos have to do with welfare reform?" they asked, claiming that they were being unfairly singled out and were "victims" in a political fight that did not involve them. The "victim" argument worked, and the plan was never introduced in Congress, a clear case of agenda denial (DeParle 1994, A1).

A final attack strategy is the use of deception. Several activities can be included under this heading: lying, spreading false rumors, or planting false stories in the media. Deception involves the dissemination of materials known to be inaccurate or of questionable veracity. This can be a particularly potent weapon when the media reprint the material. A disputant may, in fact, distort its own position or that of an opponent. The tactic of distorting one's own position works best when it is sheathed in a scientific facade. One of the best examples of this tactic is the tobacco companies' attempt to avoid legislative initiatives aimed at exposing nicotine as a health risk. For three decades, they distributed "scientific reports" showing that nicotine is a harmless, nonaddictive substance not requiring regulation. Many in the media reported these studies, and the tobacco companies' allies in Congress used this research to prevent public health issues from being placed before the committees responsible for writing legislation. Recent investigations showed that chief executive officers of tobacco companies had such studies altered or stopped as far back as the 1960s. In addition, an actor can spread lies about its opponent. For example, any whistle-blower who attempted to state that a tobacco company's claims were inaccurate was the subject of intensive background investigations and the leaking of unfavorable information or innuendos to the media. Such a climate of fear made individuals less likely to testify (Hilts 1994b, A1).

Medium-cost Strategies: Symbolic Placation

An alternative to attacking initiators is for opponents to turn to symbolic placation, an alternative set of medium-cost strategies. With symbolic placation, opponents admit the existence of a problem but block any consideration of the initiator's proposed solution, citing reasons such as the cost or that the remedy is hopelessly naive (e.g., we can't eliminate violence from society). Instead, they try to address the grievance through visible, but not very significant, action. As a result, opponents "downsize" a problem so that few, if any, resources are allocated to deal with it. In turning to symbolic placation, opponents adopt a language emphasizing mutual interests, and the zero-sum vocabulary associated with adversarial conflict is set aside. At this point, a conflict is often characterized by caution, as each side hopes to persuade the other rather than defeat it through directly confrontational strategies. Opposition leaders may even meet with a grievance group. One outcome can be the use of sympathetic, counterrhetorical strategies, which can be effective in blunting protesters' initiatives (Ibarra and Kitsuse 1993, 38–43).[3]

Although both public officials and affected groups can engage in attack strategies, negatively impacted groups engage in such activity more often than governmental officials, who are more likely to use symbolic placation strategies. Officials recognize, often grudgingly, the existence of a problem but attempt to thwart serious consideration of the proponents' proposed solutions. One reason this occurs is that some leaders recognize the importance of giving the appearance of "coping" with a problem that people see as significant (Edelman 1964).[4] Public officials often appeal to protesters by stressing the interests of the wider community, or they may invoke community norms and values that limit actions that may be taken (Coleman 1957, 21). In the 1973 Michigan contamination case, Reich (1991, 188–90) found that the Farm Bureau Federation sought to contain the conflict by calling on the "loyalty" of its farmer members and appealing to a myth that the group was serving the farmers in an attempt to avoid litigation.[5] Symbolic placation strategies do not entail any future commitment and are most often successful in one of two situations: when the power differential between the initiators and opponents is so great that the former conclude that there is not much likelihood of success, or when commitment to wider community values is, in fact, relatively high and feelings about the issue under consideration are not.

Symbolic strategies require some actions on the part of opponents, and although they are often not very costly in material terms, they may help legitimize the initiators and the grievance they raise. However, opponents hope that by acknowledging the existence of the issue they will be in a position to control actions that are later undertaken to address it. Hence they are willing to do such things as create a committee to consider the proposed issue, showcase or create a pilot project to deal with the problem in a small area, co-opt the issue by bringing members of the grievance group into the decision-making body, stress actions already taken to address the problem, or postpone action by showing concern about the issue but suggesting that it cannot be considered at the present time for a variety of reasons.

One of the most common symbolic placation strategies is to create a committee to study the problem (Cobb and Elder 1983, 127). The committee or higher-sounding "commission" has a number of typical characteristics. Usually it is a blue-ribbon panel composed of bipartisan experts in the area with a small budget and a fixed time frame—normally six months to a year—to issue a report. As William D. Carey, former assistant director of the Bureau of the Budget, noted in congressional testimony:

> It is true that government is getting a great deal of advice, and some information from the legions of advisory bodies which it creates. I am much less clear on what happens to the advice or who is listening. I do know that very little of the advice from most Presidential advisory bodies ever seeps through to the President himself. Most of it is lost through evaporation, some leaks out on staff advisors to the President, and no one can say with certainty how much of it feeds into policy decisions. . . . In my experience, nothing was simpler than to set up an advisory group. It started wheels turning, it bought time, it was a surrogate for action, and it produced a kind of structural grandeur. It implied that someone was taking charge of the problem, and perhaps that things would work out. This is the way of governments. (Primack and von Hippel 1974, 31)

Symbolic placation through commission creation defuses a conflict and can weaken whatever momentum initiators have developed. The mere fact that these panels are composed of politically experienced people means that it is unlikely that earthshaking recommendations will be forthcoming. As Wise notes in a recent study of CIA wrongs after the Aldrich Ames fiasco, "Although its members were both experienced and distinguished, a commission made up of members of the establishment is not likely to clobber the establishment or step on many toes—and it didn't" (Wise 1996, M2, M6). By the time the study is done, other problems will have emerged, and the problem is viewed as less urgent. Often the appointment of a commission itself relieves public alarm about how to cope with the problem. This strategy is particularly effective in dealing with new protest groups with minimal resources. As Bachrach and Baratz note, "tactics such as these . . . are particularly effective when employed against impermanent or weakly organized groups (e.g., students, the poor) which have difficulty withstanding delay" (1970, 45). A prominent illustration was the Kerner Commission, which President Johnson appointed in the late 1960s to examine the causes of the inner-city riots. It identified "white racism" as a primary cause of the problem. Yet no legislation emerged from that commission's findings to deal with what it saw as the core of the problem.

Officials often find that appointing a commission is an excellent symbolic strategy; it suggests that they are addressing a problem without actually doing anything. Nixon used it for pornography, Ford for inflation, Carter for Three Mile Island, and Reagan for Central America. After the 1992 Los Angeles riots, the state legislature appointed a commission. Six months later, it concluded that the problems were the same as those that had caused the Watts riots in the 1960s. Recommendations were offered, but the report suggested that the state budget crisis made meaningful change unlikely ("New Riots, Old Story" 1992, 36).[6] On a much less volatile issue, Mahon and McGowan show in chapter 4 how the accounting industry resorted to commissions to study the problem of regulating the industry. Several blue-ribbon commissions were impaneled over the years, and few recommended any governmental regulatory actions.

Showcasing or tokenism is a symbolic placation strategy in which opponents focus on one small part of a problem to show their commitment to dealing with it. For example, police departments often dramatize their effectiveness by focusing on crimes such as prostitution, gambling, begging, and drug abuse. As police make a symbolic sweep in a particular crime area, the action is often accompanied by media attention. By doing this, the pressure on police to address deeper concerns of upset local residents is mitigated, and the chance of these concerns being placed on the agendas of local officials is lessened.

Sometimes showcasing or tokenism occurs when public officials redefine a problem narrowly and then deal with only those who qualify for aid as the problem is now defined. For example, when the contamination of the feed supply in Michigan could no longer be defined as a nonproblem, action was needed. The state agriculture department redefined the problem as an agricultural, not a public health, issue. Officials defined the problem as involving "only one feed, affect[ing] mainly cows on a few farms" (Reich 1991, 70). This redefinition confined the issue's impact to fewer people, and the agricultural bureaucrats used a test to detect the level of the dangerous chemical in cows' milk. Those farmers whose milk had chemical readings above a certain number were given help; those with readings below the number were not. However, the level was set so high that few qualified. This arbitrary standard was based on uncertain scientific data, yet it gave the appearance of meaningful action for those few farmers who met this stringent technical criterion (Reich 1991, 184–5).

Symbolic placation also occurs when actions that appear on the surface to deal with the problem are really nothing more than superficial actions that make no difference. Lopez and Reich provide two examples of this strategy in chapter 8. The El Paso Public Service Board rescinded its "no water outside the city" policy, which appeared to give colonias greater access to water. However, in reality, only two of the many colonias were impacted. Second, the state legislature created a local water district authority to serve the colonias but gave it no resources to provide water when the board dropped its opposition to it.

"More of the same" is another symbolic placation strategy in which what has been done in the past is done at a heightened level. In doing this, an opponent demonstrates good faith by increasing the level of activity, but the heightened pace of activity closes the door on what initiators want to consider doing. It looks, however, like the problem is being addressed. Hall and Jones in chapter 3 report that the SEC used this strategy during the 1960s and 1970s after it was criticized for inactivity, increasing the number of regulatory reporting releases filed by the commission. The greater use of disclosure gave the impression that the SEC was dealing with the issue of financial mismanagement.

Co-opting prominent people from initiating groups is another symbolic approach to weaken the claims of initiators. Offering a position to the leader of an outside group can reduce the effectiveness of its appeal (Coleman 1957, 17). For example, consider the case of the America Beverage Institute (ABI), a trade group representing breweries and restaurants. It is working against efforts to tighten state drunk-driving laws, and issue activists are seeking to lower the legal intoxication level from 0.10 to 0.08. Currently, ABI is fighting to keep the issue of lower blood alcohol readings as an indicator of drunk driving off state legislative agendas. One way that ABI is attempting to defuse the issue is by hiring Candy Lightner, the founder of Mothers Against Drunk Driving (MADD), as a lobbyist. She opposes the lower limit because she believes that it will have no impact on drunk driving. She argues that "her enemies were still drunk drivers but not restaurants" (Lewin 1994, A7).

In addition to co-opting people, opponents can co-opt an initiator's symbols and associate them with their own actions. Good examples of symbolic co-optation are found in the environmental area, where many symbols associated with the environment are viewed favorably. For example, a recent Gallup poll showed that 63 percent of Americans considered themselves environmentalists and that by a margin of sixty-two to thirty-four, Americans would give priority to the environment over economic growth (Fritsch 1996, A12). This has political consequences for those battling over the use of public lands. Davis (1995) reports an intriguing use of symbol co-optation in his study of how logging interests have tried to keep environmentalists' grievances off the formal agenda in establishing Oregon's forestry policy. Timber interests refer to themselves as "environmentalists" and are "associated with the symbols of environmentalism such as abundant wildlife, healthy forests and wise stewardship" (Davis 1995, 38–9). In addition, they never call their opponents environmentalists but the more strident "preservationists" (Davis 1995, 38–9).

In fact, the use of environmental symbols by its natural adversaries (e.g., developers, loggers) has become so widespread that environmental groups have developed a name to describe it: "greenscamming." Now opposition groups routinely take environmental names to mask their mission to keep environmental groups' key proposals off the formal agenda. Big utilities under attack for reducing the fish population have set up a cover group called Northwesterners for More Fish. A mining company that wants to create a large landfill bills itself as the Friends of Eagle Mountain (Fritsch 1996, A1). Co-optation of language is also seen in the conflict over the bovine growth hormone. In chapter 5, Plein shows one of the most powerful weapons that bST opponents used was the idea that cows' milk was being technologically tainted and that the rhythms of nature were being altered. To combat this, the pro-bST forces co-opted the symbol of nature, arguing that bST was a natural hormone that cows already produced and that there was nothing unnatural in its use.

Postponement is a symbolic placation strategy in which an opponent argues that although the initiator has a valid grievance, constraints such as time, money, and personnel make action impossible at the moment. This strategy is similar to one that Ibarra and Kitsuse call "declaring impotence," which registers sympathy with the cause while "pointing to an impoverishment of resources at hand for dealing with the issue" (1993, 39). Since 1988, Presidents Bush and Clinton have both done this, arguing that there are many problems that deserve governmental action, but the fiscal resources are simply not available to deal with them.

Finally, symbolic placation can involve offering a litany of past accomplishments in concert with postponement. The argument goes something like this: although we cannot act on your behalf now because of constraints, our past record is excellent. In most areas, public officials can point to actions taken on behalf of most socially aggrieved groups dating back to the Great Society. Stressing a past record of accomplishments gives the impression of credibility in taking further action (Cobb and Elder 1983, 128-9). The Federal Aviation Agency (FAA) was created to promote and maintain airline safety, but in the few past years, safety advocates have been critical of the agency, arguing that it focuses on airline promotion rather than safety. Proposals to limit the scope of the agency have been discussed but never seriously considered. Why? The FAA has stressed its past record and fiscal constraints. The agency's response to such criticism has been to show statistics indicating that crashes are rare and to provide documentation that airlines are continuously monitored in terms of safety procedures used. FAA officials claim that more would be done to promote safety if additional funds were available. Only when an airplane crashes with a loss of life is that defense challenged (Wald 1996, A12).

High-cost Strategies

The last group of strategies are those that involve a great expenditure of the opponent's resources. Although both sides stand to lose from such tactics, as in a negative-sum game, opponents clearly believe that they will lose relatively less than the initiators in the long run. For this reason, such strategies are not used lightly and are generally brought into play only after other less costly efforts have clearly failed and when the issue is sufficiently important to the opponents to continue opposing its consideration. High-cost strategies involve electoral, economic, and legal threats, as well as economic sanctions or legal actions, arrest, imprisonment, and organized violence directed against the initiating group.

Affected groups may direct actions toward elected public officials, threatening to withhold a group's support for a particular official or to actively support an opponent. An increasingly common threat is that if the outside group does not desist, it will be sued and face the prospect of a costly legal battle (Lipsky 1968). Land developers often want to build new projects that could threaten the environment. Local environmental groups try to get on the local formal agenda to block such efforts. Developers have used Strategic Lawsuits Against Public Participation (SLAPPs) against environmentalists to keep them from placing political obstacles in the way of their desired projects. Indeed, the Sierra Club has been the "nation's leading SLAPP target" (Pring and Canan 1996, 85). Public officials have used the tactic against citizens who criticized their conduct at public meetings. SLAPPs have also been used by companies to intimidate consumers and threaten those who complain about unsafe working conditions (Pring and Canan 1996, 128–42). Boyle notes that "SLAPPS seem to be proliferating almost everywhere. Police, teacher, and other public employee organizations are SLAPPing critics . . . [and] landlords are SLAPPing tenants." The overwhelming majority of SLAPPs are eventually dropped or thrown out of court, but "the average case dragged on for three years, costing defendants time, money and emotional stress" (Boyle 1991, 4).

Using electoral sanctions against initiating groups can often be done effectively only by the most powerful opponent groups. Over the past thirty years, gun control has been part of the public agenda (Page and Shapiro 1992, 94–7), yet the item has rarely made it onto the formal agenda of the U.S. Senate. One of the reasons is that the opposing group, the National Rifle Association (NRA), has been successful in threatening and targeting legislators and subsequently defeating them for not being vigilant in protecting its interests. In great part, the NRA's power as an opponent group is rooted in legislators' reelection fears and how the NRA's three million members and $100 million annual budget will be used (Puga 1994, B6).

The threat of economic sanctions is sometimes used to oppose consideration of an issue. Jackman, in chapter 6, shows how antiabortion forces threatened a Catholic hospital boycott of pharmaceutical products made by European pharmaceutical producers Hoechst A and Roussel Uclaf, which manufacture the RU 486 abortion pill, to prevent Food and Drug Administration (FDA) consideration. In fact, for several months, threats of possible boycotts dominated the debate over importing this European abortion pill to the United States.

In addition to suing people for exercising their First Amendment rights, opponent groups are taking the strategy of suing initiators to another level. They are trying to defuse critics' efforts by precluding them from speaking out in the first place. Food producers are increasingly coming under the scrutiny of consumer groups and nutritionists concerning the extent to which their claims about food products are accurate. In an effort to silence these critics, twelve states have passed (and four states are considering) "food disparagement" laws. These laws make it a crime to criticize perishable items without having a carefully re-searched scientific basis. As one lobbyist for the food industry said, "The food industry is tired of being the target of any activist with the price of a full-price ad, activists who decide to scare the bejesus out of the public." In most states where these laws are in effect, those convicted can go to prison for a year and may have to pay the plaintiff for financial loss (Oldenburg 1996, 2A).

One way to attack issue initiators is to pass a law making their issue illegal. For example, in Michigan, Dr. Jack Kevorkian has attained worldwide attention since his first successful effort to help a seriously ill patient commit suicide in 1990. He advocates a legal right to die for patients. After Kevorkian helped a number of individuals end their lives, Michigan passed a law against medically assisted death specifically to stop Kevorkian's efforts. In this case it was unsuc-cessful, because it failed to deter Kevorkian, and state judges found the law un-constitutional. However, this action forced Kevorkian to devote some of his lim-ited resources to fighting the legal challenge (Lessenberry 1994, 5).

Public officials sometimes use incarceration or the threat of incarceration to cause problems for initiating groups that use extralegal tactics such as sit-ins or street blockades to draw attention to a grievance. This strategy taxes the commit-ment of initiators and their ability to provide substitute leadership while their leaders are in jail. In addition, they must have the money to obtain legal assis-tance. This can be expensive and time-consuming, depending on the charges that the arresting officers make. Detention has a risk for the opponent group, however. It can make martyrs out of those arrested and increase the commitment of the aggrieved group to its cause.

At the far end of the continuum are threats involving physical force against either specific individuals or large groups in the population. Such threats are hardly made casually, and opponents are usually aware of the risks to their own images in the wider population if they actually implement them. The deterrent effect, however, is often outweighed by the desire to destroy supporters of a new issue, as the frequent use of political violence and repression in the world attests. Jackman shows in chapter 6 that antiabortion groups made such threats to keep RU 486 off the market. Given the previous use of violence by groups such as Op-eration Rescue, the threat was credible. As the more militant wing of the anti-abortion movement became interested in the RU 486 issue, the impact of this threat was considered carefully by all parties involved in the conflict.[7]

Finally, the ultimate strategy is physical beating and death. Opposition groups have used terror for several hundred years in the South to keep blacks from mobilizing to place their grievances on the formal agenda. Similar violence has characterized union development and the suppression of other minority groups. However, opponents face the danger that if the attendant publicity places the outsider in a victimized status, their tactics will not sustain public support for long. For example, media attention finally forced southern sheriffs to aban-don this tactic in dealing with civil rights supporters in the 1960s, as the federal government intervened in local conflicts where it had previously ignored them (Garrow 1978).

The array of tactics that opponents can use to keep new issues off the formal agenda is summarized in Table 2.1. Normally, the least costly strategies are tried first; then a gradual escalation occurs that involves greater opponent commitment and investment in time and other resources. If all these strategies fail and public officials and private opponents cannot keep an issue off the formal agenda, they will continue to oppose it in other arenas. However, most opposition strategies—even if they do not work in the long run—will keep initiating groups' issues off the formal agenda for a while and raise the cost to initiators.

CONCLUSION

One of the major battles in politics is who will control the political agenda. Agenda conflicts are about what issues government will act on; they are also about alternative interpretations of political problems and the acceptance and rejection of competing worldviews. In agenda conflicts, there are two main groups of actors: the initiators and the opponents. The former represent the possibilities for change in the political system. They express grievances by naming problems, blaming the forces that cause them, and claiming a need for public action to galvanize political support. In this way, the political system can be responsive to the grievances of disadvantaged peoples that need to be addressed. However, there is another group that represents opposition to political change and has a commitment to the status quo. They are the opponents, who have a vested interest in keeping the political agenda limited to those issues that are currently being discussed and not including any new items. As long as the agenda is not altered in any significant way, their material and symbolic positions will not be affected.

The political process involves a continuing conflict between these two forces. The name and the content of the issues change, but the main characteristics of the two sides do not. In most cases, the forces for the status quo are victorious and the political agenda continues, with battles over recurrent but few new issues. The problems facing issue innovators are many. They lack political funds, experience, and large numbers of dues-paying supporters. In most instances, those elements can be found in the arsenal of the opponents. However, initiators often have other weapons that the opponents cannot match, such as intensity or commitment to a cause.

Faced with a challenge, an opponent seeks to respond strategically while using resources as efficiently as possible. In fact, resources alone are often insufficient to blunt a demand. What is required is to meet a set of words and themes with a counter set of ideas. The contest is first one of nonrecognition, and when that is no longer possible, it becomes one of problem definition in which each side elaborates a set of themes that resonate with the mass public. The contestant that

Table 2.1. Strategies Used to Deny Agenda Access

Low-cost Strategies

    Nonrecognition of a problem

    Denial that a problem exists

    Refusal to recognize the groups that are pushing an issue

Medium-cost Strategies: Attack

    Reversal of roles: claim victim status

    If group legitimacy is low: discredit the group advocating the issue

        Link it with unpopular groups

        Question ethics, behavior of leaders

        Blame group for problem

        Use deception: release false information

    If group legitimacy is high: discredit the issue itself

        State that issue is not a legitimate public concern

        Dispute facts of the case

        State that concerns are isolated incidents

        Raise fears of the general public

        Focus on problem definition by stressing issue characteristics that buttress the opponent:

            Ambiguity: raise fears

            Socially significant impact that is negative (many people harmed)

            Negative spillover (generations to come will pay)

            Clear precedent (current policy adequate)

            High complexity (people can't comprehend it)

Medium-cost Strategies: Symbolic Placation

        Invoke community norms, such as loyalty

        Showcase by narrowly defining the problem

        Co-opt leaders or group's symbols

        Create a commission to study the problem

        Postpone

High-cost Strategies

        Electoral threats or withholding of support

        Economic threats or actual sanctions

        Legal threats or actions (laws, suits, incarceration)

        Physical threats or actions (physical beatings, murder)

does the better job of linking its issue position to culturally rooted worldviews is usually victorious. This involves the use of cultural strategies, associating a proposal with powerful values and symbols. The opponent has a wide variety of strategies that can be used to reduce the impact of the initiator's argument. If effective, this will limit the intensity of the issue innovator to its own small core of adherents and preclude the initiator from attracting others to the cause. This set of tactics, when combined with the resource potential of the opponents, makes it clear why so few issues ever make it onto the formal and public agendas.

This discussion of agenda conflicts has two related goals that are demonstrated in the remaining chapters and to which we return in the concluding chapter. The first is to better understand the politics of agenda setting. Most prior work stressed the perspective of those working for the active consideration of new issues. Although it has certainly acknowledged the importance of opponents' strategies, the perspective tended to present opponents in one-dimensional terms. It is important to emphasize that opposition is often rooted in the deeply felt fears that new proposals engender and that the intensity of opposition is tied to the specific material interests at stake, as well as to the deeply held threats to identity that the worldview of initiators and their proposals embodies.

The next seven chapters examine cases of agenda denial in which each author provides details about how agenda denial occurred and directly addresses issues central to the themes raised in this chapter. In the final chapter of the book, we return to these questions and attempt to draw lessons concerning the conceptual value of our scheme based on the contributors' cases. Medium-cost symbolic strategies are particularly common among opponents, and high-cost strategies involving severe threats and the use of violence are relatively infrequent. We hypothesize that this is a crucial feature of policy conflicts in contemporary U.S. politics and not just a function of the cases presented here, and we suggest why this is the case.

The second goal we emphasize is recognition of the importance of identity politics in each of the agenda conflicts presented. One does not have to look at dramatic issues such race or gender politics to find identity politics. Even apparently technical matters such as securities regulation or the use of bovine growth hormone engage identity issues that shape the outcome of the conflict.

NOTES

1. In the case of ambiguity, opponents attempt to blur the issue by raising extraneous concerns. Other issue characteristics are reversed. Issue opponents argue that the issue does not have social significance (i.e., does not affect everyone, or not many beyond the initiating group) or temporal relevance (i.e., has no spillover potential and will not influence the future). They also use complexity (i.e., argue that the issue is much more complex

than the initiators realize) and categorical precedence (i.e., the issue is not unique and has already been dealt with).

2. Terms of attack include any negatively perceived groups, such as "polluters," "exploiters," "homosexuals," "quacks," or "antifamily groups." One of the most effective strategies is to deny the link to a positive symbol. This makes the initiating group "anti-American" or "un-American."

3. Mahon and Waddock (1992, 27–8) argue that symbolic action normally precedes substantive actions or attempts to deal with a problem. This is possible but is not a matter that we consider here.

4. Edelman (1964, 82) argues that Hoover's denial that there was a depression deprived him of the ability to take credit for any government actions to battle it. Roosevelt, in contrast, by promising vigorous, albeit vague, action to cope with the widely perceived crisis, gained widespread support during the 1932 election campaign.

5. This strategy enjoyed limited success.

6. That is not to say that all commissions are symbolic overtures. Many of the policies of Lyndon Johnson's Great Society were originally developed through the use of a series of task forces (Wood 1993). The National Commission on Social Security Reform appointed in 1981 by President Reagan did not create a solution for dealing with the needs of the elderly, but it helped create a contrived situation out of which significant legislation emerged to deal with the issue in 1983 (Light 1985).

7. Pruitt and Rubin (1986) point out that a great advantage of credible threats is that they cost nothing to those who make them if they produce the desired response from an opponent. In contrast, promises are problematic when the promiser has to deliver.

REFERENCES

Alabama requires boaters to get license. 1994. *New York Times,* April 29, p. A14.

Bachrach, P., and M. Baratz, 1970. *Power and poverty.* New York: Oxford University Press.

Boyle, R. H. 1991. Activists at risk of being SLAPPed. *Sports Illustrated,* March 25, pp. 4, 6–8.

Cobb, R. W., and C. D. Elder. 1983. *Participation in American politics: The dynamics of agenda-building.* Baltimore: Johns Hopkins University Press.

Coleman, J. 1957. *Community conflict.* New York: Free Press.

Davis, S. 1995. The role of communication and symbolism in interest group competition: The case of the Siskiyou National Forest, 1983–1992. *Political Communication* 12:27–42.

DeParle, J. 1994. Casinos become big players in the overhaul of welfare. *New York Times,* May 9, pp. A1, A9.

Downs, A. 1972. Up and down with ecology: The issue attention cycle. *Public Interest* 28:38–50.

Edelman, M. 1964. *The symbolic uses of politics.* Urbana: University of Illinois Press.

Eyestone, R. 1978. *From social issues to public policy.* New York: Wiley.

Fritsch, J. 1996. Nature groups say foes bear friendly names. *New York Times,* March 25, pp. A1, A12.

Garrow, D. 1978. *Protest at Selma.* New Haven, CT: Yale University Press.

Hilts, P. J. 1994a. Tobacco company was silent on hazards. *New York Times,* May 7, pp. 1, 11.

———. 1994b. Tobacco maker studied risk but did little about results. *New York Times,* June 17, pp. A1, A22.

Ibarra, P. R., and J. I. Kitsuse. 1993. Vernacular constituents of moral discourse: An interactionist proposal for the study of social problems. In *Constructionist controversies: Issues in social problems theory,* edited by G. Miller and J. A. Holstein. New York: Aldine de Gruyter.

Iyengar, S. 1991. *Is anyone responsible? How television frames political issues.* Chicago: University of Chicago Press.

Kolbert, E. 1993. New arena for campaign ads: Health care. *New York Times,* October 21, pp. A1, A20.

Lessenberry, J. 1994. Kevorkian says he'll form group, rules for aiding suicides. *Boston Globe,* May 5, p. 5.

Lewin, T. 1994. Founder of anti-drunk-driving group now lobbies for breweries. *New York Times,* January 15, p. A7.

Light, P. 1985. *Artful work: The politics of social security reform.* New York: Random House.

Lipsky, M. 1968. Protest as a political resource. *American Political Science Review* 62:1144–58.

Mahon, J., and S. Waddock. 1992. Strategic issues management: An integration of issue life cycle perspectives. *Business and Society* 31(1): 19–32.

New riots, old story, panel finds. 1992. *New York Times,* October 4, p. 36.

Oldenburg, A. 1996. Industry turns to laws on "food disparagement." *USA Today,* March 27, pp. 1A, 2A.

Page, B., and R. Shapiro. 1992. *The rational public: 50 years of trends in American politics.* Chicago: University of Chicago Press.

Primack, J., and F. von Hippel. 1974. *Advice and dissent: Scientists in the political arena.* New York: Basic Books.

Pring, G. W., and P. Canan. 1996. *SLAPPs: Getting sued for speaking out.* Philadelphia: Temple University Press.

Pruitt, D., and J. Rubin. 1986. *Social conflict: Escalation, stalemate and settlement.* New York: Random House.

Puga, A. 1994. After gun vote, the postmortem: Can NRA revive? *Boston Globe,* May 8, p. B6.

Radin, C. A. 1994. Denial of acid rain dissolving in Japan. *Boston Globe,* April 2, pp. 1, 11.

Reich, M. R. 1991. *Toxic politics: Responding to chemical disasters.* Ithaca, NY: Cornell University Press.

Stone, D. 1988. *Policy paradox and political reason.* Glenview, IL: Scott, Foresman.

Wald, M. L. 1996. An F.A.A. reluctant to change. *New York Times,* June 24, p. A12.

Wise, D. 1996. A report that blesses espionage-as-usual. *Los Angeles Times,* March 17, pp. M2, M6.

Wood, R. 1993. *Whatever possessed the president? Academic experts and presidential policy, 1960–1988.* Amherst: University of Massachusetts Press.

PART II
The Securities and Exchange Commission

3

Agenda Denial and Issue Containment in the Regulation of Financial Securities: The SEC, 1933–1995

Billy R. Hall Jr. and Bryan D. Jones

The Securities and Exchange Commission (SEC) has been touted as the most successful regulatory agency in the federal government. One might view this reputation in two separate lights: It may be the case that the SEC is successful in meeting its objectives. However, it may also be the case that the agency is extremely adept at defending its approach to regulating the nation's capital markets, an approach that centers fundamentally on disclosure rather than proscription.

In this chapter, we examine securities regulation historically, beginning with the conditions that led to the establishment of the basic national framework for securities regulation in the 1930s. Since then, the SEC and its allies have generally been able, through a variety of strategies, to preclude serious agenda access to reform proposals demanded by critics on the Left, who claim that the SEC is too protective of exploitation in the nation's capital markets, and by those on the Right, who claim that the SEC interferes too much in the markets, harming the capital formation process.

The history of the SEC can be divided into four periods. The first and most crucial period was the era of formation, in which the basic framework for securities regulation was put into place. Given the hostility toward corporate capitalism at the time, government supervision of the capital markets was a real possibility. Instead, Congress opted for a disclosure-enforcement framework, in which the capital markets remained private and no securities instruments were outlawed. Rather, issuers were required to follow disclosure procedures that, if violated, could result in civil or criminal proceedings.

Once the major framework was put into place, it became a powerful instrument for the defense of minimal influence in the capital markets. Indeed, the second period in the development of securities regulation was one of quiescence and capture, with the SEC acting so passively that Marver Bernstein, in his classic *Regulating Business by Independent Commission* (1955), predicted its demise. Instead, scandals and Democratic administrations revitalized securities regulation. By the mid-1970s, Democratic critics were calling for a national market system, threatening the existing exchanges. SEC bureaucrats successfully contained the issue, working within the disclosure-enforcement framework and bringing the major exchanges on board with incremental reforms. Finally, the modern era has been characterized by a Right-based attack on the regulatory framework, with Republican congresspeople calling for an abandonment of the neutral disclosure-enforcement framework in favor of an orientation that would promote the formation of capital.

The SEC, then, has developed its own set of procedures, complete with an agenda for action and justifying ideology. Disclosure-enforcement merges with an ideology supportive of capitalism to produce an agenda for action that emphasizes maximizing the flow of information for investors and minimizing interference in the securities markets. The linkage between ideas and procedures produced an extraordinarily successful policy monopoly (Baumgartner and Jones 1993) that has put opponents of the system continually on the defensive. Indeed, throughout most of the history of the SEC, reform proposals, mostly from the Left but more recently from the Right, have been denied agenda access. That is, proposals are often dismissed out of hand, not taken seriously because of the perceived unassailability of the disclosure-enforcement framework.

Nevertheless, the issue of securities regulation has occasionally reached the formal agenda of the policy-making branches of government, often because of a scandal in which an unregulated or lightly regulated aspect of securities markets has led to problems. This indicates that the SEC's success in warding off serious reform has not been because of the absence of problems in the regulatory environment but because of the manner in which the SEC and its allies in Congress and elsewhere have responded to the challenges. In general, issues have been limited to incremental adjustments to the basic framework.

In accounting for the success of various strategies directed at agenda control, it is important to factor in the macropolitical environment. We focus here both on periods of quiescence in the agency's environment, during which a combination of disinterest on the part of opponents and active agenda denial took place, and on more turbulent periods, during which the agency and its allies engaged in strategies of issue containment. Given the historical perspective we take in this chapter, it is sometimes difficult to distinguish between active strategies to deny agenda access and apathy on the part of agency critics. However, historical records suggest that when the agency becomes lethargic in its enforcement duties and fails to defend adequately its fundamental disclosure-enforcement framework, it may suffer attacks that are at least successful in getting the issue of securities regulation on the agenda and may actually result in changes in the securities laws.

When it is under attack, however, the agency has been extraordinarily successful in what it has had to yield. During periods of turbulence, the agency defends its disclosure-enforcement framework through two major strategies. First, the agency is adept at what Cobb and Ross in chapter 2 call symbolic placation strategies. In the case of the SEC, threats to the regulatory framework are met by warnings that regulation can impede or even destroy the capital markets, with dire consequences for economic activity in the United States. The second major strategic device used by the SEC is a variant of what Cobb and Ross call showcasing. That is, it is rare for the SEC to try to defeat the reformists in high-cost, head-on strategies. Rather, there is a tendency to admit the problem and offer incremental regulatory solutions within the basic framework. This generally defuses the critics, but it also means that the agency has had to compromise, and this set of compromises over time has created a stable, but not toothless, regulatory operation.

This successful regulatory agency contrasts vividly with the subsystems studied by Baumgartner and Jones in *Agendas and Instability in American Politics* (1993). The episodic interruption of the regulatory subsystems centering on industry and commerce that they describe does not characterize securities regulation. Although major challenges have been mounted, the SEC has adjusted and survived with enhanced reputation. In great part, this success has resulted from the SEC's ability to make attacks on its general framework unthinkable and, when the unthinkable occasionally becomes thinkable, to contain the larger issue through incremental adjustment.

Successful regulatory actions over long periods of time require the ability to both undermine the confidence of opponents that their attacks are worthwhile, thereby effectively denying them agenda access, and contain the damage when opponents' concerns do gain access to the agenda. The SEC has been perhaps the most successful of the nation's regulatory agencies. How can we account for this success? We show in this chapter that the regulatory framework adopted in the early years of the SEC, the disclosure-enforcement framework, has served as a powerful defense to demands for both more and less regulation of the financial securities markets (on disclosure-enforcement, see Khademian 1992). This approach is based on the notion that regulators ought not interfere with markets themselves, but they ought to ensure that investors have the full information necessary to make rational decisions. If companies fail to disclose the proper information, the basis for enforcement actions exists.

The disclosure-enforcement framework is a regulatory process, but it is much more. It is fundamentally an ideology of government actions in capitalist markets. Over time, it has become powerful and persuasive—more powerful, we argue, than the specific realpolitik of interactions among participants in the securities regulation subsystem. The power of this framework has been instrumental in denying agenda access to such Left reforms as government supervision of a national exchange system and Right reforms such as the use of the SEC to promote capital formation (rather than be a neutral arbiter), and it is the power of this policy monopoly that has allowed SEC regulators to work with the major exchanges to make incremental changes in the existing laws and regulations, such as regulations relating to insider trading. This joint strategy of agenda denial to radical proposals and issue containment when proposals do emerge is primarily responsible for the incremental nature of securities reforms.

SUBSYSTEMS AND POLITICAL CHANGE

Subsystems are defined as "clusters of individuals that effectively make most of the routine decisions in a given substantive area of policy" (Ripley and Franklin 1987, 8). Subsystems may become established for the express purpose of regulating an industry, or they may result from explicit subsidy or promotional activities by government. In both cases, there has been a tendency for affected industries, congressional policy makers (especially those occupying key committee and subcommittee positions), and executive agency bureaucrats to establish formal and informal networks of communication that support the status quo.

This policy network operates mostly out of the limelight of the national political agenda, a behind-the-scenes policy style that insulates the subsystem from outside interference. The result is an arrangement that acts to protect a mutually beneficial policy arrangement (Bosso 1987; Browne 1986; Cobb and Elder 1983; Dodd and Schott 1979; Freeman 1965; Griffith 1939; Jenkins-Smith, St. Clair, and Woods 1991; Maass 1951; Redford 1969). These relationships bring stability to an issue area. When threatened, participating institutions rally around the policy-making status quo. Because of the power of subsystems to stabilize an issue area, scholars have inferred a whole system of government based on mutually noninterfering subsystems, a system that is highly resistant to democratic change (Lowi 1979).

Financial securities regulation seems to fit the classic subsystem pattern. With financial securities issues, control of the regulatory process is not lodged solely with the government's Securities and Exchange Commission. It is divided between the SEC and a number of self-regulatory organizations, such as stock exchanges and the National Association of Securities Dealers (Ratner 1988, 193). The exchanges have a great deal of discretion in regulating the markets. This opportunity to participate in market regulation demonstrates why commercial groups pledge their support. Regulated firms gladly tolerate constraints and, once established, would protest their removal out of fear of market disarray. Members of legislative committees tend to follow the lead of their subsystem constituents. When challenges come from the outside—whether from the executive, the media, or public attention in general—each member of the subsystem rallies in support of the policy framework.

The problem with finding explanations of policy stability within a mutually reinforcing network of noninterfering subsystems is that the facts contradict such explanations. Subsystems in the United States are not incrementally drifting clusters of legislators, bureaucrats, and interested parties who operate at local equilibria. Interventions by the macropolitical institutions (Congress, the president, and the political parties) have been regular historical occurrences in U.S. politics (Redford 1969). Waves of dramatic change have both created the political environments conducive to the establishment of subsystems and torn down the institutional structure supporting other subsystems (Baumgartner and Jones 1993; Mayhew 1991). Actors must then forge new institutions and thus new subsystem relationships.

Securities regulation, however, has experienced no major disruption in its basic nature since its founding in the 1930s (although certainly an occasional threat has emerged on the national policy agenda). So the question we pose is this: why has the securities regulatory subsystem conformed so closely to the classic stability-enhancing subsystem while so many other subsystems have been wracked by major changes?

We propose two general explanations that can potentially account for the success of the securities regulatory subsystem in the United States. One explanation concerns the unique position of financial regulation in the capitalist economy. It is therefore a *structural* explanation. The second concerns the strategies and tactics employed by subsystem participants to deny agenda access to reformers and to contain issue expansion once a reform proposal has reached the agenda. This is a *strategic* explanation.

Financial securities provide unique challenges to regulators, challenges that could account for differences in subsystem histories. A security has no intrinsic value in itself, but represents rights in something else. Securities are created rather than produced, and they are not used or consumed by their purchasers (Ratner 1988, 1–3). The rights of ownership (for stocks) or repayment with interest (for bonds) are bought and sold in complex financial markets, as are more exotic rights such as options and futures. These financial markets offer efficient mechanisms for raising capital for business expansion and for handling complex transactions that could not be performed without the buying and selling of pieces of paper (today, simply electronic notations). Unlike any other regulatory target, financial securities are essential to the operation of modern capitalism. As a consequence, they occupy a favored place in the regulatory structure of government.

There is no reason that the particular system of securities regulation that has developed in the United States is necessary for the conduct of capitalism. Indeed, markets in other nations are both more and less regulated than those in the United States, depending on the nation. So it seems that one must turn to more strategic-type explanations to understand the particular successes of the securities regulatory system in the United States. In doing so, we turn first to a brief overview of the history of securities regulation in the United States.

THE SECURITIES MARKETS AND THE NATIONAL POLICY AGENDA

The key issues for this chapter are how the members of the securities regulation subsystem are able to keep out of the national limelight and how, if public attention does focus on the subsystem, the issue is contained. It is important at the outset to distinguish between two key concepts. First, Cobb and Elder (1983) distinguish between the *public* and the *formal* agendas. In the following discussion, we define the formal agenda as attention to securities matters by Congress; the public agenda is indicated by coverage by major newspapers. We use coverage in the *Washington Post* and the *Wall Street Journal* to indicate public agenda access, with the *Wall Street Journal* being more indicative of the specialized public focusing on capital market activities. We also examined the historical record for indications of agenda concern.

Second, it is important to keep in mind Kingdon's (1994) distinction between problems and solutions. To some extent, solutions and problems are separate. Because a problem is put on the agenda does not imply that a solution will be attached to the problem. Indeed, a major strategy of the leadership in the securities regulatory subsystem has been to immediately offer a solution to any problems that emerge in the financial markets. This problem-solution package, the disclosure-enforcement framework, becomes a bulwark in the defense of the subsystem. Jones and Bachelor (1993) termed such problem-solution packages *solution sets*.

The ability to offer a set solution to problems as they arise on to the public agenda means that issues may be more readily contained than if there were no ready answers to the problem. Moreover, to the extent that solution sets fit with powerful prevailing ideologies, they may serve to deter erstwhile reformers from raising other possible solutions in the first place. Although defenders of a policy arrangement may be unable to block the ascendancy of the problem to the agenda, they may be able to forestall the emergence of solutions that would not be in keeping with the prevailing policy arrangement. In the case of securities regulation, the symbolic power of disclosure-enforcement has thwarted efforts to initiate more regulation of markets in the face of scandals, market manipulations, and market collapses, but that same symbolic power has also deterred major scaling back of market regulation in the broad-scale deregulation movement. Agenda denial has occurred, but so has issue containment. When reform proposals have gained momentum, the SEC and its supporters have generally countered with modifications in the disclosure-enforcement framework that allegedly solve the problem.

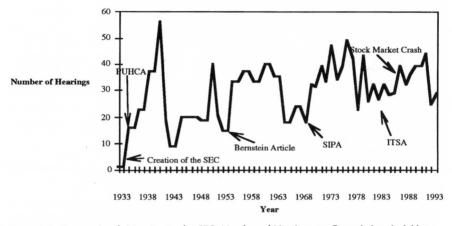

Figure 3.1. Congressional Attention to the SEC: Number of Hearings on Commission Activities. Source: Congressional Information Service.

The Initial Ascendancy to the National Agenda (1932–1940)

By the 1920s, certain problems that were seemingly endemic to unregulated markets were becoming evident. These problems included price manipulation, the excessive use of credit to finance speculative activities, and the misuse of corporate information by insiders. State governments became concerned with certain deceptive practices regarding so-called bucket shops and, in the absence of federal interest, passed the so-called blue sky laws to regulate them. The first serious federal interest in securities regulation came in the wake of the 1929 stock market decline and subsequent economic depression.

Figure 3.1 presents the number of congressional hearings that focused on issues of securities regulation.[1] The figure shows that in 1932, congressional committees began an extensive period of hearings on securities activity. Congressional interest peaked in 1940 and has never been as high since, even though congressional capacity to hold hearings has generally expanded greatly over the years. This period of intense interest corresponds to the establishment of the subsystem.

In March 1932, the Senate, still under the control of the Republicans, passed a resolution allowing the Banking and Currency Committee to investigate the securities industry (Skousen 1991, 6). These hearings uncovered numerous fraudulent practices. For example, stock pools regularly employed publicists to plant news tips with journalists during pool operations. Later, the committee would write that "the annals of finance present no counterpart to this enormous decline in security prices" and market trust (Seligman 1994, C1).

Franklin D. Roosevelt, in his first inaugural address in 1933, denounced the financial industry: "Practices of the unscrupulous money-changers stand indicted in the court of public opinion, rejected by the hearts and minds of men" (Levitt

1994, C8). He hoped to bring the markets under federal supervision. One of the first matters of business in the first hundred days of Roosevelt's New Deal was the Securities Act of 1933. This legislation focused on the initial distribution of securities to the public (Coleman 1985, 156). It was designed to protect investors from false claims (which abounded before the stock market crash) by regulating the initial offering and actual sale of securities through the mail system. Often referred to as the "truth in securities" law, Skousen argues that its basic objective is "to ensure that investors are given full and fair disclosure of all pertinent information about a firm" (1991, 22).

With the issue of securities regulation firmly on the national agenda, opponents of regulation turned to strategies of issue containment. Wall Street hoped to block any new legislative attempts and to dilute the provisions of the 1933 act. Richard Whitney, president of the New York Stock Exchange, led the opposition. When he saw that a new law creating a special regulatory agency was likely to be passed, Whitney shifted strategies to influence the resulting legislation—in particular, to include industry representation and self-regulation by the established stock exchanges. The Securities and Exchange Commission was created at the conclusion of the Senate Banking and Currency Committee's 1932–1934 investigation of stock exchange practices. Unlike the initial 1933 Securities Act, which is restricted to initial offerings, the 1934 Securities Exchange Act extends the full and fair disclosure doctrine to companies with securities regulated on national exchanges (Skousen 1991, 26).

The SEC's authority was extended in the Public Utility Holding Company Act of 1935; the Maloney Act of 1935, which mandated self-regulation of over-the-counter trading; the Trust Indenture Act of 1939; and the Investment Company Act of 1940. The ICA was the last act in the flurry of New Deal securities regulation; it applied the disclosure framework to mutual-fund companies.

The 1930s was a period of vigorous national governmental activity, and financial regulation was no exception. The frameworks for national regulation of financial operations—banks, savings and loans, and the financial markets—were put into place. Business interests, discredited by the recession, fought a rearguard, on-the-agenda action to weaken regulation as much as possible and to include business interests within the regulatory frameworks. The list below summarizes the major legislation affecting the regulation of securities. More than half were passed between 1933 and 1940.

Securities Regulation: Major Acts

1933	Securities Act
1934	Securities Exchange Act
1935	Public Utility Holding Company Act (PUHCA)
1935	Maloney Act
1939	Trust Indenture Act
1940	Investment Company Act (ICA)

1964	Securities Act Amendments
1970	Securities Investor Protection Act (SIPA)
1975	Securities Act Amendments
1977	Foreign Corrupt Practices Act (1977)
1984	Insider Trading Sanctions Act (ITSA)

Source: Hall 1995.

By 1940, the subsystem's regulatory framework was in place, and its benefits were becoming obvious to participants (Khademian 1992, 57). SEC founders realized that for a competitive market to function well, buyers need sufficient information. The rationale for government action rests on the belief that competitive pressures are not adequate to provide the consumer with reliable detail. Thus, the SEC was created to review the issuance of securities through disclosure. Regulators focus on the disclosure of relevant information and use their enforcement powers against the manipulation of disclosure requirements.

At its inception, the Securities and Exchange Commission lacked the resources to oversee industry activities. The SEC opted for neither a huge regulatory bureaucracy nor an aggressive attack on predatory corporations. Rather, the agency worked with the exchanges, with corporations, and with private-sector accountants to forge a mixed public-private system of regulation (Stillman 1992). Regulators decided to focus on the disclosure of relevant information and to use enforcement actions against the manipulation of these requirements. Under the tutelage of Chairman James Landis (1936–1938), this initial cooperative approach helped the SEC oversee the market and adapt to a dynamic environment (Kohlmeier 1969; Pointer and Schroeder 1986; Khadamian 1992).

Quiescence and Capture (1940–1960)

A void in securities legislation should not be surprising in time of war. World War II brought growth in the regulatory powers of the federal government (Lieberman 1991, 67). However, a wartime economy hampered the commission's ability to initiate legislation. More than one-third of the agency's staff was drafted (Khademian 1992, 58). The SEC's budget was cut significantly. Figure 3.2 shows a drastic drop in the budget as a percentage of federal outlays from 1940 to 1945, a drop from which the commission never recovered. Government was growing after the war, but so was the economy; clearly, securities regulation had been crowded off the national agenda by other matters. Congressional hearings dropped to an all-time low during the war and stabilized at a low level from 1942 through 1955 (with the exception of 1950).

Even if the SEC had remained at full funding levels, the agency likely would not have expanded its mandate. Dwight D. Eisenhower entered the White House with a charge to cut government spending and reduce regulation (Eisenhower

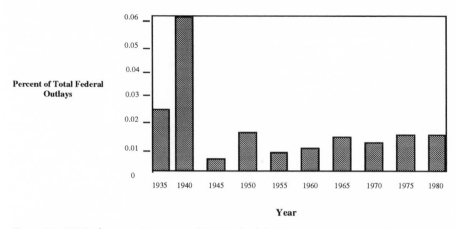

Figure 3.2. SEC Budget as a Percentage of Total Federal Outlays. Source: SEC Annual Reports.

1960). SEC Chairman Ralph Demmler, nominated by Eisenhower in 1953, shared the administration's agenda (Khademian 1992, 58). In 1953, 1954, and 1955, the Budget Bureau recommended reductions in the budget. Therefore, reduced funding levels, coupled with the loss of personnel, hindered the commission from promulgating any new regulations.

Although established regulatory responsibilities were secure, SEC attentiveness to market fraud was lethargic during the period. In the 1950s, a classic Wall Street stock market manipulation was carried out on the American Stock Exchange (Kohlmeier 1969, 237). Certainly those in charge of the American Stock Exchange were at fault, but the SEC also shirked responsibility in detecting the fraud. There were numerous other cases in the 1950s in which obvious manipulation of corporate finances occurred, and the commission was simply not able, or did not feel that it was able, to act aggressively to protect shareholders. Phillips and Zecher found that, throughout the 1940s and 1950s, the scholarly community reported that the SEC had disappeared from the regulatory scene (1981, 13). The enforcement rate throughout the period remained at the same level as when the commission was created, yet the budget of the SEC actually shrank until the 1960s.

The typical commission response was to retreat to the disclosure-enforcement framework, with an emphasis on disclosure. The security regulatory laws, according to the regulators, did not make the SEC "arbiter as to whether corporations should or should not do certain things. Its mission is basically to see that they tell the public what they are doing" (Fortune 1959, 88). Markets worked best if left alone, and the commission should do no more than require disclosure.

Figure 3.1 is indicative of the considerable congressional concern about securities scandals during the 1950s, with hearings almost doubling during the latter part of the decade. However, no corrective legislation was passed into law, and there is little evidence that the commission became more aggressive in using the regulatory powers it possessed. The appeal to the sanctity of markets and the claim that rational investors would make correct decisions if the information were available served to dissuade erstwhile reformers from even raising issues of increased legislative powers or more aggressive enforcement. This period of quiescence allowed subsystem participants to use what Cobb and Ross in chapter 2 identify as low-cost strategies. Clearly problems existed, as the scandals of the mid-1950s indicated. However, reform efforts were weak and desultory, allowing the use of low-cost strategies by opponents of reform. Supporters of the status quo argued that disclosure was enough and that more regulatory activity could harm the market. The claim that policy initiatives can have dire unintended consequences is a common strategy among opponents of regulation. This appeal "to the market" raises powerful symbolic associations—so powerful that reform opponents may have to resort to modest containment strategies such as symbolic placation or showcasing.

This was the situation that Marver Bernstein encountered when he predicted the death of the SEC in 1955. Bernstein saw an agency captured by industry. He proposed a historical pattern that commissions follow from birth to decay and argued that evolutionary history is divided into four periods: gestation, youth, maturity, and decline. The fourth stage of the life cycle is old age passing into death, which is where he placed the SEC.

Containing Left Reform (1960–1980)

Captured agencies are, however, particularly vulnerable to reformist criticism. By 1960, the macroenvironment of securities regulation was on the verge of a dramatic shift. As the 1950s ended, the United States was about to embark on a period of intense governmental activism, lasting from the inauguration of President Kennedy in 1961 to the middle of the Carter administration (about 1978). This period of governmental activism, and the consumer movements that flowered in the late 1960s, changed the macropolitical environment for the securities regulatory subsystem. It was a period that produced the disruption of many industrial-regulatory subsystems (such as nuclear power) and the birth of new-style regulatory subsystems that were far less business-friendly (such as the regulation of consumer products and job safety).

The election of Kennedy in 1960 and a stock manipulation scandal (again on the American Exchange) at about the same time thrust the SEC back into the spotlight. In 1961, Congress began an investigation into stock market regulation, and the 1962 market decline following three years of speculative frenzy in glamour stocks (Skousen 1991, 9) added urgency to the effort. By 1963, the investigation produced the most extensive analysis of the stock market since the 1930s. The result was a revitalization of securities law, including the closing of major loopholes in the disclosure format relating to insider trading. The commission moved to encourage regulatory reforms on the exchanges and recommended that the disclosure format be extended by legislation to the over-the-counter securities markets (which were self-regulated under the 1938 Maloney Act). Congress passed amendments to the Securities Act in 1964 that authorized this.

By the 1970s, there was harsh criticism from the business community about business regulation by government, and Presidents Nixon, Ford, and Carter appointed chairmen of the major regulatory commissions who favored regulatory restraint. The rhetoric to reform congressional and regulatory commission action (Needham 1983, 395) created an interest-group wave of enthusiasm to deregulate the regulated industries in government (Lieberman 1991, 68). The SEC, however, was largely bypassed by the deregulatory fervor—perhaps because of the perceived sanctity of its disclosure-enforcement framework. Indeed, Congress pressed for increased investor protection. The Securities Investor Protection Act of 1970, an amendment to the Securities Exchange Act of 1934, created the Securities Investor Protection Corporation (SIPC). Congress also updated the 1940 Investment Company Act at the suggestion of the SEC. The Securities Act was amended once again in 1975 to extend the SEC's regulatory authority over over-the-counter securities trading.

The commission pursued enforcement in earnest throughout the decade. A declining market, failures on Wall Street, public dissatisfaction, and criticism from Congress pushed the agency into more aggressive enforcement. Some indication of the agency's aggressiveness can be gleaned from an examination of regulatory reporting releases filed by the commission. Reporting releases are prescribed methods of disclosure and SEC filing requirements. They have become the major public-sector pronouncements for fields such as financial accounting. Figure 3.3 shows a significant jump in reporting releases filed by the commission in the 1970s and, incidentally, indicates how passive the agency was during the 1950s and early 1960s. The increased activity can also be seen as part and parcel of a long-run strategy to contain Left reformist zeal through more aggressive use of the disclosure-enforcement mechanism. At the same time, it would not be correct to call this action what Cobb and Ross in chapter 2 term showcasing, for the actions were incremental modifications of the existing framework.

Another threat to the SEC and its enforcement framework occurred in 1975. The commission advocated a national market system to standardize individual stock exchange policies. Instead of threatening markets such as the New York Stock Exchange, the idea and its plan for implementation evolved under SEC guidance from within the industry. The post-Watergate Congress, heavily Democratic, was dissatisfied with this approach, however, and pushed the commission with 1975 amendments to take a more activist role and restructure the markets. Khademian explains that the legislation, "in addition to a mandate for structural reform, increased the SEC's power to oversee regulation, enhanced the SEC's preemptive rule-making authority, and increased the agency's enforcement capabilities" (1992, 82). A relaxed implementation of these directives by the SEC, which worked with the exchanges to garner approval on steps to expand author-

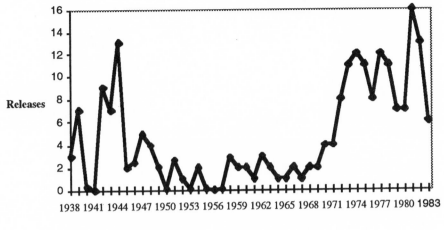

Figure 3.3. SEC Reporting Releases. Source: Pointer and Schroeder, 1986.

ity, limited the expansion of the issue as congressional attention turned to other matters.

Some idea of the intense political environment faced by securities regulators can be gleaned from an examination of Figure 3.4. There we tabulate the number of stories in the *Wall Street Journal* and the *Washington Post.* First, note that the *Journal* provides far more intensive coverage of the SEC than does the *Post,* but the series tend to rise and fall together.[2] In both papers, the mid to late 1970s were a high point of media interest. *Post* reporters wrote almost two hundred stories about the SEC in 1976 but by 1982 wrote fewer than ten. In 1960, the *Wall Street Journal* offered fewer than ten stories but offered an incredible six hundred in 1975. During the 1980s, coverage in the specialized press remained high—around two hundred per year until the late 1980s—but far less than at the high-water mark of the mid-1970s. General press coverage almost disappeared in the early 1980s.

The ebb and flow of media attention to securities regulation are one indicator of changes in the macropolitical environment of the subsystem. Clearly the agency operated in a different political environment in the 1970s than in the 1950s, 1960s, or 1980s. As a consequence, it adopted a more aggressive regulatory stance but continued to work closely with the securities industry and to defend the disclosure-enforcement framework.

Challenges from Left and Right (1980–1994)

Whereas the 1970s were a time of increased activity and exposure, with pressures to expand regulatory activities, the 1980s brought challenges from both the Right and the Left. The financial environment was one in which mergers and ac-

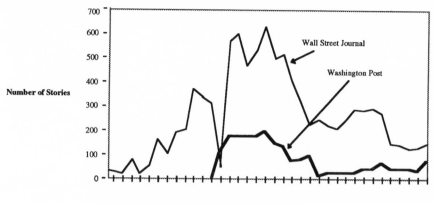

Figure 3.4. Media Coverage of the SEC.

quisitions, hostile and negotiated, flourished as never before (Fleischer and Fraidin 1994, C1). The Republican administration demanded deregulated financial markets, but Congress and vigorous consumer groups demurred. Despite vigorous deregulation efforts by the Reagan administration, "the scope, content, and consequences" of securities regulation increased in the 1980s (Wright 1988, 103). For example, the Insider Trading Sanctions Act was passed in 1984.

The most damaging case ever to face the SEC occurred late in the decade— the case of Ivan Boesky. Boesky was an arbitrageur convicted of trading on non-disclosed information, but not before he had bilked individual investors out of millions of dollars. The SEC engineered a settlement that most thought was too light. Congress criticized the commission to such an extent that it slowed down other important investigations, especially that of the junk bond scandal.

In this environment, the SEC adopted a survival approach (Fleischer and Fraidin 1994, C1–3). The agency vigorously enforced its ban on insider trading, attacking several high-profile targets, and it adopted investor protection rules. However, it maintained a neutral stance between bidder and target in the takeover wars of the 1980s. The agency generally maintained a conservative stance, conducting studies but not pushing for additional legislation. As in the past, when under pressure, the agency highlighted its adherence to the principle of free flow of information under its disclosure guidelines. When violations occurred, such as insider trading, the agency acted aggressively. When other alleged problems emerged, such as corporate takeover bids, the agency remained neutral and sought only to make sure that disclosure procedures were followed.

Perhaps even more indicative of the power of the disclosure framework was legislative response to the 500-point decline in the Dow-Jones industrial average on October 18, 1987. The collapse of 22.6 percent was far greater than the 12.8 percent decline of 1929. The causes were probably related to the speculative frenzy that continued in the face of rising interest rates, but many saw the use of new, exotic securities derivatives as a contributory factor. Congress held hearings but failed to produce legislation, as SEC staff argued that the disclosure framework would protect investors and that further intervention could cause additional market problems. The markets recovered, and congressional attention turned elsewhere.

The Modern Attack from the Right

For the first time in the history of the SEC, critics in 1995 demanded that the agency not only limit its regulation of the capital markets but also become an active promoter of capital formation. Republicans, having captured control of both houses of Congress in 1994, were determined to push financial deregulation. The centerpiece of the attack was a bill introduced by Democrat Jack Fields of Texas, chairman of the Telecommunications and Finance Subcommittee of the House Commerce Committee. Fields vowed that his bill would "bring the most sweeping reform of securities laws in the past 40 years" (Knight 1995). The bill required the SEC to not only protect the investing public but also promote "efficiency, competition, and capital formation" (Lowenstein 1995).

Key provisions of Fields's bill included cutting the Securities and Exchange Commission from five members to three, privatizing the SEC's corporation records computer system, ending federal regulation of borrowing by securities firms, and exempting mutual funds and other institutional investors from some commission investor protection rules. Most critically, the bill attacked the well-established disclosure-enforcement framework that provided the backbone of the SEC's regulatory strategy. That strategy hinges on full disclosure of activities and assumes that investors will digest the information and use it in their investment decisions. Fields's bill limited certain important disclosure requirements, including one involving takeover activity.

When committee hearings opened in November, however, the House plan looked much different. SEC allies had attacked the initial provisions in the securities law rewrite, and state securities regulators—the majority of them appointed by Republican governors—had organized resistance to the GOP proposal. The revised plan called for statutes that would actually strengthen existing SEC controls, such as giving the commission broad new authority to grant exemptions from outdated securities laws. Fields admitted that his committee was now looking at "a far less ambitious and far less speedy revision of the rules of Wall Street" (Knight 1995). Nevertheless, Congress passed, and overrode President Clinton's veto of, an act that significantly limited the ability of investors to sue companies when future earnings had been deliberately overestimated—a limitation on the disclosure-enforcement approach.

THE DISCLOSURE-ENFORCEMENT PROCESS AS AN AGENDA DENIAL AND ISSUE CONTAINMENT MECHANISM

Our brief overview of the securities regulation framework indicates the remarkable success of the system. Since its implementation, no major market disruptions have occurred, and there has been no widespread public antipathy toward market capitalism. Although scandals have wracked the exchanges, the securities regulation subsystem, through a combination of agenda denial and issue containment strategies, has been able to ride out the extensive public criticism and the many serious reform proposals from both the Right, with demands for deregulation and the active promotion of capital markets, and the Left, with demands for tighter regulation beyond the disclosure-enforcement framework.

The glue holding the securities subsystem and its policy resolution together has been the acceptance of and support for this disclosure-enforcement framework. The impact of a powerful enforcement idea, when associated with a subsystem, is great. Indeed, one of us has applied the term *policy monopoly* to policy subsystems in which a powerful idea has buttressed the typical realpolitik of subsystems. The core belief about process is communicated through both image and rhetoric (Baumgartner and Jones 1993, 7). If participants remain convinced that the process is necessary for a market's survival, the policy monopoly can sustain itself during periods of threat. Indeed, if the idea is powerful enough, it may dissuade reformers from even mounting an attack. A lobbyist supporting recent Republican reform efforts said, "Let's face it, this [the SEC] is an organization that is in many ways exemplary" (Lowenstein 1995).

Rourke (1984, 20) states that "nothing contributes more to bureaucratic power than the ability of career officials to mold the views of other participants in the policy process." The disclosure basis of investigatorial and prosecutorial actions in the securities subsystem rallies market participants to support agency decisions. Disclosure-enforcement can explain overall system resilience, as well as many individual issues that occupy the daily activities of securities policy participants. The institutions supporting this regulatory arrangement may be unstable and evolve with changing events and conditions, but they have found protection in a disclosure-based schema. The disclosure-enforcement process is the product of decisions by various parties. Experts and regulators, legislators and their constituents, and the administration all have preferences and political priorities regarding the regulation of securities, and all have various means of influencing the final outcome (Khademian 1992, 43). Yet the rule of the game for securities policy continues to be disclosure-enforcement.

PATH DEPENDENCE IN POLICY MAKING

William O. Douglas once commented that "the great creative work of a federal agency must be done in the first decade of its existence if it is to be done at all. After that it is likely to become a prisoner of bureaucracy and of the inertia demanded by the establishment of any respected agency" (Karmel 1982, 77). Douglas was right and wrong in the case of the SEC. He was wrong, because the SEC has demonstrated a vitality that allowed it to prosper and revitalize itself after a period of moribund capture in the 1950s. He was right, because the basic framework of the agency was established in its first decade, and its resiliency is very much due to the propitious choice of regulatory framework in those years.

All policy subsystems are *path dependent* (Jones 1994). That is, their current policy patterns are more heavily influenced by early events in their history than by later ones. Early in an agency's history, administrators must establish a framework for proceeding, a process that governs subsequent actions. The framework for these decision patterns provides a context, which in turn limits the number of alternatives to solving a problem. This rather narrow set of options then becomes controlling through case decisions (MacAvoy 1979, 24). The issues confronting the subsystem continually change, but the process that frames the detection of issues remains constant.

The Great Crash of 1929 left industry, government, and public confidence at an all-time low. Public involvement in the market reached a no-confidence status, allowing new subsystem relationships to replace those being destroyed (Wessel 1991). Congress and the early SEC commissioners had many strategic choices available to rebuild the markets. With its broad discretion, the agency could have stepped in and taken over the exchanges. However, the disclosure process strategy encouraged industry to participate in its own regulation.

When regulators rally around a dominant enforcement technique, that formula impacts the scope, style, and likelihood of success of investigatory efforts. Disclosure in this sense is not a policy choice; it is a process. Prosecutorial victims may argue against a particular interpretation, but they accept the overlying process structure. The market support for enforcement protects the subsystem from controversial action.

Affected interests become locked into the subsystem issue-framing process and thereby become path dependent, using communication avenues that are favorable to its enforcement image (Baumgartner and Jones 1993, 107). Decisions by the securities subsystem revolve around disclosure-based regulation. The commission's diligence and effectiveness in establishing a popular mode of enforcement, sustaining its mandate, and pursuing successful policy make the SEC a model regulatory agency for the federal bureaucracy (Bruck 1980, 16; Cary 1964, 661; Karmel 1982; Mayhew 1991; Ratner 1988).

Path dependency, however, can be broken, as it has been in many regulatory agencies. In the case of the SEC, process has become a buttressing ideology—an idea so strong that one of us has referred to the resulting system as one of process-induced equilibrium (Hall 1995).[3] Congressional investigations conducted in the 1960s, 1970s, and 1980s raised serious questions about the effectiveness of disclosure as a regulatory model (Skousen 1991, 10). The SEC not only endured these challenges but, over the last sixty years, has expanded its disclosure-based mandate of power.

The formative securities statutes of the 1930s mandated a "thoroughgoing disclosure of information by corporations, forbade numerous specific abuses in securities trading, and gave the SEC broad powers over governance of exchanges and the securities industry" (McCraw 1984, 185). As the early drafters realized, an equally important part of enforcement strategy could not be set down in words but would have to come from the commission's practice in administering the enabling legislation. Disclosure-enforcement not only sustained implementation patterns; it remains the setting for strategic decisions that guide the commission daily.

CONCLUSION

The SEC was created to save an industry. Although its responsibilities have expanded over the years, the SEC's objectives remain unchanged: "to prevent misrepresentation in corporate financial statements and in the sale or exchange of securities" (Coleman 1985, 156–7). Today, the commission caters to the same constituency as when it was created and maintains its core structural relationships. Challenges continue to test the subsystem's survival, but it endures. In an era when more and more critics point to government ineffectiveness, partisanship, and competing interests, the SEC and its allies are hailed as a success. Our analysis suggests that this success is not a result of the power of subsystem participants, the professionalism and efficiency of the agency, or even the cultural appeal of capitalist markets in the United States. All these factors are, of course, important. However, the key is the slavish devotion to a process, disclosure-enforcement, that has reached the level of ideology. Perhaps more than anything else, this ideology has fostered the ability of subsystem participants to deny agenda access to reform ideas and to contain them when they do reach the agenda.

In modern democracies, neither agenda denial nor issue containment is easy. An open system fractured with numerous overlapping policy venues allows reformers to capture a single venue and wage battle from that vantage point. The same system allows the defeated to survive, in reduced form, to fight another day. In such decentralized, open systems, issues are difficult to control and manage and most assuredly cannot be managed through exercises in political influence alone (Baumgartner and Jones 1993).

Yet as this volume amply demonstrates, both agenda denial and issue containment are part of the complex relationships that characterize U.S. politics. Our study of the regulation of financial securities suggests that managing the agenda status of an issue is indeed a complex process. Over a long period of time, the macropolitical environment will change, as will the abilities of regulatory agency leaders. The key to successful management, by which we mean the ability to sustain a vibrant regulatory subsystem in the face of reform efforts from the Left and the Right and attempts by industry at outright capture, is a connection between buttressing idea and regulatory process. For the SEC and subsystem participants, disclosure-enforcement is a regulatory process, but it is more. It is an ideology of how governments and markets work best together.

One of the real benefits of our historical overview is how vividly it demonstrates that this relationship is not (necessarily) one of industry capture. During the 1950s, the agency was captured—it did little to threaten the securities industry (indeed, it did little at all). However, the SEC, with the urging of Congress, remade itself beginning in the early 1960s—hewing to the basic regulatory framework all the while. Whereas this framework served to stave off Left reform in the 1970s, it is currently being employed to defuse Right reform. It is difficult not to adopt an organic metaphor: neither an agent of Congress nor a tool of industry; rather, the subsystem has life on its own, all the while adjusting to changes in the macropolitical environment.

NOTES

1. We used a keyword approach to survey hearings, tabulating all hearings in which "Securities and Exchange Commission" was discussed. This is a moderately conservative approach to sampling. We have found that a keyword approach in essence oversamples an issue. If one were to use "financial securities" as a keyword, for example, one could pick up many incidences of simple mentions of financial securities. Using the particular agency minimizes this problem, but it underestimates the initial access of the issue to the national agenda.

2. We used keyword searches of computerized databases to construct these series. The databases covered different time periods.

3. The term is used to distinguish it from the more familiar structure-induced equilibrium.

REFERENCES

Baumgartner, F. R., and B. D. Jones. 1993. *Agendas and instability in American politics.* Chicago: University of Chicago Press.

Bernstein, M. 1955. *Regulating business by independent commission.* Princeton, NJ: Princeton University Press.

Bosso, C. J. 1987. *Pesticides and politics: The life cycle of a public issue.* Pittsburgh: University of Pittsburgh Press.

Browne, W. P. 1986. Policy and interests: Instability and change in a classic issue subsystem. In *Interest group politics,* 2d ed. Edited by A. J. Cigler and B. A. Loomis. Washington, DC: Congressional Quarterly.

Bruck, C. 1980. Waning days for the zealot at the SEC. *The American Lawyer* 11:16–30.

Bureau of the Census. 1994. *Statistical abstract of the United States.* Washington, DC: U.S. Department of Commerce.

Cary, W. L. 1964. Administrative agencies and the Securities and Exchange Commission. *Law and Contemporary Problems* 29:653–62.

Cobb, R. W., and C. D. Elder. 1983. *Participation in American politics: The dynamics of agenda-building.* Baltimore: Johns Hopkins University Press.

Coleman, J. W. 1985. *The criminal elite: The sociology of white collar crime.* New York: St. Martin's Press.

Congressional Information Service. Annual. *CIS/annual: Abstracts of congressional publications and legislative citations.* Washington, DC: CIS.

Dodd, L., and R. Schott. 1979. *Congress and the administrative state.* New York: Wiley.

Eisenhower, D. D. 1960. *Public papers of the presidents of the United States.* Washington, DC: U.S. Government Printing Office.

Fleischer, A. Jr., and S. Fraidin. 1994. M&A era thrust in spotlight. *National Law Journal,* July 18, p. C1.

Fortune Report. 1959. The SEC: Caveat emptor. In *The independent federal regulatory agencies,* edited by L. I. Salomon. New York: H. W. Wilson.

Freeman, J. L. 1965. *The political process: Executive bureau–legislative committee relations.* New York: Random House.

Griffith, E. S. 1939. *The impasse of democracy.* New York: Harrison-Hilton.

Hall, B. R. 1995. *Unlocking government gridlock: The process strategy of financial securities regulatory law.* Ph.D. diss., Texas A&M University.

Jenkins-Smith, H. C., G. K. St. Clair, and B. Woods. 1991. Explaining change in policy subsystems: Analysis of coalition stability and defection over time. *American Journal of Political Science* 35:851–80.

Jones, B. D. 1994. *Reconceiving decision making in democratic politics.* Chicago: University of Chicago Press.

Jones, B. D., and L. Bachelor. 1993. *The sustaining hand,* 2d rev. ed. Lawrence: University Press of Kansas.

Karmel, R. S. 1982. *Regulation by prosecution: The Securities and Exchange Commission vs. corporate America.* New York: Simon & Schuster.

Khademian, A. M. 1992. *The SEC and capital market regulation.* Pittsburgh: University of Pittsburgh Press.

Kingdon, J. W. 1994. *Agendas, alternatives and public policies.* New York: HarperCollins.

Knight, J. 1995. GOP pares securities revisions. *Washington Post,* November 15, p. C1.

Kohlmeier, L. M. Jr. 1969. *The regulators: Watchdog agencies and the public interest.* New York: Harper & Row.

Levitt, A. 1994. SEC chairman: Investor protection is main goal. *National Law Journal,* July 18, p. C1.

Lieberman, C. 1991. *Making economic policy.* Englewood Cliffs, NJ: Prentice-Hall.

Lowenstein, R. 1995. House aims to fix securities laws, but, indeed, is the system broke? *Wall Street Journal,* August 10, p. C1.

Lowi, T. 1979. *The end of liberalism,* 2d ed. New York: Norton.

Maass, A. 1951. *Muddy waters: The army engineers and the nation's rivers.* Cambridge: Harvard University Press.

MacAvoy, P. W. 1979. *The regulated industries and the economy.* New York: W. W. Norton.

Mayhew, D. 1991. *Divided we govern.* New Haven, CT: Yale University Press.

McCraw, T. K. 1984. *The prophets of regulation.* Cambridge: Belknap Press of Harvard University Press.

Needham, D. 1983. *The economics and politics of regulation: A behavioral approach.* Boston: Little, Brown.

Phillips, S. M., and J. R. Zecher. 1981. *The SEC and the public interest.* Cambridge: MIT Press.

Pointer, L. G., and R. G. Schroeder. 1986. *An introduction to the Securities and Exchange Commission.* Plano, TX: Business Publications.

Ratner, D. L. 1988. *Securities regulation.* St. Paul, MN: West.

Redford, E. S. 1969. *Democracy in the administrative state.* New York: Oxford University Press.

Riker, W. H. 1982. *Liberalism against populism.* Prospect Heights, IL: Waveland Press.

Ripley, R. B., and G. A. Franklin. 1987. *Congress, the bureaucracy, and public policy.* Chicago: Dorsey Press.

Rourke, F. E. 1984. *Bureaucracy, politics, and public policy.* Boston: Little, Brown.

Seligman, J. 1994. Agency born amid scandals. *National Law Journal,* July 18, p. C1.

Skousen, K. F. 1991. *An introduction to the SEC.* Cincinnati, OH: South-Western Publishing.

Stillman, R. J. 1992. *Public administration: Concepts and cases.* Boston: Houghton Mifflin.

Wall Street Journal index. Annual. New York: Wall Street Publishing.

Washington Post index. Annual. Woodbridge, CT: Research Publications.

Wessel, D. 1991. The bond club: Treasury and the Fed have long caved in to primary dealers. *Wall Street Journal,* September 25, p. C1.

Wright, D. 1988. *Understanding intergovernmental relations.* Pacific Grove, CA: Brooks-Cole.

4

Making Professional Accounting Accountable: An Issue Doomed to Fail

John F. Mahon and Richard A. McGowan

> *Accountants essentially regulate themselves in curious ways with what appears to be a minimum level of discipline. The whole thing is conducted in the same manner as necromancy and sorcery in the Dark Ages—in the dark of the moon with very few attendees.*
>
> —Rep. John Dingell (Gaines 1985, 3)

Alistair Cooke, the recently retired host of *Masterpiece Theater* and keen observer of U.S. society, observed that Columbus had a twofold intention as he embarked on his voyage: "For Gospel and for Gold" (Cooke 1973, 32). Ironically, Columbus became famous as neither a missionary nor a merchant, but as an explorer.

Professionals also profess to have a dual purpose for using their expertise: to maintain the public good and to serve the interests of their clients or customers. Many professionals have been able to avoid direct public scrutiny of their actions and practices for a long time. Because of their professed goals, professionals have a unique relationship with government that allows them to be self-regulating and self-policing. They offer the following arguments for this unique relationship: (1) because they employ an expert body of knowledge to accomplish their tasks, only other professionals in their field possess the knowledge and skills to evaluate a professional's performance; and (2) since the goal of professionals is to serve the public's interests, why put additional burdens on professional practitioners as they go about their work of service?

Yet it is somewhat ironic that during the last twenty years of active deregulation, many professions have come under increasing pressure to justify their privileged relationship with government and society as a whole. Since most professionals no longer operate as sole practitioners, but as part of a group or partnership whose sole purpose appears to be no different from that of any tradi-tional corporation, why should these professionals remain self-policing? Indeed, does this form of regulation best serve the public interest?

In this chapter, we examine how the accounting profession dealt with calls for further regulation. This examination provides the reader with insights into issues facing other mainly self-regulating professions, such as law and medicine, and suggests strategies and tactics that these professions are likely to pursue to deny agenda status to proposals that might erode their autonomy. We first offer an overview of accounting as a self-regulating profession from the 1930s. By the 1970s, several visible scandals involving major accounting firms' malpractice brought demands for federal regulation of the industry. Yet despite the fact that several powerful members of Congress initiated hearings into accounting mal-practice, no legislation was ever reported out of committee or discussed on the floor of either house. The profession and its allies employed low- and medium-cost strategies to blunt demands for reform. First, they denied that there was a significant problem, arguing that the scandals misrepresented the work of the overwhelming majority of accounting professionals. Then the industry created its own commissions, which proposed cosmetic changes in accounting practices and gained SEC endorsement for continued self-regulation. Together, these were suf-ficient to keep the issue of accounting reform off the formal agenda.

SELF-REGULATING PROFESSIONALS: THE CASE OF ACCOUNTING

The professions have traditionally including the following occupations: phy-sicians, lawyers, architects, dentists, engineers, teachers, clergy, and accountants. Although many of these professions have experienced extensive growth, the number of accounting professionals has tripled over the past forty years—a truly remarkable growth, as shown in Figure 4.1. Although the other professions have also grown, this explosive growth in the number of accountants poses some inter-esting problems for the profession.

According to Friedson (1986), the two distinctive characteristics of a profes-sion are a body of expert knowledge and authority over clients. If these two characteristics exist, the profession has an autonomy that normally results in self-regulation and a strict licensing procedure for its practitioners. When a profes-sion cannot meet these standards, Friedson predicts that the profession will be subject to a "deprofessionalization" process undertaken by various governmental agencies.

The first line of defense for accounting, as for any profession, in denying agenda access to regulatory claims is to assert that the profession's own self-policing mechanisms are more than sufficient. However, in order to make that claim effectively, the profession must maintain legitimacy by possessing both ex-pert knowledge and autonomy from client influence. If this is not done, an oppor-

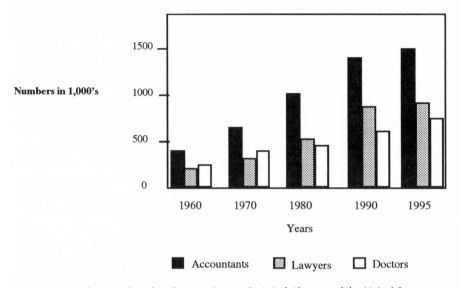

Numbers in 1,000's

Figure 4.1. Number in Selected Professions. Source: Statistical Abstracts of the United States (1975, 1985, 1992, 1996).

tunity will develop for opponents to demand government regulation of the profession. Attacks on a profession first identify or name an injurious problem that needs fixing (Felstiner, Abel, and Sarat 1980–81, 635). Blaming occurs when an aggrieved individual or group attributes an injury to another individual or organization. Only after a problem has been named and blame has been attributed can "claiming" occur, as an aggrieved individual or organization seeks a remedy (Felstiner, Abel, and Sarat 1980–1981; Mahon 1993).

Although this framework analyzes the process of dispute development, it is an incomplete account of how problems get on the formal agenda of a governmental agency or legislative body. In addition to naming, blaming, and claiming, supporters have to attract attention and adherents (Cobb and Elder 1983; Mahon 1989). It is easiest to expand support when a problem has a simple definition, broad appeal, unique aspect, serious concern, and action component. If an issue meets these criteria, the likelihood that it will achieve formal agenda status is enhanced but by no means guaranteed.

A Body of Expert Knowledge?

Critics of the accounting profession have attempted to name a problem by attacking the field's claim to have a body of expert knowledge. This attack focuses on two major points. Whereas accountants maintain that they have a body of non-routine expert knowledge, critics contend that the information they rely on is capable of being routinized, as in computerization. A second point that critics use to attack accountants' claim to expertise involves public accounting firms' loss of their monopoly as providers of accounting services. Increasingly, information specialists or management information specialists have begun to encroach and expand into areas that accountants traditionally claimed as their domain. The National Society of Public Accountants (NSPA) is an association of unlicensed accountants who are actively engaged in providing bookkeeping and tax services to clients but do not perform opinion audits. Since the traditional public account- ing firms do not pretend to offer assurances of reliability to third parties in many of their activities, the NSPA has pressured many state legislatures to permit an- other sort of licensing procedure besides the traditional certified public account- ant (CPA) exam. Similar problems exist in work performed by paralegals and for- mer legal secretaries. These individuals have begun to provide services that are capable of being routinized through technology (e.g., wills, simple property transfers). Lawyers recognize that such work by nonlawyers could call into ques- tion their designation as a profession and have vigorously fought such activities. This particular issue does not engender a great deal of public support and debate, because it involves a limited number of parties and is not perceived as having great consequences for the society as a whole.

Authority over Clients?

The second characteristic of a profession is the professional's independence or autonomy from any demands that a client might make on that professional's opinion or judgment. Representative Dingell, a Democrat from Michigan, stated this question of autonomy succinctly when he observed: "How can the inde- pendent auditor on the job be expected to maintain independence when his or her personal success is linked to attracting clients and enhancing revenues?" (Johnston 1985, 1). Note that Dingell's interest in this particular problem is a new challenge for the profession because of his position as a powerful, articulate in- dividual serving as an agent for the general public's interest.

In the case of accountants, their independence is being questioned in two ways. First, the consumers of accounting services have gotten into the habit of shopping around for auditors. A firm or corporation pays for an auditor's opinion, but it wants that opinion to confirm its version of the health of the firm. If the firm does not get the opinion it wants, it goes out and finds a public accounting firm that will give it a clean bill of health. A classic example of this type of behav- ior involved a small Oklahoma bank, Penn Square, which federal regulators had to close in July 1984. This bank eventually forfeited on over $2 billion in risky loans to oil speculators using funds from such prominent banks as Chase Man- hattan Corporation and Continental Illinois National Bank. Where were the auditors? Penn Square had received a qualified opinion of its financial statements from Arthur Young because of a lack of adequate reserves for possible loan losses. So Penn Square fired Arthur Young and hired Peat, Marwick, Mitchell &

Co., which gave Penn Square a clean bill of health. Peat, Marwick, Mitchell & Co.'s opinion preceded the collapse of the bank by only three months (Belkaoui 1989, 117). Although this is an extreme case, it is not uncommon. In 1993, the number of publicly held firms that fired their auditors jumped 48 percent, from 298 to 442. In the vast majority of cases, these firms were not only able to switch firms but also able to have qualified opinions switched to clean opinions (Carmichael 1994, 85). This auditor "shopping" supports comments made by Robert Chatov in 1985:

> If one were starting from point zero today, I think that it would be judged madness to invent a system where the one to be audited hired the auditor, bargained with the auditor as to the size of the fee, was permitted to purchase other management services from the auditor, and where the auditor in turn had the prime responsibility for setting the rules and for enforcing them and applying sanctions against themselves. (Klott 1985, 22)

A more recent example in which the conduct of an accounting firm appears to have been influenced by the desire to keep a client satisfied involves Coopers and Lybrand. In 1990, Mitsubishi Motors bought control of Value Rent-a-Car. Value Rent-a-Car's 1989 financial statement, which Coopers and Lybrand had certified, stated that its net worth was a negative $5.9 million. However, after Mitsubishi took over Value Rent-a-Car, its real net worth was actually closer to negative $10 million. Mitsubishi sued Value Rent-a-Car's owners and Coopers and Lybrand, accusing it of letting Value Rent-a-Car hide its poor financial status.

As Mitsubushi pursued its case, it requested Coopers and Lybrand's audit working papers. Mitsubushi made an interesting discovery: the working papers that it received from the accounting firm differed from those it had obtained from Value Rent-a-Car. In other words, it appears that Coopers and Lybrand revised its working papers a year after the audit to make it look as if it had been tougher on Value Rent-a-Car than it actually had been, to protect itself from charges of neglect (Berton 1995, A1).

Although this case is still being decided by the courts, it appears that the temptation to alter working papers is rising. Since courts accept these papers as proof of an audit's soundness, these charges not only have serious legal implications but also show just how far public accounting firms are willing to go to provide opinions that will please their clients, maintain their relationship with clients, and lead to both retained and increased future business. Abraham Briloff of the City University of New York and an accounting professional has been very critical of his profession. He has characterized accounting as a "private priesthood" that routinely fails to provide the rigorous independent standards implicit in an audit. He has argued that an audit has become a commodity for sale and that accountants should adopt a skull and crossbones logo for their audits as a warning to the public. Briloff has also argued that accounting firms should be prohibited from offering peripheral services to their clients (Johnston 1985; Klott 1985).

Dingell has used the examples noted above (and others) to strengthen his position for governmental oversight of the profession and to increase the general public's concern about this issue. He is clearly using a symbolic strategy here by highlighting spectacular and widespread failures. Dingell attempted to show the widespread impact on society and that the problem is not likely to go away without some action, because the accounting profession is unable to police itself. He attempted to expand the conflict by bringing the media and the general public into it to support his position. The accounting profession countered his claims by noting that many of these scandals were the result of individual actions and not the actions of the profession as a whole (a low-cost strategy of "antipatterning"). In addition, accountants argued that many of these actions were illegal and covered by other existing laws, so no new action was required.

Another reason that critics of the accounting profession question its autonomy and authority over clients is the increasing consumerism of public accounting firms. No longer are the "Big Six" interested in providing just auditing services. For the past twenty years, revenues from the auditing portion of accounting firms have been either stable or declining. At the same time, these firms have had to hire specialists and in general support bigger staffs. Thus, in order to supplement declining revenues from the audit function (and in some cases to turn a profit), accounting firms have expanded their activities beyond auditing and now provide consulting and other managerial services for their clients. Arthur Anderson has been the most aggressive in this area, but most of the other Big-Six firms are following Anderson's lead. As a result, the conflict of interest between the accountant's duty to accurately represent the client's financial position and the accountant's desire to please that client in order to secure additional engagements is clearer.

Establishment of the Securities and Exchange Commission

The coming of the depression in 1929 brought demands that business reform itself and that government be involved in the process. The creation of the Securities and Exchange Commission (SEC) in 1934 clearly established the idea that government would try to provide greater protection for investors than it had in the past. The SEC also raised the specter of greater federal intervention in other areas of corporate establishment. The appointment of Joseph P. Kennedy as the first chairman of the SEC allowed the business community to breathe a sigh of relief, since he was "one of their own" and would understand their concerns. Kennedy's appointment signaled to business that although reforms were necessary, the general inclination of the SEC would be to keep regulation of business and corporate affairs to a minimum.

In trying to protect the public from unsafe securities, one problem that confronted the SEC was the establishment of a uniform accounting theory and principles for every corporation in the United States. The question was how these uniform standards ought to be established. Should the government or the private sector set the standards? With Kennedy in command of the SEC, there was little doubt that the issue would be solved in favor of the private sector. The argument that won the day centered on the professional nature of accounting work. Only accountants would understand the intricacies of setting and maintaining the rules and regulations needed to ensure that the public was being protected from unscrupulous business interests. Business threw its weight behind this solution, realizing that it preferred to hire private accounting firms rather than foot the bill to train and maintain government auditors. The complexity of the issue and the lack of public interest supported the argument for allowing the accounting profession to set the standards instead of government. The practices of the accounting profession are a result of a series of compromises among business, government, and society over time and are a monument to the American preference to avoid governmental interference if at all possible.

The Accounting Profession on the Defensive: 1976 to the Present

Although government and the business community initially fostered the accounting profession's activities, in recent years, government's attitude toward accounting has become increasingly ambiguous. The various agencies (Cost Accounting Standards Board [CASB], Financial Accounting Standards Board [FASB], Internal Revenue Service [IRS], and SEC) have some influence over the environment in which the accounting profession operates, but they have little desire to expand their control. Congress, however, has been increasingly critical of the performance of the accounting profession, in particular, Democrat John Moss of California and Dingell.

In 1977, Congress enacted the Foreign Corrupt Practices Act, which forbade U.S. corporations to make payments to foreign officials in order to ensure that they would get contracts from various foreign governments. The fact that these illegal payments had been undetected for many years raised questions about the CPAs' effectiveness in identifying and disclosing fraud by management. This question about the quality of accounting services led to the House Commerce Committee's Subcommittee on Oversight and Investigations' examination of the SEC's oversight of the accounting profession. Moss, who chaired the hearings, and other critics of the accounting profession maintained that the profession had not established, and appeared unwilling to create, institutions and sanctions that would ensure adequate protection of the public's interest (Previts and Merino 1979, 318).

In late 1976, Moss introduced a bill whose official title was the Public Accounting Regulatory Act (more commonly known as the Moss Act), which stated as its goals:

To establish a National Organization of Securities and Exchange Commission Accountancy, to require that independent public accounting firms be registered with such an Organization in order to furnish audits reports with respect to financial statements filed with the Securities and Exchange Commission, to authorize disciplinary action against such accounting firms and principals in such firms. (H.R. 13175, 94th Congress)

Other provisions of the bill included:

- Only one member of the commission's five-member board could come from a public accounting firm.
- The new commission would review the work of every accounting firm every three years. The primary focus of the work would be the "public interest."
- CPA firms' liability would be greatly increased. Under this act, they would have been liable even when a business deliberately intended to defraud or mislead the auditors.

Needless to say, the accounting profession saw this bill as a great threat. In response, it mustered all its forces to oppose serious consideration and enactment of the bill. On the side of industry once again was the complexity of the issue and the general public's disinterest. The industry mobilized its allies to state in writing and in testimony before Congress that no such change was necessary, as adequate protections already existed—that is, there was ample legislation already in place, and no new legislation was needed.

Marshall Armstrong, chairman of the FASB, was outraged by congressional actions against the accounting profession and led the counterattacks on this legislative incursion into accounting. He argued that the House Commerce Subcommittee's report was "highly misleading" and that the subcommittee "failed to comprehend the difficulty of achieving agreement on accounting concepts" (Andrews 1976a, 55). As an example of this failure to comprehend the complexity of accounting, Armstrong noted that the subcommittee confused "accounting with auditing and wrongly blamed accounting standards for corporate fraud and illegal payments" (Andrews 1976a, 59). Armstrong received support on this issue of complexity and misunderstanding from Wallace E. Olson, chairman of the American Institute of Certified Public Accountants (AICPA). Olson observed: "They [Congress] tell us our arguments are far too complex, too complicated" (Andrews 1976b, 1). Another observer of this unfolding conflict noted that Congress seemed "somewhat mystified as to precisely what it is that accountants do" (Andrews 1976b, 1).

This approach to the issue—on grounds of complexity and misunderstanding—was not the only tactic that the industry pursued. In a direct attack on the subcommittee's credibility, Armstrong derided its overreliance on a single accounting witness's testimony. He argued that this testimony was a "mess of misinformation" and that the "typically cautious and complicated arguments" would be lost in high-level Washington politics (Andrews 1976a, 55). Finally, the industry attempted to blur the issue by arguing that the problems with accounting were a result of the distorted legal system, which allowed accountants and auditors to be sued for malpractice for making honest errors. To solve some of the problems with accounting, the legal system's approach to malpractice would have to be changed (Ronen 1977, 14).

Moss retired from Congress before any action was taken on his proposal. At the time of the Moss hearings, Democratic Senator Lee Metcalf of Montana held hearings and came to a very different conclusion. His committee report recommended that the private process be allowed to continue as currently constituted. The SEC, however, was perhaps the profession's most valuable ally in opposing this bill, even though it would have gained a great deal of power from its enactment. The SEC argued that it had undertaken a record number of disciplinary actions against accountants in the past and had barred several large public accounting firms from taking additional audits from SEC clients. In essence, the SEC argued that it would be no more capable of detecting fraud than were public accountants, and the SEC certainly did not want to be the target of the public's ire by giving its seal of approval to an audit that later proved to be faulty. In this conflict, the accounting profession generally employed low-cost strategies, particularly using the support of Metcalf and the SEC in articulating a powerful position that no serious problem existed that could not be dealt with through self-regulation.

The accounting profession also sought to placate Moss by requiring all members of the AICPA to undergo peer review every three years. Another public firm would conduct this review to ensure compliance with AICPA quality-control measures. Thus, by enacting self-regulatory measures, the accounting profession satisfied congressional concerns. Accountants recognized that "quick action was necessary to forestall imminent legislation aimed at imposing governmental control on the profession," but they also knew that "some semantic sleight-of-hand" was necessary to get the proposals passed (Rankin 1977, 57). These measures would be much less costly than government control and would also assure the public that the profession was taking steps to protect the public's interest. Note, however, that this was a clever strategy on the part of the accounting profession to offer a relatively cheap, symbolic fix (tokenism) to the problem by adding yet another layer of self-regulation.

Upon Moss's retirement and Metcalf's death, congressional interest in accounting regulation diminished. Although Senator Thomas Eagleton, a Democrat from Missouri, held additional hearings in 1979, the profession mounted a spirited counterattack, including public support and testimony from the chairman of the SEC for continued self-regulation and oversight by the SEC (Lee et al. 1988). At this point, congressional critics were in a difficult situation. The very agency that could be more active in regulating the accounting profession continued to side with accountants on these issues and argue for self-regulation.

A new line of criticism of the accounting profession began to emerge in 1987, less than ten years after the failure of the Moss bill. Dingell, the new chair of the House Commerce Committee's Subcommittee on Oversight and Investigations, conducted hearings that centered on the independence of public accounting firms from their clients. The collapse of the Wedtech Corporation, a Bronx-based defense contractor, in December 1987 was the scandal that provided the impetus for these hearings. The company was charged with and admitted forging over $6 million in invoices submitted to the federal government. As the story was told, there was evidence of political payoffs as well as accounting sleights of hand. Again, the question was asked: how could this corporation receive a clean bill of health from its auditors? It appears that Wedtech was able to get cooperation from the accountants when the partner of KMG, the accounting firm that conducted Wedtech audits, was offered the presidency of the firm, along with $1.5 million in stock and a $900,000 loan (Belkaoui 1989, 115).

Dingell used the Wedtech case to launch hearings on the independence of accounting firms from their clients. The accounting profession easily countered, saying that the case was atypical, employing its antipatterning argument. Although the independence issue was connected to audit failures resulting from faulty accounting procedures and standards, Dingell quickly challenged another facet of the independence question, namely, the scope of services being offered by accounting firms. By the 1980s, the accounting profession had invested heavily in its consulting "product" line, and while audit services were barely registering growth, the consulting part of public accounting firms was growing at an annual rate of 20 percent. Indeed, the largest consulting firm in the United States was Andersen Consulting, which was part of a major public accounting firm, and four of the top ten consulting firms were connected with public accounting firms. Therefore, any attack on the independence of public accounting firms was also an attack on the area that provided them with their greatest opportunity for growth.

Dingell proposed legislation under which public accounting firms would have been prohibited from offering consulting services to their audit clients. Once again, the SEC came to the rescue. It maintained that the Dingell proposals were too draconian and that the benefits that clients received from the detailed knowledge of its auditors outweighed any possible negative effects on the auditors' objectivity—an argument raising fears that the "fix" would make the existing situation worse. The accounting profession made some token concessions, offering to prohibit consulting services if the consulting fee was 50 percent of the audit fee and barring accounting partners from taking executive positions with their clients (Previts 1985, 131).

The profession also continued to advance some of the themes argued earlier in the Moss debates and to expand the potential concerns that Congress would have in the future. The problem with accounting, accountants said, lies in the legal system and liability laws. "If a solution to the liability problem is not found soon, some accountants fear that there will not be enough auditors to do the kind of investigations necessary to issue an opinion on a public company. If that happens, the financial information that investors depend on could be much less reliable" (Berg 1987, 4). Accountants cleverly argued that failure to address the problem with the legal system could have spillover effects in the investor community. Accountants continued to highlight the failure of the public and Congress to understand the complexity of the profession. For example: "it is impractical for auditors to check a company's every transaction, and since the auditors must ultimately rely on the basic integrity of management, it is impossible for auditors to catch every case of cheating" (Berg 1987, 4).

The profession shifted the blame for its problems from accounting and auditing to the credibility and honesty of management. Bob Ellyson, managing partner of the Miami office of Coopers and Lybrand, stated the problem simply and succinctly: "We've tried to explain to Chairman Dingell and to the public that there is an expectations gap. People really don't understand what accountants do. They incorrectly assume that a business failure must mean that there was an audit failure as well" (Feinberg 1987, 9). As in the Moss situation earlier, accountants rushed to offer new self-regulatory proposals to "defuse criticisms in Congress that many C.P.A.'s have been lax in audits of public companies" (Berg 1988, D2).

Once again, the accounting profession had survived a rigorous attack from powerful congressional critics. The SEC, the very agency that Congress had given the power to regulate the accounting profession, turned down yet another opportunity to gain and wield power over this profession. Meanwhile, the accounting industry was able to make minor changes to mollify its congressional critics while still maintaining its basic self-regulatory stance and independence from government and from any major changes in its policies and procedures.

THE POLITICS OF AGENDA DENIAL

This short history of the accounting profession provides an overview of its successful four-decade effort to deny serious agenda consideration of challenges to the profession. Considering all the scandals over the last two decades (Baldwin-United, Continental Illinois, Drysdale Governmental Securities, Penn Square, United American Bank, Value Rent-a-Car, and Wedtech) in which the accounting profession was involved, the lack of significant, substantive overhaul of the regulation of the profession is remarkable. How has the profession been able to resist erosion of its position?

Source of the Issue

Where did the issue of accounting regulation come from? The legislators who named the problem seemed to be in a position to render a decisive defeat to the industry. Yet Dingell, Eagleton, and Moss were unable to define the issue in a way that attracted sufficient support from other key stakeholders—including the media and those governmental agencies responsible for oversight. As a consequence, it was difficult for them to build the coalition necessary to get the issue on the agenda for serious consideration.

Dingell had prior investigatory successes: forcing an Environmental Protection Agency administrator (Burford) from office, having a presidential adviser (Deaver) convicted, catching the founder of the nuclear submarine (Rickover) in questionable deals, exposing waste in the Pentagon, and revealing corruption in the generic drug industry. Yet reputation is not the same as political effectiveness, and the strategies he pursued against the accounting profession were easily blunted. Not that he did not emphasize the seriousness of the problem. In fact, Dingell emphasized that the issue was a new one that harmed many people. He portrayed the accounting profession as an industry out of control, with widespread and frequent failures, and as a monopoly requiring closer regulation in the public interest.

Saying who was responsible for the problem—blaming—was complex, just as the question of what constituted an audit failure was technical, making it hard to engage the public. Many of the situations involving accounting firms also involved individual or corporate misbehavior, and it was not clear whether these were exceptional instances of wrongdoing or a systematic industrywide pattern. In addition, those most likely to be harmed in the future (corporations) were wary of additional governmental involvement in their businesses. Finally, when specific demands were made on government by these legislators, the agency most likely to be supportive of such actions, the SEC, rejected the idea of increasing its authority, power, and visibility. Much of the momentum for change was lost when the SEC supported the accounting profession's position of continued self-regulation.

In short, the issue of regulating the accounting profession never progressed farther than congressional hearings. The supporters of change in accounting regulation were never able to demonstrate, in Cobb and Elder's (1983) terms, the social significance and relevance of the issue in nontechnical terms that had appeal to the general public and the media. Indeed, the very existence of the SEC and of the accounting profession's self-regulatory mechanisms served as effective barriers to the categorical precedence argument that was raised.

Agenda Setting, the Role of Symbols, and Strategies Pursued by the Accounting Profession

Regulating the accounting profession does not intuitively appeal to many political actors. The congressional leaders involved were never able to mobilize widespread support for the issue, and the attentive public and the general public were never involved at all. The accounting profession seized the high ground and was able to obtain the support of the attention groups most likely to be affected by any changes in the status quo—the business community and the governmental agencies charged with oversight. As a result, the legislative initiatives simply collapsed and never moved beyond the subcommittee or committee hearing stage.

The accounting profession had three related arguments to use against increased federal government involvement that were also powerful symbols themselves. The first was that the industry was already subjected to a great deal of oversight from both the government and private oversight groups, in addition to self-regulation. Accountants argued that regulation and oversight from the SEC, IRS, CASB, and FASB and state involvement in certification and education were sufficient for one industry. Second, they asserted that a significant portion of self-regulation is based on state-mandated certification and licensure and that federal regulation would infringe on powers reserved to the states. Finally, although never raised directly, the specter of the federal government and its agencies having access to firm-specific data raised the fears of the business community, which was more worried about increased governmental knowledge of company operations and financing than about potential errors and problems caused by the accounting profession.

As a result, the accounting profession was able to use low-cost strategies to attack the proponents' reform proposals, arguing early and often that there was no systematic problem to deal with. As a consequence, the accounting profession initially pursued strategies of nonconfrontation, opting to have friendly legislators such as Metcalf and the SEC argue its case. The effective use of low-cost strategies placed legislators such as Dingell and Moss in an awkward position. In order for them to win on the issue, they would have to raise their level of involvement and enlist the support of a broader set of stakeholders. Yet in order to be successful, they would have to define the issue in such a way as to appeal to a broader constituency and possibly dilute the focus of their attack.

Eventually, the accounting profession's refusal to admit the existence of a problem proved insufficient, when scandals involving Penn Square, Value Rent-a-Car, and Wedtech received press attention. Then the profession moved to an antipatterning strategy, agreeing that these cases revealed a problem, but defining them as isolated instances. The industry pursued other medium-cost attack strategies that proceeded on several fronts simultaneously and were the key to the industry's continued success in denying agenda access. Accountants argued that proposed changes were built from faulty premises. The general performance of the accounting profession was excellent, they said; isolated examples of problems did not demonstrate a pattern requiring major overhaul of the current system. Tweaking of the system was all that was needed. Accountants also argued that further involvement of the government would undoubtedly add costs to the auditing process that would have to be borne by the client (and, in all likelihood, passed on to the firm's customers), with no appreciable difference in performance over what was currently available. Interestingly, the industry was careful never to engage in a direct attack on either the SEC or a member of Congress trying to regulate it. Accountants never placed blame on lax SEC oversight, not wanting to create a powerful enemy of an agency that has consistently served the industry's interests. Nor did they want to antagonize representatives whose ire could cause future problems.

In addition to pursuing these attack strategies, the industry used symbolic placation strategies, such as creating committees to study the problems. Commissions that have been established over the years to investigate problems and issues with accounting include the Cohen Commission, which studied the responsibilities of auditors; the Treadway Commission, which looked at fraudulent financial reporting; and the Anderson Committee, which developed recommendations for mandatory quality reviews (Bollinger et al. 1993). Each of these commissions or committees was considered a blue-ribbon panel, and each of them recommended changes to be undertaken by the accounting profession. They also, in some cases, recommended specific legislative and regulatory actions to be undertaken by the government. However, few, if any, of the recommended governmental or regulatory actions were ever implemented.

The profession frequently argued that the errors and problems noted in its own self-regulation were gross exceptions and therefore did not require draconian responses. Finally, the profession was able to co-opt a potential strong supporter of change—the SEC. In each and every case that we reviewed, the SEC was either silent on any proposed change or strongly supportive of the accounting profession's stand on the issue. This deprived Congress of a strong and influential ally in altering the legislative and regulatory framework for oversight of the accounting profession.

CONCLUSION

The accounting profession has been extraordinarily successful in turning back proposals that would subject it to federal regulation, which would erode its professional status and independence. It has done this by forming a long-standing alliance with the SEC and having the SEC serve as the industry's agent in resisting major change to the regulatory status quo. This alliance with the SEC has allowed the accounting profession to blunt the impact of any potential legislative interference. The industry has cleverly managed the agenda denial process by arguing that the very complexity of the auditing function is best left to those with the expertise to understand it, by the effective use of symbolic arguments and focused attack strategies, and by co-optation of a key player in any future change in the legislative and regulatory environment (the SEC). The inability of the industry's major critics to craft an appeal to broader stakeholders has contributed enormously to the accounting profession's ability to deny agenda access to regulatory proposals.

The primary focus of the accounting profession's critics is the independence issue, which has become an even greater concern as more accounting professionals have joined firms or partnerships. It is interesting to note that all the regulatory reforms in the last twenty years have been aimed at accounting firms rather than individual professionals. Hence, it appears that the independence of a profession is linked to the economic structure of the industry. We hypothesize that the more a profession is organized around firms and partnerships, the more likely the public is to question its professional status and perhaps seek renewed investigations.

As with any industry, the accounting profession has to be concerned with any high-visibility scandals that will cause the public to question its ability to self-regulate. In our view, the essential ingredient in achieving success in changing the oversight of a profession and gaining access to the agenda is the capture of the general public's interest and support of such change. This undoubtedly requires a simplification of the issue for the public's consideration and strong support from the media in publicizing the issue and expanding it beyond the ability of the profession to control it.

REFERENCES

Andrews, F. 1976a. Accounting board assails criticism of its rule making. *New York Times,* October 21, pp. 55, 59.

———. 1976b. Spotlight on the accountants. *New York Times,* November 14, sec. 3, p. 1.

Belkaoui, A. 1989. *The coming crisis in accounting.* Westport, CT: Greenwood Press, Quorum Books.

Berg, E. 1987. Critics fault accountants for not blowing whistles." *New York Times,* July 5, sec. 4, p. 4.

———. 1988. C.P.A. group votes to alter membership criteria. *New York Times,* January 14, p. D2.

Berton, L. 1995. Ledgerdemain? *Wall Street Journal,* November 2, p. A1.

Bollinger, G. M., S. G. Bonta, T. J. Flynn, R. L. Gray, L. A. Turman, and W. M. Primoff. 1993. View point: Legislating liability reform. *Journal of Accountancy* (July): 53–8.

Carmichael, D. R. 1994. What does the independent auditor's opinion really mean? *Journal of Accountancy* (November): 83–7.

Cobb, R. W., and C. D. Elder. 1983. *Participation in American politics: The dynamics of agenda-building.* Baltimore: Johns Hopkins University Press.

Cooke, A. 1973. *America.* New York: Alfred Knopf.

Feinberg, A. 1987. Accountants try to put a little kick in their image. *New York Times,* September 27, sec. 3, p. 9.

Felstiner, W. L. F., R. I. Abel, and A. Sarat. 1980–1981. The emergence and transformation of disputes: Naming, blaming, claiming. . . . *Law and Society Review* 15:631–53.

Friedson, E. 1986. *Professional powers.* Chicago: University of Chicago Press.

Gaines, S. 1985. CPA audit failure: Tainting by the numbers. *Chicago Tribune,* April 7, p. 3.

Johnston, O. 1985. Self-policing of auditing industry hit; SEC criticized for reluctance to govern accounting firms. *Los Angeles Times,* February 21, p. 1 (Business section).

Klott, G. 1985. Accounting role seen in jeopardy. *New York Times,* February 21, p. 22.

Lee, B. Z., T. C. Barreaux, J. F. Moraglio, and D. H. Skadden. 1988. AICPA in Washington: Success stories: Because members deliver. *Journal of Accountancy* (September): 82–83.

Mahon, J. F. 1989. Corporate political strategy. *Business in the Contemporary World* 2(1): 50–63.

———. 1993. Shaping issues/manufacturing agents: Corporate political sculpting. In *Corporate political agency: The construction of competition in public affairs,* edited by B. Mitnick. Newbury Park, CA: Sage Publications.

Post, J. E., and J. F. Mahon. 1980. Articulated turbulence: The effect of regulatory agencies on corporate responses to social change. *Academy of Management Review* 5(3): 399–407.

Previts, G. 1985. *The scope of CPA services.* New York: John Wiley & Sons.

Previts, G., and B. Merino. 1979. *The history of accounting in America.* New York: John Wiley & Sons.

Rankin, D. 1977. Accountants adopt self-regulation in revamping plan. *New York Times,* September 9, p. 57.

Ronen, J. 1977. Who should audit the auditors? *New York Times,* May 8, sec. 3, p. 14.

Statistical abstract of the United States. 1994. Washington, DC: U.S. Government Printing Office.

U.S. House. 1902. *Final report of the Industrial Commission.* House Document 380, 57th Cong., 2d sess.

U.S. Senate. 1976. *The accounting establishment: A staff study, prepared by the Subcommittee on Oversight and Investigation of the Interstate and Foreign Commerce.* 94th Cong., 2d sess., Washington, DC: U.S. Government Printing Office.

PART III
The Food and Drug Administration

5
Strategies of Agenda Denial: Issue Definition and the Case of bST

L. Christopher Plein

Regulatory decisions entail political risks. This is one reason that elected officials have seen fit to delegate much responsibility to bureaucratic actors (Bryner 1987; Kerwin 1994; Schoenbrod 1993). The broad regulatory statutes enacted by Congress regarding such areas as public health, product safety, environmental protection, and workplace safety leave much interpretation and implementation discretion in the hands of administrators. Over time, regulatory policy arrangements have evolved to deal with both technical and political dimensions of regulatory policy enactment and enforcement. These arrangements often reflect mutual accommodations reached between regulated interests and regulators. The hallmarks of such relationships include a dependency on voluntary compliance with regulatory procedures, reliance on regulated interests for information used in administrative decisions, and the use of technical and scientific procedures and criteria for assessing health and environmental risks.

It should come as little surprise that, given the prominent role of regulatory arrangements, both decisions and the decision-making processes involved can be a source of concern and debate. A new product or practice submitted for regulatory review can attract attention if its novelty and potential societal effects are perceived to be significant. Although new products and practices are often popularly framed in terms of social progress, controversies over advances in biomedicine, nuclear energy, data processing, and agricultural practices illustrate the political conflict often associated with such technological developments. Debate involves the call for more stringent and comprehensive government regulation to take into account the social and economic consequences of new technologies.

Pending regulatory decisions can be the triggering mechanism for agenda fights. These focus attention on the issue at hand, such as the review of a new drug. However, they also provide an opportunity to challenge *how* decisions are made in the regulatory arena. This chapter investigates such an experience and documents the use of agenda denial tactics to fend off challenges to existing regulatory arrangements. In particular, this chapter examines how the Food and Drug Administration's (FDA's) assessment of bovine somatotropin (bST) provided an opportunity for critics to express concern over the lack of social and economic impact criteria in the regulatory review process. Perceiving a challenge not only to a product but also to the integrity of established regulatory arrangements, the FDA, private interests, and various governmental actors engaged in concerted efforts to deny challengers and their policy proposals agenda access. These responses often made use of symbolic and culturally salient images and rhetorical appeals to shape issue perceptions in such a way that reforms of FDA practices would not be considered.

The bST controversy illustrates how both substantive and procedural matters can become intertwined in issue debates. The FDA's and its allies' priority was to preserve existing regulatory procedures and arrangements—even if this meant deferring a decision on the approval of bST. The bST controversy created an opportunity for critics to challenge not only a product but also the process by which that product was reviewed by regulatory authorities. Because the regulatory review process was a relatively closed system, critics sought to advance their cause through forums outside the FDA, such as state legislatures, congressional hearings, and the mass media. In this manner, they hoped to exert pressure on the regulatory review process, gain footing in the policy arena, and force changes in the manner in which FDA reviews were carried out. For these interests, success involved greater weight being given to the social and economic impact of new technologies.

As long as bST remained the rallying cry for those seeking to upset existing regulatory arrangements, rendering an administrative decision on the product posed the risk of political backlash. Champions of the existing system realized that a decision on bST could not be tendered until challenges to regulatory procedures were successfully countered. In essence, the objective for the FDA and its supporters was to diminish the utility of the bST controversy as a vehicle for expressing more abstract concerns about the dangers of technology and the shortcomings of regulatory safeguards. They feared that successful articulation of these concerns might spell trouble for existing regulatory arrangements, and they used a variety of specific agenda denial tactics. These included framing powerful images from cultural and socially relevant themes, attacking critics of bST and of the review procedures, depicting bST as a benign product, and emphasizing the efficacy of regulatory arrangements through rhetoric, symbolic actions, and endorsements.

FOCUS OF CHALLENGE: FDA REGULATORY REVIEW PROCEDURES

In November 1993, the Food and Drug Administration gave final approval to the adoption and use of bST, a biotechnologically derived growth promoter, in dairy operations.[1] This decision brought a sense of closure, at least within the policy arena, to an issue that had been under regulatory review for close to a decade. The bST experience is illustrative of contemporary issue controversies driven by perceptions of risk and negative externalities. The bST issue served as a vehicle for those troubled about the pace of technological development and the ability of regulatory safeguards to properly manage progress. Thus, although bST was at the *center* of the controversy, it was not essentially at the *heart* of the debate. In other words, bST became a controversy because it provided a dramatic and relatively well defined vehicle for those seeking to advance a broader agenda of more stringent regulatory processes that focused on the social and economic impacts of new technologies. In the end, established regulatory actors and regulated interests were successful in fending off this challenge.

Although the most relevant formal agenda for dealing with bST was the administrative review process of the FDA's Center for Veterinary Medicine, opponents of the product and existing regulatory arrangements raised the issue in a number of other forums, including the public arena, state legislatures, and Congress. By heightening public awareness, mobilizing sympathetic interest groups, and prompting congressional intervention, critics hoped to alter existing regulatory policy procedures. Specifically, critics held that the potential economic effects on the dairy industry were not adequately considered in the animal drug review process. They held that bST would benefit large-scale dairy operations and drive family farmers out of business and undermine rural communities. In addition, these critics held that increased milk supplies would put additional burdens on taxpayers to fund federal dairy price programs. Furthermore, bST was portrayed as an unwanted and potentially unhealthy additive imposed on consumers. The FDA's response emphasized bST's safety and maintained that it was beyond the purview of the agency to determine the social and economic consequences of new technologies (U.S. Congress 1986, 66). If such economic impact criteria were included in FDA review procedures, not only would bST be doomed to fail, but the entire regulatory process would be upset—thus threatening established actors and arrangements. These actors, which included federal regulatory authorities and a clientele base made up primarily of the pharmaceutical industry, research interests, and the veterinary medicine community, mobilized resources, often in concert, to fend off this challenge.

Given that the decision-making power rested in the FDA's hands, a simple agenda denial strategy would have been for the review and approval of bST to be expedited, thus laying the controversy to rest. This would have allowed bST to come to market and would have set a precedent for regulating new biotechnologies. By establishing this precedent, arguments for new regulatory procedures aimed at biotechnology in general and calls for the review of socioeconomic impacts might be defeated. But the FDA was not in a position to exercise this option. The nature of regulatory politics, the FDA's past history, and larger social and political factors prevented such actions from being taken, highlighting the importance of agenda denial tactics in policy debate.

Regulatory decisions are not made in a vacuum. If the issue under consideration has been subject to political and public scrutiny, administrative authorities will display a great deal of sensitivity to institutional and social factors. This is particularly true for the FDA, an agency whose actions have often come under the microscope of congressional scrutiny and the spotlight of public attention. As a number of scholars have observed (Foreman 1988; Bryner 1987; Wilson 1989), the FDA often gets it from both sides for being too slow, too quick, too lax, or too strict when it comes to regulatory review. Regulated interests complain of onerous information requirements and a lengthy review process, and champions of the public interest often fault the FDA for being too permissive and too accommodating to industry demands. These debates often play out in congressional committee hearings and deliberations.

For members of Congress, there are rewards for serving as effective brokers or mediators in regulatory controversies. Thus, they can work as ombudsmen for regulated interests that feel that the system is too burdensome and bureaucratic, or as champions for consumers, citizens, and constituents when risk or threat seems apparent. They also provide guidance to agencies through policy signaling and oversight activities (Foreman 1988). This function is particularly important, because Congress has tended to cede considerable discretion to the FDA under broad and ambiguous statutes (Wilson 1989). Because attention tends to be on the review of products rather than on procedure, many committees can claim jurisdiction over FDA matters. Increasingly, the role of broker is one that the White House sees for itself as well (Plein 1992; Friedman 1995).

In the case of the FDA, regulated interests enjoy a high level of access and involvement in the regulatory review process. The costs of product review and compliance are an expensive and bitter pill that private interests realize they must endure. However, there are benefits as well, since a complicated regulatory process serves as an effective barrier to entry for newcomers, hence providing some market protection. In addition, a positive FDA determination is a seal of approval that can win investor interest in product development, secure consumer confidence in the marketplace, and provide legal indemnity from product failure. In short, it is in the interest of the regulated to forge effective working relationships with regulatory authorities. Indeed, the regulatory review process for new animal drugs reveals a close working relationship between regulators and the regulated. It follows, then, that calls for significant changes in the way the review procedures are carried out may be unwelcome to both regulated interests and government regulators.

The review of drugs for animals is conducted by the FDA's Center for Veterinary Medicine and involves a two-step process. The first is an application to conduct product research. When this approval is given, the applicant conducts extensive research to determine the safety and efficacy of the new drug and submits the data and analysis for FDA review. To encourage candor and protect proprietary information, reports may be exempted from public scrutiny under "confidential business information" criteria. Once these studies are completed, an application is made for final approval to market the drug. During the investigation, decisions are made to determine the safety of consuming products from drug-treated animals. For example, in 1984, the FDA approved studies for animal safety and efficacy and allowed the marketing of milk from bST test herds (U.S. Congress 1991, 44). In sum, the established procedure for reviewing new animal drugs, such as bST, turns on four criteria: human safety, animal safety, efficacy and consistency in drug production and results, and environmental safety (U.S. Congress 1992a, 2–3).

Overall, the animal drug review process appears to be a relatively closed policy-making arrangement. There is significant reliance on regulated interests to provide the relevant data, and the scope of review is limited to efficacy, potential environmental risks, and human and animal safety. This process emphasizes scientific methodologies and analysis; larger questions of the possible economic and social consequences of new drugs are excluded. Confidential business information requirements may serve to protect petitioners from unwanted public scrutiny over the quality and findings of research studies. Public participation is limited to the deliberations and meetings of the Veterinary Medicine Advisory Committee (VMAC), a body made up primarily of researchers who offer evaluations and recommendations on drug reviews. Meetings of these groups provide limited opportunities for public input. Like other federal advisory committees (see Lowrance 1986; Dickson 1988), the VMAC has been criticized for being too representative of scientific and industry interests at the expense of those voicing broader social and economic impact concerns.

Given the limited opportunities for access to the review process, those calling for changes in regulatory procedures seek other forums and rely on intermediaries, such as affected groups and institutional supporters. Affected groups are those that have standing, in a legal or de facto sense, vis-à-vis a pending regulatory action. For example, during the 1970s, the use of court injunctions became a popular tool to delay or block the implementation of agency rulings. In the past, standing was frequently granted to those with an indirect tie to the issue at hand (see Kerwin 1994, 254–6). However, achieving such status has become more difficult in an era of conservative judicial appointments. As a result, process-oriented interests may seek linkages to those with *substantive* concerns. In the case of bST, these parties were first identified as small-scale dairy farmers, and later consumers. It was hoped that institutional representatives of these interests, such as members of state legislatures and sympathetic members of Congress, would articulate these concerns in the policy arena and spark movement toward new regulatory requirements.

bST: THE MAKING OF A PUBLIC POLICY ISSUE

The emergence of bST as a vehicle to promote social impact assessment in regulatory review satisfies the three criteria for expecting an issue to attain agenda status identified in chapter 1 by Cobb and Ross and elsewhere by others (Stone 1988). First, statistical models of the potential impact of bST detailed how the product would drive small-scale farmers from the dairy sector. Research studies at Cornell University (Kalter et al. 1984) received wide circulation in academic, media, and policy circles. Second, emerging controversies over product adoption and accompanying press attention raised the issue quickly and sharply for the public. Third, social impact criteria developed in Western Europe for new agricultural technologies set precedents for similar actions in the United States. These issues came into sharp focus once bST left the laboratory and was submitted for regulatory review. The review and pending decision on bST provided an opportunity for the challenge to FDA procedures to emerge and for the actions of the FDA and its supports to deny agenda access to these questions.

In their agenda-setting efforts, bST's critics developed two issue images. One centered on the threat that new biotechnologies, such as bST, posed to family farmers and rural communities. This image relied on the cultural saliency of pastoralism, as traditionally expressed in the agrarian myth and manifested in the ideal of the American family farm. After having limited success with this image, a new issue image portrayed bST as a threat to consumer health. For challengers, the use of evocative images, such as the demise of the family farm and the threat of hormone-laced milk, was effective in translating ambiguous concerns about unchecked and underregulated technological developments and their social and economic effects. As a result, a technically complex and relatively narrow matter was transformed into a broader policy issue that posed challenges to existing policy and institutional arrangements.

At one level, the contest was over whether federal regulatory procedures should take into account social and economic impact issues, but the bST debate was played out on many fronts, as champions for social impact assessment sought to raise public awareness. In particular, the debate found purchase in the legislatures of a few dairy states, where activism led to the introduction of legislation aimed at banning or otherwise disabling the marketing of bST. For example, in 1989, the Wisconsin state legislature considered legislation calling for the labeling of dairy products derived from bST-treated cattle. Similar measures were considered in the Minnesota and Vermont legislatures ("Three States Consider bST Bills" 1989a, 6). In the first half of 1991, both Wisconsin and Minnesota passed temporary moratoriums on the sale of bST-treated milk (Schwarze 1990, 6). The same year, the Vermont legislature passed a resolution calling for Congress to study the "economic effects of growth hormone on the farm, on consumer preference, and on the dairy industry" prior to regulatory approval ("Three States" 1989, 6). Grassroots groups, working under the guidance of Washington-based environmental and public-interest advocates, supported these bills at the state level. Supporters of bST had a difficult time in these state battles. For example, in Wisconsin, the Monsanto Company committed considerable money and time to combat the state labeling initiative, only to be defeated in a committee vote (Sawyer

1989b, 1A; Sawyer 1989a, A16). As one industry official perceived the situation, state legislatures lacked political complexity, allowing well-organized advocates to engage in "public policy terrorism," where actions are driven more by perception than by fact (IBA 1989a, 10).

Initially, the most vocal opposition to bST came from small networks of dairy farmers and rural lifestyle advocates who saw the product as just the latest in a series of capital-intensive production techniques characteristic of modern agriculture (see Browne 1987). These interests saw bST as a threat to small-scale or family farming. Because the controversy emerged during a period of farm crisis unrelated to the product, the prospect of another nail in the coffin for family farming had an apparent appeal for issue-definition efforts aimed at thwarting bST's adoption. This debate caught the attention of a loose coalition of public-interest advocates concerned about the pace of technological change and the capacity of regulatory arrangements to prevent disruptive social and economic consequences. The bST debate gave these policy process interests a measure of standing in state legislatures. It also gained these groups limited entrée at the federal level, as can be seen in the congressional testimony from a representative of the Humane Society of the United States: "Such a revolution in the dairy industry will mean the extinction of small- and mid-sized family dairy farm operations. Diversity is important because it is an integral aspect of an ecologically sound and economically stable and democratic agriculture. If BGH is marketed, it will stimulate the trend toward monopolistic 'super farms' " (U.S. Congress 1986, 276).

The controversy generated attention in such national media as the *Wall Street Journal* and the *New York Times*.[2] State-level activity provided opportunities for bST's opponents to receive press coverage and generate awareness of the issue. The threat that bST posed to traditional farming was sharply drawn in a *New York Times Magazine* article, which stated, "Bovine Growth Hormone is perhaps the clearest example of the raw power of new technology, and the increasing swiftness of the changes it is likely to produce" (Schneider 1988, 47). The implications for family farming were recognized in both the popular media and academic circles (Kalter et al. 1985; Comstock 1988). Also significant were actions that Western European countries and the European Economic Community took in delaying the adoption of bST until social impact consequences could be assessed.[3]

Interestingly, those who had the greatest immediate stake in the dairy market implications of bST—that is, dairy farmers—displayed ambivalence toward the new production technique. Although there was noticeable resistance to the product among small-scale dairy producers in such states as Wisconsin, Vermont, and Minnesota, mainstream dairy farmers and their trade organizations tended to take a hands-off approach to the debate. For example, a March 1989 poll found that 75 percent of dairy farmers opposed bST, but only 28 percent stated that they would not use the new product. The poll also found that levels of support for bST

were lower among small-scale farmers than among owners of large dairy operations ("Those Who Oppose bST" 1989, 6). In the larger agricultural community, support for bST split along lines of operational scale. The National Farmers
Union, a 300,000-member association made up primarily of small-scale farmers,
expressed opposition to bST. The American Farm Bureau Federation, the nation's largest agricultural association, representing larger-scale agricultural operations, expressed support for the adoption of bST and other agricultural
biotechnologies (Sauber 1989, 24). One trade journal expressed dismay over the
National Milk Producers Federation's lack of leadership and neutral position toward bST, sensing indecisiveness about the consequences of new technologies
("Where Is the Industry's Leadership?" 1990, 111). In short, there appeared to be
an atmosphere of resignation among many in the dairy industry that bST, like
other new dairy technologies, was inevitable and that the cross-pressures meant
that major dairy trade associations sought to remove themselves from the fray of
debate (Scott and Plein 1988). However, their potential mobilization in the debate remained a pressing concern for bST's champions.

TURNING BACK THE CHALLENGE:
THE USE OF AGENDA DENIAL TACTICS

The bST controversy caught both regulators and the regulated flat-footed.
Originally, those firms that had developed bST were more interested in being the
first to bring the product to market and perceived one another as competitors.
That these firms would join together to promote bST and defend existing regulatory arrangements testifies to the seriousness of the emergent challenges. Sensing
a threat to the regulatory review process, the FDA and other vested public and
private interests realized the importance of mounting a response to growing concerns manifested in state legislative activity, press coverage, and congressional
hearings and investigations. The decision to counter the regulatory system's critics required the commitment of resources on the part of both regulators and the
regulated. Most significantly, the decision acknowledged that the challenge could
not be ignored. They wanted an aggressive defense of the FDA involving attack,
counterattack, and alliance building toward their goal of agenda denial. Such an
effort required the development of both agenda denial strategies and tactics.
Strategic decisions focused on two aspects of agenda denial: identifying and
framing issue messages to specific audiences and players, and building and maintaining sources of support for agenda denial efforts. Tactical responses involved
what Cobb and Ross term medium-cost strategies. In the case of the bST debate,
the opponents of consideration used strategies that included placing the issue in
the context of the larger social and cultural milieu, discrediting opponents, asserting that the issue under debate was not worthy of attention, and emphasizing the
efficacy of existing institutional arrangements.

Identifying Relevant Players and Audiences:
A Strategic Perspective in Agenda Denial

Agenda denial success is shaped by resource usage. In the case of the bST controversy, those seeking to thwart agenda challenges identified three key audiences. One was the general public. As voters and consumers, the public could pose a threat in both the marketplace and the policy arena. The other key audiences in the debate were the dairy sector and the commercial biotechnology research and industry community. The former would pose a significant political threat if it mobilized against bST. The latter was perceived as essential to mobilizing support in fending off challenges to both the product and the regulatory process. In dealing with the public, agenda denial efforts depended on *broadcasting* efforts. In dealing with targeted audiences, agenda denial depended on *narrowcasting* efforts.

Defenders of bST and existing arrangements saw that it was necessary to broadcast issue images to prevent the public from becoming sympathetic to the plight of dairy farmers and concerned about the potential consumer health risks associated with bST. Thus, issue definition activities focused on conveying the positive benefits of bST, stressing that the product was not a threat to the family farmer, and emphasizing the safety of the product. Both government agencies and private interests were involved in these activities. For example, the U.S. Department of Agriculture (USDA) sponsored public conferences and distributed news items emphasizing the positive benefits of new agricultural biotechnologies such as bST (USDA 1987, 1988). Both the FDA and the National Institutes of Health provided information on the safety of bST through press releases and other outlets (Corey 1990). Among bST's developers and those in the biotechnology industry, public information campaigns were launched, aimed at providing briefing materials to major newspapers and other media outlets (Animal Health Institute and Industrial Biotechnology Association 1989).

The practice of narrowcasting also figured prominently in agenda denial activities. Throughout the debate, a key targeted audience was the dairy industry. Both regulated interests and government actors crafted messages aimed at minimizing concerns in the dairy industry over potential sectoral impacts and consumer backlash. Given its long-standing position in the agricultural policy arena, had the dairy industry mobilized against bST, the prospects for congressional review and regulatory change would have been considerable. Therefore, proponents of bST sought to convince the dairy industry that the product would be beneficial to the dairy sector. Fortunately for bST's developers, a number of key players within the agricultural policy arena, located in Congress, the USDA, and the FDA, were supportive of new agricultural biotechnologies (Plein 1991). This support was essential not only to allay dairy industry fears but also because bST's manufacturers were dependent on third-party support, as they were legally enjoined from advertising bST until they obtained formal FDA approval.

Apart from seeking to prevent the mobilization of dairy sector resistance, narrowcasting techniques were used to shore up and build support within the biotechnology industry and among governmental actors. The efforts of individual private interests and industry trade groups to link bST to the fortunes of commercial biotechnology helped strengthen support. Industry efforts to portray bST and other agricultural biotechnologies as a tool for progress and economic development also generated governmental backing. This message found resonance and acceptance among federal policy makers in Congress, the White House, and administrative agencies (Plein 1991). Thus, narrowcasting achieved the strategic ends of both easing dairy sector concerns and strengthening alliances.

Fighting Fire with Fire: Crafting Cultural and Symbolic Counterimages

Evocative images are central to issue expansion and agenda setting, as the engine of public and political awareness is built on the foundations of drama and stark contrasts (Cobb and Elder 1983; Eyestone 1978; Nimmo and Combs 1980; Stone 1988). In an effort to gain attention and encourage policy action, advocates of a ban on bST frequently resorted to the use of dramatic and culturally salient images to raise consciousness. In responding to these challenges, bST's champions offered alternative interpretations of the broad images presented. This agenda tactic marks a divergence from conventional wisdom, which holds that defenders of existing arrangements will seek to limit debate, and suggests that public and policy attention on bST quickly reached a level where the low-cost denial option was no longer viable.

In the face of the evocative image of bST undermining a foundation of U.S. culture—the family farm—bST's champions and their allies fashioned a counterimage of the decline of family farming. This image embraced the notion of the family farmer but sought to remind the public that it was essentially a vestige of the past. Instead, it emphasized how U.S. agriculture could be a bellwether for progress and provide both economic and social rewards. In this formulation, those emphasizing the endangered family farm were doing so for ulterior motives—not to protect the farmer, but to advance a radical platform aimed at turning back modern progress and economic development (U.S. Congress 1986, 297, 301). Those favoring the adoption of bST and the advancement of agricultural biotechnology often sought to place bST in the context of larger forces sweeping U.S. agriculture and society. In this way, an appearance of sympathy toward the decline of family farms could be conveyed, while a message of practical realities could be reinforced. For example, an editorial in the trade journal *Bio/Technology* surmised:

> Just as environmentalists value the pure qualities of the natural world, Americans value the traditional family farm and all that the image conjures

up. There are those who worry that the emergence of genetic engineering and the other tools of biotechnology heralds a downfall of this idealized, romanticized American institution. These concerns are genuine yet, at the same time, the trend toward consolidation that has affected American farming patterns has emerged independent of biotechnology. Economies of scale demanding significant capital investment offer monetary advantages to the larger operations. (Blair and Rowan 1989, 840)

This theme, that biotechnology and bST were part of larger forces changing the face of agriculture, was frequently emphasized in congressional testimony, public-relations materials, government reports, and other outlets (U.S. Congress 1986; USDA 1987, 1988). Such a posture provided a justification that bST, and indeed biotechnology, was no different from past agricultural technologies and hence should not be judged by different standards in the regulatory process.

"Latter-Day Luddites": Discrediting Opponents

The trade-off between preservation and progress was a price too dear for many supporters of the family farm ideal, considering international competitiveness issues, economic development concerns, and world food demands. Although our culture celebrates the traditional and the pastoral found in the agrarian myth, it also criticizes those who fail to adapt to a changing world. This countervailing tendency often focuses on agriculture (Hofstadter 1955). The realist stance taken by protectors of existing regulatory arrangements—that change in U.S. agriculture is inevitable—provided a springboard from which to launch attacks aimed at discrediting challengers. Focusing on the actions of a Wisconsin dairy producers group (and exaggerating their influence), Republican Representative Dick Armey of Texas wrote:

> This last possibility—that even a single farmer might quit farming—haunts some farm legislators. The guiding spirit of much of our farm policy seems to be the desire to freeze the farm economy in time—to stop all change, prevent all efficiencies—out of fear that somebody in the farming business might have to switch jobs. . . . More recently, a milk producers' lobby opposed the use of a hormone that would vastly increase production of milk. As we move into the competitive 1990s, one of America's largest industries is being run by "latter-day luddites." (Armey 1990, 29)

Similarly, in testimony before a committee of the Wisconsin state legislature, the Industrial Biotechnology Association (IBA) attacked those that it saw as seeking to halt progress and embrace a romantic vision of the past. Such champions of the idealized past were characterized as out of touch with the mainstream American values of technological progress and free market principles. In testimony before a Wisconsin legislative committee regarding proposed legislation to ban bST, an IBA representative noted: "We suggest that this action is the very antithesis of the American free enterprise, entrepreneurial system which encourages each producer to turn out a superior product at a lower price. It is, in a sense, an attempt to make time stand still and to cement the status quo in place— perhaps, forever" (IBA 1989b, 8).

Efforts to discredit opponents involved an us-versus-them strategy that dovetailed well with an effort to ally dairy and biotechnology interests. One tactic focused on portraying researchers and dairy interests as united in a collective stance against those forces seeking to stop progress and economic development. At a dairy industry meeting, a representative for American Cyanamid, one of the companies involved in bST research and development, warned of those who were "trying to make the dairy industry a pawn in their broader fight against all technology" (Annexstad 1987, 24). In these efforts to win over, or at least placate, those in the dairy industry, bST's proponents found a useful ally in the U.S. Department of Agriculture. The USDA provided promotional activities and conducted economic research suggesting that bST was not a revolutionary new technique that would change the face of dairy farming but just the latest in a series of advances in dairy technologies (USDA 1987, 1988).

Discrediting opponents as an agenda denial tactic endured throughout the bST debate. Later in the controversy, opponents raising human health concerns were also portrayed as extremists turning back the tides of progress. For example, in 1989, after anti-bST groups secured temporary agreements from some grocery store chains to ban the selling of dairy products from bST-treated test herds, an FDA official branded a leading critic as practicing "scare tactics," while a representative of the Monsanto Corporation likened him to an "anti-biotechnology zealot" ("Store Bans Milk" 1989, C1). One champion of bST claimed that the product was being used as a "Trojan horse" to advance various causes not directly linked to the dairy industry.[4] Responding to milk labeling proposals in Wisconsin, a Monsanto representative commented, "If we let the Luddites of this country determine our agricultural policy and or biotechnology policy, we're all in trouble" (Sawyer 1989a, A16). Attacks were also made on other groups and individuals mobilized against bST, including research scientists who raised public health issues (Scheid 1990).

bST as a Benign Technology: Defusing Controversy

From a resource utilization perspective, the process of discrediting opponents was relatively inexpensive and risk free. However, such actions signal to others that a controversy is afoot. Thus, it is a tactic that is most effective when used in concert with other agenda denial techniques. A complementary tactic involves efforts that portray an issue as familiar, incremental, commonplace, and risk free, challenging claims to an issue's novelty and significance. The portrayal of bST as a benign dairy technology countered negative criticism and attention.

Securing dairy industry acquiescence, if not acceptance, of bST was no easy task, in great part because of the challenges that bST's developers had helped create. In their efforts to gain attention and herald the development of a new dairy production technique, bST's developers initially emphasized the production gains achievable through its use. This was not exactly welcome news to the dairy industry, since it is underwritten by an economically and politically sensitive price support system. Some feared that bST would upset their subsidies. Critics of bST seized upon this fear, emphasizing that the drug would increase milk production and set off a downward spiral in revenues, contributing to the decline of family farms and causing greater taxpayer burdens for the financing of price floors on dairy commodities.

Sensing concern among dairy farmers that bST would upset milk price support systems and perhaps drive smaller operations out of business, its producers moved from the rosy scenarios of greater milk production to more mundane relative efficiencies of dairy herd operations through the use of the product. In other words, increased per cow production meant that fewer cows would be needed. For example, the Animal Health Institute (AHI), a trade association made up of agricultural biotechnology and pharmaceutical concerns, reported that bST "makes dairy cows more efficient" (AHI 1989, 3). This sentiment was echoed in a Monsanto brochure, which explained, "As a management tool, bST will allow dairymen to produce their current amount of milk with fewer animals, reducing their costs and increasing their profits" (Monsanto n.d., 6). Efforts were also made by the industry to emphasize that bST was relatively scale-neutral, allowing smaller operations to adopt the product just as easily as large-scale operations. As one industry representative observed in testimony at a congressional hearing, "bST will provide important economic benefits for all dairymen, small as well as large. Unlike most other technological advances, bST's benefits will be available equally to smaller family farms" (U.S. Congress 1986, 291).

Realizing that the key to both political and market acceptance of bST was preventing widespread opposition in the dairy industry, bST's supporters sought to blunt the sharp edge of the family farming issue by emphasizing the scale neutrality and the incremental nature of the product. Individual pronouncements of biotechnology firms, statements by government officials, scientific research, and government studies and reports all served to reinforce this image. However, such an effort was more than the aggregate of individual actions taken by those supportive of bST; it was also the product of coordinated actions. For example, in March 1987, the five major producers of bST and the AHI teamed up for a public information initiative called the bST Public Information Working Group. The primary target of the initiative was the dairy industry, followed by academic dairy researchers, veterinarians, and government officials at the state and federal levels (Klausner 1987, 663).

bST Safety and Regulatory Efficacy: Public Reassurance

In an attempt to widen the scope of conflict, critics of FDA regulatory procedures also sought to raise concerns over health risks associated with bST. On the surface, the image of consumer risk portrayed by bST's detractors was indeed evocative. The image of contaminated milk had a resonance that could not be matched by parallel developments in biotechnology, ranging from the development of leaner pork to herbicide-resistant crops to new strains of tomatoes (Martin 1990, 186). In 1990, a coalition of bST opponents kicked off a publicity effort under the provocative title the Pure Milk Campaign. As part of their efforts, they assembled television announcements, organized boycotts by well-known restaurant chefs, and reached agreements with supermarket chains to ban the sale of bST-treated dairy products (Hoyle 1992). In addition to this effort to expand the bST issue, charges were leveled at the FDA for lacking scientific objectivity and covering up the human health risks of bST. Ironically, however, by emphasizing the consumer risk issue, opponents of bST and champions of regulatory change played into the hands of those protecting existing regulatory arrangements. A challenge to the FDA was a challenge to the regulatory system in general, and any effort to frame criticism based on risk to human health invited the FDA and its allies to marshal scientific evidence to the contrary.

In an effort to dampen potential consumer fears, proponents stressed that bST was a naturally occurring product. In the same vein, the industry consciously changed references to the product from bovine growth hormone (bGH) to bovine somatotropin, distancing the products and negative perceptions associated with hormone use in drugs and food products. Before this shift in terminology, the USDA's Public Liaison Office emphasized that bovine growth hormone was a *"natural hormone* that cows produce already" and would merely "supplement" the cow's hormone levels (USDA 1987, IV-3). The point that bST was no different from naturally occurring bovine somatotropin was expressed in hearing testimony and public-relations materials as well (U.S. Congress 1986, 5; Sawyer 1989a, 16A). Industry and government officials also stressed the safety of the product. One FDA official commented at a USDA conference that bST was one of the "most benign drugs" ever reviewed (Scheid 1990, 17).

To counter charges that bST was unsafe and that the FDA was somehow derelict in its review of the drug, the agency engaged in a number of actions departing from established procedures. For example, at the FDA's request, the National Institutes of Health (NIH) convened a public conference on bST and human safety in December 1990 (U.S. Congress 1992b, 21). A summary session of the conference, geared toward the public and the media, reiterated previous findings that bST was safe for human consumption. This endorsement provided legitimacy to the FDA's tentative decision made some six years earlier. During this time, the FDA also published a peer reviewed article in a scientific journal, providing data and analysis that bST was safe for human consumption. This was unusual, since the FDA generally refuses to publish data until drug approval reviews are complete (U.S. Congress 1992b, 21). The FDA and the NIH also prepared articles and press releases for general public circulation supporting the safety of bST.

In short, many of the actions taken to deflect safety concerns and assert the credibility of the FDA had a symbolic flavor. Changing references from bovine growth hormone to bST was a relatively low-cost tactic providing distance from a negative term. Acquiring endorsements from the NIH and publishing findings in a peer reviewed journal were symbolic acts aimed at establishing the scientific credibility of the review process. In the closing months of the bST controversy, the FDA engaged in symbolic actions to convey the image that it was sensitive to consumer concerns. These involved deliberations of the VMAC on the need for labeling of bST-treated milk and a final FDA decision to allow those who did not adopt the product to advertise their products as bST free. Obviously, such action served to protect the FDA but did little for those seeking to market the product. These actions met with disapproval by bST's developers and by the larger biotechnology community, illustrating that agenda denial actions are not always taken in unison (Hoyle 1993a, 1994).

Alliance Building and Risk Minimizing: The Strategic Dimension of Coalition Support

Many who rallied to the defense of bST feared that its defeat would cloud prospects for the biotechnology industry or signal the beginning of new regulatory schemes based on social and economic risk criteria. These interests included members of the research community; the nascent biotechnology industry, which included established pharmaceutical and chemical concerns; and federal officials. When Richard Godown, president of the industry's lead trade organization, responded to proposed legislation before the Wisconsin legislature, he summed up the willingness of the industry to become involved in the bST debate: "IBA opposes the bST ban because it would be a bad precedent for future biotechnology products, singling them out as a result of allegations of economic damage not afforded past technological advances" (IBA 1989b, 8).

Alliance building is a strategic component of agenda denial efforts. By building a broad base of support, those involved in agenda denial can share the political and tangible costs involved. Not only those with an immediate stake in bST, but also those mobilized to defend existing regulatory arrangements, such as researchers, other biotechnology-related firms, and government officials, were engaged in agenda denial activities. For example, bST developers drew on the expertise and energies of two trade associations, the IBA and the AHI, to lobby and campaign to defeat calls for a ban on bST and an overhaul of regulatory review procedures. These groups tried to convey a positive image of bST. These associations, which drew their budgets from a much broader membership base, were also able to shield particular companies from controversy by taking the lead in the debate. bST's developers also found welcome assistance from government agencies. The USDA's publicity campaigns helped communicate the industry's message that bST was an incremental, benign, and useful product for use in the dairy sector. Various FDA pronouncements on bST and other agricultural biotechnologies helped reinforce this message. In fact, it can be argued that those private interests championing bST were able to achieve cost savings from a de facto public subsidy. Apart from providing a conduit for advancing issue images, the involvement of government actors in the agenda denial process also lent an air of legitimacy to the bST developers' position. To strengthen this legitimacy, the industry also sought out scientific backing for its position—a common tactic in contemporary policy debate (Lowrance 1986).

Initially, bST supporters framed the debate as a make-or-break issue to mobilize support. However, with awareness of the potential damage to regulatory arrangements and industry plans, efforts turned to minimizing the consequences of the outcome. Instead, the bST debate was framed as one of a number of challenges to the fortunes of the biotechnology industry and served as a reminder of the need to preserve regulatory arrangements in the face of opposition. In short, we can tender a generalization that the dynamics of agenda debate and the risks of participation lead to a cycle in which established interests are first slow to respond due to fears of risk and exposure, next seek to build support once participation is committed through dramatic portrayals, and then seek to minimize the risks of participation in order to maintain a coalition organized against an agenda challenge.

To maintain a base of support over the long haul of an issue debate, both sides engaged in the strategic assessment of relative opportunity costs. For defenders to sustain support, possible defeat had to be defined to minimize potential losses. It is one thing to activate supporters in the face of immediate danger but another to sustain their interest. Rhetoric changed during the course of the debate, transforming bST from a safety issue to a challenge facing commercial biotechnology and existing regulatory arrangements. Concern over the relative risks posed to various actors can be seen throughout the debate. At times, industry leaders sought to distance themselves from debate (McCormick 1993) and from the rumblings of discontent over the impact that a negative outcome would have on nonagricultural biotechnology interests (Plein 1991). The FDA engaged in symbolic activity that was not always in concert with industry interests. In agenda denial alliances, individual self-preservation may become a centrifugal force that can fray a coalition's unity.

However, risk and opportunity cost calculations are an important tool in turning back challenges. After gauging the level of challengers' commitment, appropriate agenda denial tactics can be crafted. This becomes a particularly important concept when assessing the role of those oriented around the procedural rather than the substantive dimensions of debate. As Kingdon (1994), Sabatier (1991), Baumgartner and Jones (1993), and others have observed, today's policy arena is often characterized by issue-oriented actors and coalitions in search of a policy niche in which to advance their causes. They will, at times, make their cause fit another set of circumstances and concerns unique to the context of current events or a particular policy venue.

THE bST ENDGAME: POLITICAL PRESSURES AND DELAY

When bST was first submitted to the FDA for regulatory review in 1984, it was generally assumed that the course of approval would be completed sometime in the late 1980s. Yet in the spring of 1993, the product had yet to win formal approval, despite research that appeared to satisfy safety and efficacy requirements. On review, it is apparent that a lack of positive policy signaling from Congress and the White House explains the delay in the FDA approval process. During the late 1980s and early 1990s, legislators from dairy states acquiesced to constituent pressures and sent negative signals to the FDA. In the closing months of the bST debate, it was the Clinton White House, seeking to establish its regulatory agenda, that communicated the need to delay a decision on bST.

When facing controversial issues, administrative actors usually seek political endorsement before taking action, to avoid political risks. Through the late 1980s and early 1990s, Congress sent mixed signals regarding the regulation of biotechnology in general and bST in particular. On the one hand, both Republican White Houses and a Democratic Congress expressed broad support for the development of biotechnology (Plein 1990). In Congress, the rush to embrace biotechnology took the form of legislative calls to enhance commercial development through regulatory coordination and research support, the formation of a legislative organization to promote biotechnology, and the commissioning of Office of Technology Assessment reports that often reflected favorably on the industry (Plein and Webber 1992). On the other hand, when discussion moved from the abstract to specific product applications, congressional support had a habit of shifting from ambivalence to resistance. Thus, such issues as the patenting of transgenic animals, the use of genetically engineered microbes in crop science, and the use of gene therapy and mapping in human health sometimes sparked controversy in committee hearings. The case of bST was no exception, and although Congress was far from considering legislation aimed at altering existing regulatory arrangements, there were calls for the FDA to conduct more research on human safety issues and to defer making a determination.

In the spring of 1993, the FDA again formally reiterated the human safety of bST through recommendations offered by the VMAC. This pronouncement raised industry expectations that a formal decision would be forthcoming (Fox

1993b; Hoyle 1993a). However, action did not follow, leading to speculation that the White House was putting direct pressure on the FDA to delay approval. The motives for the delay seemed to be twofold. First, a delay would allow the Clinton administration to clarify its own stance on biotechnology regulation and commercial promotion. By espousing both a pro-technological and pro-environmental agenda, the Clinton administration was walking a tightrope. Second, it appeared that the Clinton administration was hoping that the European Economic Community would reverse its ban on bST, thus paving the way for a U.S. decision that would defuse possible domestic backlash and smooth agricultural trade negotiations (Hoyle 1993a, 978). Such hopes were in vain.

What finally paved the way for the formal approval of bST was a symbolic gesture that appeased congressional detractors and conveyed a sense of responsiveness on the part of the Clinton administration to the larger social and economic impacts of bST. In August 1993, the Clinton White House accepted a tacit bargain with Senator Russell Feingold of Wisconsin that in return for his vote on the Clinton budget and deficit reduction plan, there would be a ninety-day moratorium on the sale of bST after the date of the formal FDA determination (McCormick 1993; Fox 1993a; Hoyle 1993a). Ostensibly, the purpose of this delay was so that the USDA could conduct studies of bST's economic impact on the dairy industry. This allowed a freshman dairy state senator to claim a symbolic, if hollow, victory for his constituents. The bargain also signaled that a positive FDA decision was all but guaranteed, and in fact, this action gave the green light for FDA approval. The agency wasted little time, and in November 1993, FDA gave formal approval to Monsanto to market bST.

The trade journal *Bio/Technology* observed, "With FDA approval, the longstanding controversy over bST will soon shift to the marketplace, where critics are promising to stage mass boycotts of the milk and other products derived from bST-treated animals" (Fox 1993a, 1502). However, with few exceptions, consumer response to bST has not been as controversial as originally expected. Because the FDA allowed milk producers to label dairy products that had not been treated with bST, there was some concern that consumers would boycott bST-treated milk. In fact, a number of milk and dairy product producers advertised their goods as bST free when the product began to be used in dairy operations. However, rather than creating widespread consumer demand, bST-free labeling created a special market niche for more expensive dairy products. As a result, large-scale dairy processors such as Land O'Lakes, which uses bST-treated milk in its dairy products, also developed a specialty line of bST-free products. The upshot of all this was that by early 1995, 95 percent of the company's milk sales came from bST-treated cows, and 5 percent of its products were bST free. Ironically, under such market arrangements, previously threatened small-scale dairy farms might well prosper as bST-free boutique operations (Hoyle 1995b, 14). An important constituency of the anti-bST coalition could well be taken out of the picture.

In 1994, bST use was reported in more than 8 percent of the U.S. dairy herd of 9.5 million cows, and growing (Hoyle 1995b, 15).

CONCLUSION

Political victories are achieved at a cost. In this case, regulatory arrangements were preserved at the expense of delaying a determination on bST. The submission of bST for review helped create conditions sufficient for a challenge to regulatory policy arrangements. Those allied against bST, not so much for what it was but because it represented a means of expressing concern over the lack of social and economic impact criteria in regulatory assessments, were successful in raising concerns but failed in their efforts at policy change. Both the regulated and the regulators clearly perceived these actions as a threat and engaged in a protracted agenda denial effort aimed at fending off these challenges. In the end, these interests were able to delay the decision on bST in order to preserve a process that they had developed through mutual accommodation and cooperation.

This case provides insights into the complexities of the agenda denial process more generally. Events and outcomes were neither quick nor clear, but instead involved a wide range of actors with differing and sometimes contradictory motives. A review of the experience allows us to offer a few generalizations regarding agenda denial tactics. First, contrary to conventional depictions of issue containment and control strategies that emphasize the limitation of conflict, the use of counterimages crafted from cultural themes illustrates how agenda denial can involve issue expansion. In such circumstances, the aim is to convince a wider audience, such as dairy producers and the public, that an agenda challenge threatens their welfare. Second, the conflict involved both those with a stake in the new product and those concerned primarily with the efficacy and utility of existing policy arrangements. Third, agenda denial depends on mobilizing and sustaining allies. Such alliances can help spread the resource burden of engaging in agenda denial activities. Finally, mobilizing and maintaining such assistance involve some measure of calculating and minimizing the relative opportunity costs and risks involved in participating in agenda denial activities.

If political victories are not clear-cut, neither are they certain. As attention increasingly turns to administrative determinations of those who win or lose in regulatory decisions, there will be challenges to existing policy arrangements. bST proved to be a convenient, albeit unsuccessful, vehicle to challenge the regulatory review process. Critics of regulatory policy may yet advance their cause under different guises and in different quarters of the policy arena. However, for those mobilized to defend bST and the animal drug review process, the battle is essentially over. The product is now widely used in the dairy industry, and consumers buy milk and dairy products made from treated dairy cattle. Whereas once the product was portrayed as a make-or-break issue for the success of biotechnology and the integrity of regulatory arrangements, in the end, the bST controversy ended in a whisper.

NOTES

1. An understanding of the bST controversy requires a brief tour through the world of biotechnology and dairy science. Bovine somatotropin, also known as bovine growth hormone (bGH), is a naturally occurring hormone found in cows. When bST is injected into lactating dairy cows, milk production increases or, at minimum, greater feed-to-output efficiencies are achieved. This relationship has been known since the 1940s. However, until the late 1970s, the only source of bST was from cows themselves, making it impractical to produce the hormone in sufficient quantity for use in the dairy industry. In 1977, a method was developed for producing bST through recombinant DNA techniques (Scott and Plein 1988). Using bacteria as a host, the gene for producing bST is replicated at a scale that makes commercial production feasible. By the mid-1980s, a number of agricultural-chemical and pharmaceutical companies realized the market potential for bST as a dairy production technology. After the research and development stage, these companies submitted their own formulations of the product to the FDA for regulatory review and approval for marketing.

2. For example, on September 15, 1989, the *Wall Street Journal* published a story entitled "Sour Reception Greets Milk Hormone" (Richards 1989). On March 27, 1990, the *New York Times* published an article entitled "Wisconsin Leaders Back Curb on Sale of Growth Hormone."

3. The primary social impact involved the implications for the structure of agriculture, especially small-farm operators. Recent actions taken by the European Community to impose a five-year ban on the sale of bST suggest that adoption prospects will be limited in the near future (Ward 1995; Hoyle 1995a). European Community officials have explicitly stated that the moratorium on bST is based on socioeconomic and economic risk criteria. One official commented, "There is little point to a product that has both the potential to destabilize the already fragile market and, in addition, the power to lower consumption levels" (Collins 1994, 744).

4. Statement of Franklin Loew in a presentation sponsored by the Biotechnology Forum, March 16, 1992. The Biotechnology Forum was created as a congressional caucus to study rapid developments in biotechnology and explore commercialization prospects.

REFERENCES

Animal Health Institute. 1988. *This is AHI.* Alexandria, VA: Animal Health Institute.
———. 1989. Genetic engineering expected to revolutionize animal protein production. *Animal Health Letter* (August–September): 1
Animal Health Institute and Industrial Biotechnology Association. 1989. Biotechnology and animal health. Pamphlet.

Annexstad, J. 1987. Here's the latest on bST. *Dairy Herd Management* (April): 23–5.

Armey, R. 1990. Moscow on the Mississippi. *Policy Review* (winter): 24–9.

Baumgartner, F. R., and B. D. Jones. 1993. *Agendas and instability in American politics.* Chicago: University of Chicago Press.

Blair, S. A., and A. N. Rowan. 1989. Social policy matters. *Bio/Technology* (August): 840.

Browne, W. P. 1987. Bovine growth hormone and the politics of uncertainty: Fear and loathing in a transitional agriculture. *Agriculture and Human Values* 4(1): 75–80.

Bryner, G. 1987. *Bureaucratic discretion.* New York: Pergamon Press.

Cobb, R. W., and C. D. Elder. 1983. *Participation in American politics: The dynamics of agenda-building.* Baltimore: Johns Hopkins University Press.

Collins, K. 1994. Letter to the editor. *Bio/Technology* 12(8): 744.

Comstock, G. 1988. The case against bGH. *Agriculture and Human Values* 5(3): 36–52.

Corey, B. 1990. Bovine growth hormone: Harmless to humans. *FDA Consumer* (April): 2.

Dickson, D. 1988. *The new politics of science.* Chicago: University of Chicago Press.

Eyestone, R. 1978. *From social issues to public policy.* New York: John Wiley & Sons.

Foreman, C. 1988. *Signals from the hill.* New Haven, CT: Yale University Press.

Foundation on Economic Trends. 1989. *BGH information package.* Press release.

Fox, J. L. 1993a. FDA finally approves bST for milk production. *Bio/Technology* 11(12): 1502.

———. 1993b. "FDA ponders labels for bST-derived foods. *Bio/Technology* 11(6): 656, 658.

Friedman, B. D. 1995. *Regulation in the Reagan-Bush era.* Pittsburgh: University of Pittsburgh Press.

Hofstadter, R. 1955. *The age of reform.* New York: Vintage.

Hoyle, R. 1992. Rifkin resurgent. *Bio/Technology* 10(11): 1406–7.

———. 1993a. Going gets weird with bST and wildlands project. *Bio/Technology* 11(9): 978–9.

———. 1993b. Will Clinton/Gore rollback recombinants. *Bio/Technology* 11(1): 24–5.

———. 1994. FDA's bST policy wreaks havoc in the market. *Bio/Technology* 12(6): 570.

———. 1995a. Biotech needs an industry/government initiative. *Bio/Technology* 13(4): 316–7.

———. 1995b. bST off to a fast start, despite early stumbles. *Bio/Technology* 13(1): 13–5.

———. 1995c. Clinton gears up for Republican deregulation. *Bio/Technology* 13(3): 214, 216.

Industrial Biotechnology Association. 1989a. IBA May meeting spotlights ag biotech. *IBA Reports* (June/July): 1, 2, 9, 10, 11.

———. 1989b. IBA testifies at Wisconsin bST hearings. *IBA Reports* (June/July): 8.

Kalter, R., et al. 1984. *Biotechnology and the dairy industry: Production costs and commercial potential of the bovine growth hormone. AER-84-22.* Ithaca, NY: Department of Agricultural Economics, Cornell University.

———. 1985. The new biotech agriculture: Unforeseen economic consequences. *Issues in Science and Technology* 11(1): 125–33.

Kerwin, C. 1994. *Rulemaking: How government agencies write law and make policy.* Washington, DC: Congressional Quarterly Press.

Kingdon, J. W. 1994. *Agendas, alternatives, and public policies.* New York: HarperCollins.

Klausner, A. 1987. bST makers team up for education program. *Bio/Technology* 5(7): 663.

Lowrance, W. W. 1986. *Modern science and human values.* New York: Oxford University Press.

Martin, M. A. 1990. Potential economic impacts of agricultural biotechnology. In *Agricultural biotechnology: Food safety and nutritional quality for the consumer,* edited by J. F. MacDonald. Ithaca, NY: National Agricultural Biotechnology Council.

McCormick, D. 1993. Bovine growth hormone and pork-barrel politics. *Bio/Technology* 11(9): 963.

Monsanto Corporation. n.d. Monsanto agricultural company. St. Louis: Monsanto.

Nimmo, D., and J. E. Combs. 1980. *Subliminal politics: Myths and mythmakers in America.* Englewood Cliffs, NJ: Prentice-Hall.

Plein, L. C. 1990. Biotechnology: Issue development and evolution. In *Biotechnology: Assessing social impacts and policy implications,* edited by D. J. Webber. Westport, CT: Greenwood Press.

———. 1991. Popularizing biotechnology: The influence of issue definition. *Science, Technology & Human Values* 16(4): 474–90.

———. 1992. Presidential policy intervention and the Council on Competitiveness. Paper presented at the annual meeting of the Southern Political Science Association, Atlanta, November.

Plein, L. C., and D. J. Webber. 1992. The role of technology assessment in congressional consideration of biotechnology. In *Science, technology, and politics,* edited by G. Bryner. Boulder, CO: Westview Press.

Richards, B. 1989. Sour reception greets milk hormone. *Wall Street Journal,* September 15, p. B1.

Rochefort, D. A. and R. W. Cobb, eds. 1994. *The politics of problem definition: Shaping the policy agenda.* Lawrence: University Press of Kansas.

Sabatier, P. 1991. Toward better theories of the policy process. *PS* (June): 146–57.

Sauber, C. M. 1989. How will consumers respond to bST? *Dairy Herd Management* (April): 18–24.

Sawyer, J. 1989a. Chemical firms lose round. *St. Louis Post Dispatch,* October 26, p. 16A.

———. 1989b. Labeled: Monsanto's milk campaign sours. *St. Louis Post Dispatch,* October 29, pp. 1A, 13A.

Scheid, Jon F. 1990. bST approval likely this year. *Dairy Herd Management* (January): 17–9.

Schneider, K. 1988. Biotechnology's cash cow. *New York Times Magazine,* June 12, pp. 44–53.

Schoenbrod, D. 1993. *Power without responsibility: How Congress abuses the people through delegation.* New Haven, CT: Yale University Press.

Schwarze, D. 1990. From the states: BGH victory. *Gene Exchange* 1(2): 6.

Scott, J., and L. C. Plein. 1988. BGH and the dairy industry: Agenda setting for adoption and control. Paper presented at the Midwest Sociological Society meetings, Minneapolis, March 23–26.

Stone, D. 1988. *Policy paradox and political reason.* Glenview, IL: Scott, Foresman.

Stores ban milk from hormone treated cows. 1989. *St. Louis Post Dispatch,* August 24, p. C1.

Those who oppose bST may use it. 1989. *Dairy Herd Management* (September): 6.

Three states consider bST bills. 1989. *Dairy Herd Management* (July): 6.

U.S. Congress. 1986. Committee on Agriculture. *Review of status and potential impact of bovine growth hormone: Hearing before the Subcommittee on Livestock, Dairy, and Poultry.* 99th Cong. 2d sess. Washington, DC: U.S. Government Printing Office.

———. 1991. Office of Technology Assessment. *U.S. dairy industry at a crossroads: Biotech-*

nology and policy choices. Washington, DC: U.S. Government Printing Office.

———. 1992a. General Accounting Office. *Recombinant bovine growth hormone.* Washington, DC: U.S. Government Printing Office.

———. 1992b. Office of Technology Assessment. *A new technological era for American agriculture.* Washington, DC: U.S. Government Printing Office.

U.S. Department of Agriculture. 1987. *Biotechnology: The challenge, proceedings from the USDA biotechnology forum.* Washington, DC: U.S. Government Printing Office.

———. 1988. *Agricultural biotechnology and the public: Proceedings summary.* Washington, DC: U.S. Government Printing Office.

Ward, M. 1995. EU agrees on patents but nixes bST for five years. *Bio/Technology* 13(3): 212.

Where is the industry's leadership in these critical times? 1990. Editorial. *Hoard's Dairyman,* February 10, p. 111.

Wilson, J. Q. 1989. *Bureaucracy: What government agencies do and why they do it.* New York: Basic Books.

Wisconsin leaders back curb on sale of growth hormone. 1990. *New York Times,* March 27, p. A7.

6

Blue Smoke, Mirrors, and Mediators: The Symbolic Contest over RU 486

Jennifer L. Jackman

Available in France since 1988, RU 486—commonly known as the French abortion pill—was not submitted for U.S. Food and Drug Administration (FDA) approval until 1996. RU 486 had been on the public's agenda in the United States since the medical method of early abortion was first introduced in France. However, placement of RU 486 on the formal agenda—consideration for approval by the FDA—required an application from the drug's patent holder. By deterring Roussel Uclaf, the French pharmaceutical firm that developed RU 486, and its German parent company, Hoechst AG, from submitting an FDA application, antiabortion forces kept the drug off the agenda in the United States for eight years. Abortion opponents helped forestall RU 486's agenda access through a series of symbolic strategies targeted at its European manufacturers—a threatened product boycott, an FDA import alert, and threats of violence. The efficacy of these strategies, however, diminished over time as RU 486 advocates, including the Clinton administration, countered with symbolic strategies of their own and as its manufacturers, which mediated the claims of both sides, decided to end the contest by transferring U.S. patent rights to the Population Council, a New York–based family planning research organization.

Used by some 200,000 women worldwide as a method of early abortion, RU 486, which also goes by the scientific name mifepristone, is an antiprogestin that blocks the action of progesterone, a hormone necessary to sustain pregnancy. RU 486 is administered in conjunction with a prostaglandin, which induces uterine contractions. Effective until the ninth week of pregnancy, the RU 486 procedure in effect causes a spontaneous abortion or miscarriage. RU 486 is also being tested as a treatment for endometriosis, breast cancer, fibroid tumors, meningioma, and several other serious diseases and conditions, as well as for labor induction (Donaldson et al. 1993).

France approved RU 486 for distribution on September 23, 1988. As a result of antiabortion protests, Roussel Uclaf pulled RU 486 off the market one month later. Threatening to remove Roussel Uclaf's patent rights if action was not taken to restore its availability in France, French Minister of Health Claude Evin forced Roussel Uclaf to put RU 486 back on the market on October 28; he declared that it was now the "moral property of women." In 1989, Roussel Uclaf's German parent company, Hoechst AG, reassured U.S. abortion foes that RU 486 would not be distributed beyond France. Further RU 486 distribution did occur, however. In 1991, it became available in Great Britain, and in 1992 in Sweden. China, which does not recognize international patent law, synthesized and now manufactures its own version of RU 486.

Only after eight years of public campaigns, political pressure, and prolonged negotiations did RU 486 gain agenda access in the United States. In May 1994, Roussel Uclaf transferred U.S. patent rights without remuneration to the Population Council. The Population Council, in turn, submitted an FDA application for RU 486 in March 1996. This chapter explores the use of symbolic strategies by antiabortion forces over the years to prevent FDA consideration of RU 486 and the responses that these strategies elicited from its advocates and manufacturers.

Opposition to RU 486 was strategic in origin. Antiabortion forces feared that the medical early abortion procedure would expand abortion access and force shifts in the abortion debate. This chapter first examines the symbolic and strategic motivations underpinning RU 486 opposition and the organizations leading the efforts to prevent agenda access. In order to understand the success of antiabortion symbolic strategies in keeping RU 486 off the FDA's agenda for eight years, I then describe the internal decision-making dynamics of the opposition's intended targets—Hoechst AG and Roussel Uclaf—and their pivotal roles as symbolic mediators in this contest. The three main symbolic strategies that RU 486 opponents directed at Hoechst AG and Roussel Uclaf—product boycott threats, a Bush administration FDA import alert, and threats of antiabortion violence—are analyzed next. I conclude with a discussion of the events that finally put RU 486 on the formal agenda, what the RU 486 case reveals about the use of symbolic strategies to deny agenda access, the mediation of symbolic strategies in political fights, the relationship between symbolism and resources, and the intrinsic vulnerability of symbolic strategies.

THE SYMBOLISM OF RU 486

For antiabortion forces, opposition to RU 486 was a natural extension of their opposition to abortion in general. They termed the compound a "death pill" and "human pesticide" and denounced it as a form of "chemical warfare against unborn babies." However, the symbolic threat that RU 486 posed to the antiabortion movement went far beyond being just another type of abortion. The virulence of opposition was motivated more by the antiabortion movement's strategic concerns than by ideological or identity issues.

As a method of early abortion that works in the preembryonic and embryonic stages of pregnancy, RU 486 challenged the very icon of the antiabortion movement: the late-term fetus. In a calculated effort to depict abortion as the murder of human infants, abortion protesters regularly featured late-term fetuses in their rhetoric and their visual imagery. As Sharon Camp, former vice president of the Population Crisis Committee, put it, RU 486 would "cut the heart out of the right-to-life movement. It ruins their visuals. You're going to put a pea-sized blood clot in formaldehyde and walk around and say, 'This is a baby' " (Rovner 1990, 598). The seriousness of this symbolic threat was not lost on abortion opponents.

Early in its campaign against the drug, the National Right to Life Committee (NRLC) conceded that RU 486 jeopardized the movement's strategic symbolism. "It's more difficult to make the case that this is a developing baby if you don't have pictures of the fetus. If you can show people fingers and toes it's dynamite ... the abortion debate won't go away [with RU 486], but we'd lose some of our best arguments," said Richard Glasow, NRLC education director (Fraser 1988, 33). By 1993, however, the NRLC was more circumspect in describing how RU 486 would influence antiabortion strategy. At the 1993 NRLC convention, Glasow told participants in an RU 486 workshop that antiabortion images would be "just as pertinent," because women would still seek later-term abortions. In addition, he advised participants to describe RU 486 as a procedure that "kills an unborn baby whose heart has started to beat and kills and injures women" in order to "humanize" the antiabortion position (NRLC 1993).

Another strategic challenge that antiabortion forces faced with RU 486 was its equation with contraception. Depending on the stage of pregnancy, RU 486 prevents implantation of the fertilized egg or dislodges the embryo by inhibiting progesterone. Its developer, Dr. Etienne Baulieu (1989, 1356), even coined the term "contragestive" to emphasize that postfertilization methods of pregnancy interruption such as RU 486 and the IUD are "natural aspects of fertility and control thereof." Antiabortion forces further feared that women could use it as a once-a-month contraceptive if they were at risk for pregnancy or as a postcoital contraceptive that could be used within several days of unprotected intercourse. Postfertilization methods of preventing pregnancy presented a strategic quandary for abortion opponents such as the NRLC, which claimed to take no position on contraception. Glasow warned that "if RU 486 becomes identified in the public's mind with contraception, then right-to-life opposition to the drug could be portrayed as 'reactionary' and 'out of touch' with the mainstream of Americans." The NRLC emphasized that RU 486 "clearly causes a chemical abortion whether it acts before or after implantation" (Glasow and Wilkie 1990).

The symbolic threat of RU 486 to the antiabortion movement was grounded in the reality that its availability would expand abortion access. Indeed, one study found that one-third of the obstetrician-gynecologists who did not currently perform surgical abortions would be likely to administer RU 486 if it received FDA approval (Kaiser Family Foundation 1995). By increasing the number of physicians who could perform abortions, RU 486 would result in "a massive increase in the number of abortions," NRLC President Wanda Franz (1994) warned Hoechst AG. Glasow (1988, 6) argued that RU 486 would "make the killing more 'private' and, potentially, much more widespread." Although physician involvement is required in the administration of RU 486, the fear that it ultimately could come under the control of women alone was never far from the surface of the antiabortion debate.

Another threat associated with the decentralization of abortion services, in the eyes of the antiabortion movement, was that availability of RU 486 would undermine its ability to identify abortion providers and to use targeted strategies of intimidation and violence. Eleanor Smeal, president of the Feminist Majority Foundation, predicted, "As a safe, private method of early abortion, RU 486 could put anti-abortion extremists out of business. The availability of RU 486 will de-escalate violence at clinics since it can be administered in any doctor's office" (Feminist Majority Foundation 1992).

Antiabortion forces again sought to downplay the strategic nature of their opposition to RU 486. They denied that more militant strategies would be thwarted by RU 486 and instead highlighted their ideological opposition to abortion. For example, Andrew Burnett, publisher of *Life Advocate* and a leading advocate of "justifiable homicide" to stop abortion, minimized the influence that RU 486 would have on clinic harassment and intimidation strategies:

> RU 486 will still have to be manufactured and distributed, giving great opportunities for boycotts. It will have to be prescribed and administered by so-called "medical providers" (protests of providers). Women will still have to go to a "clinic" to receive the drug (pickets, sidewalk counseling). In fact, other than the fact that this new killer drug accomplishes the abortion by a different means biologically, virtually everything is the same from the perspective of the pro-life activist. (Burnett 1993, 2)

STOPPING RU 486: IDENTIFYING THE OPPONENTS

Because of the drug's strategic, symbolic, and practical implications, antiabortion forces in the United States designated denying RU 486 agenda access in the United States a top priority. Beginning in the late 1980s, antiabortion organizations, the Bush administration, and antiabortion members of Congress worked in tandem to prevent FDA consideration of RU 486. The National Right to Life Committee, Robins Carbide Reynolds (RCR) Fund, the Catholic Church, and antiabortion public officials, including the Bush administration and members of

Congress, played the most prominent roles in the drive to keep RU 486 out of the country. On some occasions, abortion opponents collaborated fully on anti–RU 486 strategy. On other occasions, groups distanced themselves from one another, facilitating the use of moderate to extreme opposition strategies.

Throughout the drive to stop RU 486, the NRLC was the most widely featured opponent in the media and in congressional hearings. It was one of the first organizations in the United States to condemn RU 486. Even before it became available in France, NRLC representatives testified in Congress against legislation that would have given the Department of Health and Human Services funding to promote contraceptive development on the grounds that the bill would permit RU 486 research and development (Johnson 1988, 5). The NRLC was the only antiabortion organization allowed to testify in a series of hearings on the FDA's 1989 import alert, banning personal importation of RU 486. The NRLC was the first organization to call for a boycott of pharmaceutical companies seeking to license RU 486 in the United States, and in 1991, it announced a postcard campaign directed at Hoechst Celanese. Its national publication, *National Right to Life News,* provided extensive coverage of RU 486, from its controversial introduction in France to critiques of the drug's safety and efficacy.

Other national and international religious and right-wing organizations joined the NRLC's efforts on a consistent basis. The Eagle Forum, Focus on the Family, Knights of Columbus, Concerned Women for America, Southern Baptist Convention, and International Right to Life Federation participated in NRLC meetings with Roussel Uclaf and Hoechst AG in 1990 (Wilkie 1991, 5). After the transfer of RU 486 patent rights to the Population Council, these same organizations, along with the Family Research Council, joined the NRLC's call for a boycott of Hoechst Celanese, Hoechst Roussel, and Hoechst Marion Roussel products.

Organized by Kevin Dubin, a minister in Virginia, for the sole purpose of stopping RU 486, the Robins Carbide Reynolds Fund, which was named after three frequently sued U.S. firms—A. H. Robins, Union Carbide, and Reynolds—made direct threats against Hoechst AG. In 1988, RCR presented a "Declaration to Hoechst AG," threatening various forms of retaliation if Hoechst did not concede to its demands (Pogash 1991, 10–5). RCR pledged to provide Hoechst buyers with lists of alternative suppliers, call for a national boycott of Hoechst Roussel products, and urge members of Congress to bar abortion-related companies from bidding on government contracts. RCR also threatened everything from assisting plaintiffs in product liability suits against Hoechst AG to instigating investigations of environmental and antitrust violations to focusing the attention of women's organizations on the absence of women from senior management positions at the company (Robins Carbide Reynolds Fund 1988).

The Catholic Church attempted to derail RU 486 distribution with both public and behind-the-scenes strategies. French Cardinal Lustiger galvanized demonstrations against Roussel Uclaf after the French government approved RU

486. At the same time, Catholic physicians and hospitals threatened to boycott Roussel Uclaf if a decision were made to expand its distribution, a threat that would be repeated throughout the anti–RU 486 drive (Palca 1989). The U.S. antiabortion delegation that met with Hoechst and Roussel Uclaf officials in 1990 brought a copy of an opposition letter from Cardinal O'Connor of New York (Wilkie 1991). In May 1991, the Vatican Pontifical released a report against RU 486 (Townsend 1991, 15).

The Bush administration and antiabortion members of Congress were the other key players in the effort to keep RU 486 out of the United States. RU 486 manufacturers consistently cited the Bush administration's antiabortion stance as evidence that the U.S. political climate was not conducive to the drug's introduction and that the administration's position was a significant impediment to agenda access in the United States. Former Republican activist Tanya Melich (1996, 233–49) describes the frenzy of antiabortion activity in the executive branch following Bush's 1988 election win. By appointing only abortion opponents to important judicial and executive slots, supporting federal and state abortion restrictions, and arguing for the overturn of legal abortion before the U.S. Supreme Court, the Bush administration actively aided the antiabortion movement. Enacted at the request of Senator Jesse Helms, Representative Henry Hyde, and other antiabortion leaders in Congress, the FDA's import alert on RU 486 was another attempt by the Bush administration to satisfy abortion opponents.

The ideological unity of opposition to RU 486 within the antiabortion movement belied strategic divisions among antiabortion organizations. The NRLC consistently tried to differentiate itself from the more extreme elements and tactics of other antiabortion groups. Fearing possible conspiracy charges, the NRLC refused to affiliate with the RCR Fund in its early threats of reprisal against Hoechst AG. Later in the campaign, the NRLC distanced itself from Operation Rescue and other organizations involved with clinic harassment and violence. The NRLC refused to participate in a series of anti–RU 486 demonstrations in 1993 at French consulates and embassies and Hoechst subsidiaries sponsored by Operation Rescue, Pro Life Action League, Rescue America, and Advocates for Life. The militant antiabortion publication *Life Advocate* noted that the National Right to Life Committee had declined to be involved in these actions (deParrie 1993, 12).

RU 486 inspired opposition from the traditional antiabortion constituencies: antiabortion organizations, the religious Right, the Catholic Church, and conservative political officials. As will be discussed later, antiabortion organizations used a battery of symbolic strategies to oppose RU 486. Their opposition alone, however, could not have prevented RU 486 from reaching the FDA's formal agenda (although under the Bush administration, it might have stopped approval once an application was made). The efficacy of antiabortion strategies depended on the at least tacit cooperation of the companies holding RU 486 patent rights.

SYMBOLIC MEDIATORS:
THE COMPLEX ROLE OF HOECHST AG AND ROUSSEL UCLAF

Antiabortion strategies to keep RU 486 off the agenda can be examined only in the context of the power wielded by Roussel Uclaf and Hoechst AG over the fate of the compound. Because they controlled the decision whether or not to place the drug on the FDA's agenda with a licensing application, RU 486 manufacturers were the targets of both opponents and supporters. The opponents were dependent on Roussel Uclaf's and Hoechst AG's continued refusal to apply for a license to market RU 486 in the United States. Similarly, advocates could not submit an application for approval without the direct involvement of the patent holders. Each side sought to convince the manufacturers that it was dominant in U.S. politics. Following a pattern that best fits Zald and Unseem's model of movement–countermovement interaction (1987, 260), RU 486 foes and supporters engaged with each other "only in the sense that they attempt[ed] to undo the effects of the other." Much of this contest was conducted in the symbolic realm.

Besides the decision to deny or permit introduction in the United States being in the hands of its manufacturers, these two multinational corporations also served as symbolic mediators in the fight over RU 486. In this role, Roussel Uclaf and Hoechst AG set the terms of the symbolic debate and determined the efficacy of strategies for and against the compound. Through their interpretation, translation, and responses, the two pharmaceutical firms had the power to construct the meaning of the symbolic strategies employed by forces for and against RU 486. Moreover, the symbolic strategies of the antiabortion and abortion rights movements became symbolic resources to Hoechst AG and Roussel Uclaf as they struggled internally to determine the fate of RU 486.

Roussel Uclaf and Hoechst AG defy characterization as either opponents or proponents of RU 486. For many years, they refused to allow an FDA application to market the compound, so they certainly could not be described as RU 486 proponents. As neither public officials nor negatively affected groups, Hoechst and Roussel are not defined by the opposition categories Cobb and Ross propose in chapters 1 and 2. Yet these firms engaged in some of the same symbolic strategies to deny agenda access that characterize traditional issue opponents. They allocated and often reallocated blame for why RU 486 was not being marketed in the United States. They established criteria for U.S. introduction and decided when and if the United States had met these criteria. By using the symbolic strategies of RU 486 foes as an excuse for inaction, the two firms gave credibility to antiabortion threats. But in the end, RU 486 manufacturers proved undependable allies for the antiabortion movement, because they also were responsive to pressure from abortion rights advocates and the U.S. government, whose position shifted dramatically with the election of President Clinton.

The complexity of the roles of Hoechst AG and Roussel Uclaf in the symbolic contest stemmed in large part from the fact that the two companies could not be treated as a single entity. RU 486 was developed under the leadership of Dr. Edouard Sakiz, Roussel Uclaf's chief executive officer (CEO), who even co-authored some of the key scientific articles in the development of RU 486 as a method of early abortion (Greenhouse 1989b). Sakiz's support for developing the compound stemmed particularly from his belief that Roussel Uclaf had made the wrong decision in the 1960s when the company chose not to pursue development and manufacture of contraceptives in response to Catholic Church pressure (Greenhouse 1989b). Moreover, Sakiz and his closest colleagues were strong advocates of women's equality and women's reproductive rights. They were proud of RU 486 as a scientific achievement and as an advance for women and favored its distribution.

Although Sakiz removed RU 486 from the French market with a board vote in 1988, his decision to vote against the compound occurred only after intense pressure from Hoechst AG, as well as from antiabortion forces (Greenhouse 1989b). In fact, some claimed that the Roussel board vote against RU 486 was strategically orchestrated to shift responsibility for the decision to market the compound from Roussel Uclaf to the French government (Lader 1991, 51). In a 1988 interview with *Le Monde,* Pierre Joly, a vice president at Roussel Uclaf, said that with the French government's decision, "We are relieved of the moral burden weighing on our group. For us the problem is now solved" (Tempest 1988, 1). Indeed, much to the dismay of antiabortion forces, Roussel Uclaf elected to keep RU 486 on the market in France even though a French court ruled in 1991 that Health Minister Evin did not have the statutory authority to force Roussel Uclaf to resume marketing it. The NRLC claimed that the court decision "removed the principal excuse that the Roussel Uclaf officials have been using to disguise their strong ideological commitment to abortion" (Glasow 1991).

In stark contrast, Hoechst's CEO, Wolfgang Hilger, was identified widely as an opponent of abortion and RU 486 and a close ally of the Catholic Church (Lader 1991). In a letter to the International Federation of Gynecology and Obstetrics, Hilger wrote, "It is my conviction that Hoechst should not market it. Commercialization of a drug facilitating—and easing—abortion is against Hoechst's corporate credo" (Newman 1993, 1). Hilger also reportedly had symbolic concerns about what RU 486 would mean to Hoechst AG. He feared antiabortion analogies comparing RU 486, "the death pill," to the death gas manufactured during World War II by the German company's ancestral firm, IG Farben (Greenhouse 1989b; Lader 1991, 49).

The distinct positions of Hoechst AG and Roussel Uclaf became even more complex with leadership changes in the companies and the consolidation of the two firms' pharmaceutical enterprises in the 1990s. With the retirement of Sakiz in 1993 and Hilger in 1995, the presidencies of both Roussel Uclaf and Hoechst AG changed hands. The men succeeding Sakiz and Hilger in their respective presidencies had little ideological passion either for or against RU 486. Because of their deep personal commitment to RU 486 and the longevity of their involvement with the compound, Sakiz, now chair of Roussel Uclaf's board of supervisors, and Dr. Catherine Euvrard, director of communications and scientific relations and a member of Roussel's board of management, retained responsibility for RU 486 and ultimately executed the transfer of its patent rights to the Population Council.

Both opponents and proponents have advanced various theories to explain the reluctance of Hoechst and Roussel Uclaf to market RU 486 in the United States. Fears of an antiabortion boycott, a hostile political climate, the controversy over abortion, and product liability concerns are frequently cited reasons for the manufacturers' decision not to distribute RU 486. Others attributed this decision to Hilger's personal opposition to RU 486 and his close relationship with the Catholic Church. Still others posited market reasons, suggesting, on the one hand, that RU 486 would compete with the contraceptive market for which Roussel Uclaf manufactures ingredients and, on the other hand, that it would result in little financial gain for the companies.

Countries' inability to meet Roussel Uclaf and Hoechst AG's specified criteria for marketing RU 486 became the major public justification for limiting its distribution. A joint 1991 Hoechst–Roussel Uclaf policy outlined the criteria for RU 486 distribution:

> Firstly, the launch of mifepristone for the drug-induced termination of pregnancy can only be considered in a country where abortion is tolerated by society. What is needed is a statutory ruling on abortion determined in accordance with democratic principles. Secondly, the country in question must have an advanced medical infrastructure. This must include, primarily, the availability of prostaglandin and strictly controlled distribution and use of mifepristone as in France to preclude misuse as far as possible. Thirdly, there must be an actual wish for the licensing of mifepristone in a particular country, e.g. the form of a written request from representative, competent bodies such as the government or the health authorities. (Hoechst AG 1991, 6)

Ostensibly, these criteria standardized RU 486 distribution decisions. However, in practice, the interpretation and application of the criteria were political decisions.

Ultimately, judgments about whether the United States had met the specified criteria were subjective. Before U.S.-made Cytotec was identified as the best companion prostaglandin for RU 486, the absence of a compatible prostaglandin was identified as an obstacle to U.S. introduction. Concerns about the U.S. distribution system for RU 486 were cited frequently by the firms, whose experiences with RU 486 had been only in countries with socialized medicine and a limited number of designated abortion clinics. At other times, the requisite official U.S. government request for RU 486 was posed as the main stumbling block, even though the United States had no official apparatus for making such requests.

From 1989 to 1992, the hostile U.S. political climate, as demonstrated most vividly by the Bush administration's antiabortion actions, was articulated most frequently by Roussel Uclaf and Hoechst AG as the reason for not marketing the drug in the United States. Ariel Mouttet, a Roussel Uclaf official, explained, "Abortion is a very controversial issue in the United States. It is like a war. We feel it is not the job of our company to get involved in this war. . . . The United States has to solve the question of how it feels about abortion. We would like to market RU 486 in the U.S., but we feel it is going to be a matter of time before the political debate is settled" (Tempest 1990, A18). Representative Ron Wyden, a Democrat from Oregon, blamed Roussel Uclaf's reluctance to enter the U.S. market on "the arbitrary, political, and unscientific RU 486 policies of the FDA, and the protests that have been promised from anti-abortion groups" (Wyden 1990b, 2–3).

Others within Roussel Uclaf saw gender politics in the unwillingness of Hoechst AG to eschew this public controversy in favor of advancing science and health care for women. In one interview, Euvrard said that her male colleagues refused to recognize that "abortion is a real drama for women" and that these men are "afraid of controversy, afraid to fight. For them, it is always the problems of politics, money and corporate image" (Pogash 1991, 15). Similarly, Roussel Uclaf's medical director Andre Ulmann explained: "[Decision makers at Hoechst] are men who are often aged men, elderly men who know nothing about birth control and abortion. They are convinced it is going to bring a lot of trouble. They are told it could jeopardize their market if there is a boycott" (Pogash 1991, 14).

Roussel Uclaf and Hoechst AG—sometimes acting in concert, sometimes separately—determined the extent to which the symbolic strategies of the anti-abortion movement influenced decision making, provided a cover for inaction, justified action, and ultimately affected agenda access. The influence of symbolic strategies on whether or not the United States was deemed qualified to receive RU 486 was more contingent on the companies' posture toward U.S. distribution than on the strategies themselves. Hoechst AG and Roussel Uclaf had the power to interpret and translate the symbolic strategies of RU 486 opponents and proponents into relevant criteria.

KEEPING RU 486 OFF THE FDA AGENDA:
THE SYMBOLIC STRATEGIES OF ABORTION OPPONENTS

The most visible strategies used by antiabortion forces to wage the fight against RU 486—a threatened economic boycott, the FDA import alert, and threats of violence—were resource based in appearance but symbolic in operation. The potential economic impact of a boycott against Hoechst and Roussel Uclaf was debatable. The import alert had little value as a legal sanction, and the potency of threats of violence stemmed from violent incidents in the United

States, not from an evaluation of specific threats made against Hoechst AG and Roussel Uclaf. Nonetheless, these strategies helped keep RU 486 off the FDA's agenda for eight years. Since the power of these strategies rested with their symbolism, they were vulnerable to the symbolic counterattacks of abortion rights advocates and to the interpretive vagaries of Roussel Uclaf and Hoechst AG.

The Illusion of Economics: Boycotting Roussel Uclaf and Hoechst AG

The strongest symbolic strategy that antiabortion forces employed to prevent FDA consideration of RU 486 was the threat of an economic boycott against Hoechst AG and Roussel Uclaf. Threatened product boycotts were often cited by the media, antiabortion forces, and even many abortion rights advocates as the primary reason that Roussel and Hoechst decided not to market RU 486 in the United States. The manufacturers also publicly mentioned fears of economic reprisal by antiabortion forces as one of their main justifications for limiting distribution of the drug (Palca 1989, 1319).

Threats of a boycott dominated the struggle from 1988, when RU 486 was introduced in France, until 1994, when an actual boycott was announced. Boycott threats from U.S. antiabortion groups began when RU 486 was still in the trial stage. In his May 1988 testimony against language in the Title IX Reauthorization Act promoting the development and marketing of new contraceptives, Richard Glasow of the National Right to Life Committee threatened, "Any drug company which approaches the FDA for permission to market an abortion pill will become the target of a massive boycott by pro-life organizations and churches" (Johnson 1988, 5). Boycott threats were among the initial reasons Roussel took RU 486 off the market in France (Greenhouse 1989b).

Although boycott threats first surfaced in early 1988, threats of economic reprisal issued by Ken Dubin and his group Robins Carbide Reynolds Fund in December of that year also appeared to have been pivotal (Pogash 1991, 10–5). In powerful language, the RCR "Declaration to Hoechst" threatened a multipronged economic pressure campaign aimed at consumers, industrial buyers, and investors. Although Hoechst never met with RCR, as the group had demanded, a March 1989 telex from Hoechst executive Dr. Von Winterfeldt assured RCR that "it is not our intention to market or distribute RU 486 outside of France" (Howlett 1990). A Moral Majority news release credited the Hoechst decision to RCR's economic pressure strategies. The release stated, "We clearly communicated to Hoechst AG that if RU 486 was distributed outside of France, it would cause tremendous social upheaval including picketing and economic boycott. They have shown responsible citizenship in valuing human life over profit" (Moral Majority 1989).

In February 1989, in response to the reinstatement of RU 486 on the French market, International Right to Life called for a boycott of Hoechst and Roussel Uclaf products. The International Right to Life Canadian affiliate called for a boycott of French products, including wine (Greenhouse 1989a), and in 1990, the American Life Lobby joined the wine boycott (Eaton 1990). Hoechst Celanese, a 100 percent–owned Hoechst AG U.S. subsidiary, was the central target of the NRLC's boycott threats. Since Hoechst Celanese generated almost one-quarter of Hoechst AG worldwide profits, antiabortion forces reasoned that the U.S. subsidiary would have a substantial role in decision making about the future of RU 486 in the United States. Supporters also identified Hoechst Celanese as the primary obstacle to availability in the United States. Baulieu testified before Congress, "the real problem, as far as I can see is that the company in power in this story, in the USA, is currently the branch of Hoechst in the United States of America, Hoechst-Celanese. This industrial group is not convinced that it is good for them to have a company having that activity, introducing RU 486 which is labeled abortifacient" (Baulieu 1991, 7).

Beginning in January 1991, the National Right to Life Committee directed its primary postcard campaign at Hoechst Celanese. "If [Hoechst Celanese] received sufficient numbers of postcards, they will communicate that tide of criticism to their European bosses," reported the *National Right to Life News* (Andrusko 1991). In 1993, antiabortion groups picketed Hoechst Celanese in New Jersey, Kentucky, and Virginia (Glasow 1993a, 6). In 1994, the NRLC added Copley Pharmaceuticals, a Massachusetts firm recently purchased by Hoechst Celanese, to its list of potential boycott targets (Andrusko 1994, 13).

The boycott threats were targeted not only at Hoechst and Roussel Uclaf subsidiaries but also at any company that might consider making RU 486 available in the United States. John Wilkie, then president of the National Right to Life Committee, pledged: "It is a foregone conclusion that any company marketing an [abortion-inducing] agent in the U.S. will be hit with an instant, massive national boycott of every product they make, except those where there were no other alternative drugs" (Chapman 1989, 13). Antiabortion forces took full credit for the decision of some pharmaceutical companies not to pursue RU 486.

Roussel Uclaf gave mixed messages publicly about the boycott's potential effectiveness. On the one hand, Ariel Mouttet, a Roussel Uclaf official, said that the threat of a boycott "is something we take very seriously" (U.S. House 1991, 7). On the other hand, Tony Eaton, a manager of Roussel Uclaf UK, which began marketing RU 486 in Great Britain in 1991, told *Family Planning World,* "Everywhere RU 486 goes, anti-abortion groups say they will boycott [Roussel]. If there was a boycott, we never felt its effects" (DiConsiglio 1993, 1).

Although the threatened boycott was the most often cited reason for not proceeding with an FDA application on RU 486, abortion rights supporters sought to expose that the boycott was a symbolic excuse for inaction that had no resource base. Authors Rebecca Chalker and Carol Downer (1992, 192–3) challenged the boycott theory on the basis of the timing of Roussel's decision not to market the compound. Chalker and Downer insisted that the decision on the part of RU 486 manufacturers to limit distribution of the compound preceded boycott threats from U.S. groups. A study commissioned by the Feminist Majority Foundation found:

> Hoechst AG and Hoechst Celanese are not ideal targets for a consumer boycott. The vast majority of their products are either industrial products—like polyester fibers, fibers for tire cord, textile dyes, superabsorbers for diapers, industrial paints, and crop protection agents—or prescription drugs. . . . A boycott would thus have to be an indirect one. Consumers would have to boycott the products that use Hoechst or Hoechst Celanese materials, or pressure would have to be put on the medical profession to use alternatives. (Corporate Campaign Inc. 1992, 171)

The only credible boycott threat, in the view of many analysts, was the prospect of a boycott by Catholic hospitals of Hoechst and Roussel pharmaceutical products (Palca 1989, 1319). Lader reported that Catholic hospitals controlled one-third of U.S. hospital beds and represented 640 of 3,289 nonprofit hospitals (1995, 125). Threats of a Catholic hospital and physician boycott of Roussel products began after the French government's approval of RU 486 in September 1988. After the announcement, Roussel Uclaf received three hundred letters from Catholic doctors threatening a boycott (Lader 1991, 50). In a February 20, 1992, meeting with the Feminist Majority Foundation, a Hoechst official informed the organization that the bishop of Austria had threatened that Catholic hospitals would boycott Hoechst if RU 486 were brought into Austria.

The weakness of the general product boycott threat became especially apparent when antiabortion forces formally launched their boycott in response to Roussel Uclaf's transfer of U.S. RU 486 patent rights without remuneration to the Population Council. Informing Hoechst AG of the launch of the boycott, NRLC President Wanda Franz wrote, "You may or may not be able to escape the legal responsibility by giving the patent away, but you cannot escape the moral responsibility that will ensue. As we have repeatedly told you and the public, we hold Hoechst AG and Roussel Uclaf directly responsible for the introduction of RU 486 for use in abortion. . . . The controversy surrounding RU 486 and your companies has only just begun" (Franz 1994). However, after six years of promising a boycott, the NRLC at its June 6, 1994, press conference still did not identify which products would be boycotted.

At a second press conference a month later, the NRLC did release a boycott list of specific products manufactured by Hoechst Roussel Pharmaceuticals, Copley Pharmaceuticals, and Hoechst-Roussel Agri-Vet. The goal of the boycott, Franz said, was "to cause Hoechst AG and Roussel Uclaf to rescind the license for use of RU 486 in the United States; and second, to cause them to review their actions and to cease production of RU 486" (NRLC 1994). In 1996, the boycott was expanded to include products manufactured by Hoechst Marion Roussel, which was created by the merger of Hoechst AG, Roussel Uclaf, and Marion

Merrell Dow pharmaceutical operations ("CWA Pro-Family Groups Boycott" 1996).

Even with the launch of an actual targeted boycott, antiabortion forces still framed the objectives of the boycott strategy in symbolic terms. Antiabortion groups hoped that the boycott would deter other pharmaceutical companies that might be interested in bringing RU 486 to market, as well as change the position of Roussel Uclaf. Beverly LeHaye of Concerned Women for America (CWA) promised, "We intend that this pressure will make other pharmaceutical companies think twice before jumping on the RU 486 bandwagon" (Concerned Women for America 1994).

The symbolic strategies of abortion rights groups, which sought to convey that withholding RU 486 would have its own set of economic consequences, helped erode the symbolic power of the boycott. First, supporters demonstrated through petition drives, state legislative resolutions, and polling data the strength of their numbers, implying to manufacturers that the economic repercussions of a pro–RU 486 boycott would be greater than those of an anti–RU 486 boycott. The *Philadelphia Inquirer* editorialized, "But over time, with supporters of abortion rights mobilizing in the wake of the Supreme Court's *Webster* decision, the economics of ducking the issue may start to look worse than the economics of making the pill available one way or another" ("Abortion Pill" 1989). RU 486 supporters also galvanized visible support from scientific and medical organizations to show that those pharmaceutical firm constituencies would stand behind a decision to introduce RU 486 to the United States. Both publicly and privately, Roussel Uclaf officials encouraged the outpouring of support for RU 486 to counter antiabortion threats. An unnamed Roussel Uclaf executive told the *New York Times* (Greenhouse 1989a): "What would be needed to change the company's attitude would be very successful marketing in France and very strong support for the pill in world public opinion."

Another component of the abortion rights strategy was to show that pro–RU 486 groups had the capacity to conduct an effective boycott against the two companies. The Feminist Majority Foundation prepared and distributed "Web of Influence" materials identifying for the public the companies, unions, and financial institutions that did business with Hoechst AG and Roussel Uclaf and gave supporters the addresses of U.S. entities involved in business transactions with RU 486 manufacturers. In some cases, abortion rights supporters also made actual boycott threats. For example, physicians attending the 1988 meeting of the World Congress of Obstetrics and Gynecology threatened to boycott Roussel Uclaf's pharmaceutical products if the company did not reverse its decision to take RU 486 off the market in France (Palca 1989, 1320; Simons 1988). The National Organization for Women also pledged to lead a product boycott unless RU 486 was brought to the United States (Mathews 1990, A22)

Supporters also devised several symbolic strategies to posture themselves as competitors with Roussel Uclaf for the RU 486 market. Abortion Rights Mobilization (ARM) obtained and tested a Chinese version of RU 486. ARM then developed its own clone of the compound. The organization also announced a possible legislative strategy to remove RU 486 patent rights from Roussel Uclaf (Lader 1995). Wyden pledged to hold congressional hearings on removing RU 486 patent rights if negotiations between the Population Council and Roussel Uclaf were not concluded expeditiously.

Finally, pro–RU 486 forces challenged the efficacy and the ethics of antiabortion boycott strategies. In response to the July 1994 announcement of an antiabortion boycott against RU 486 manufacturers, Smeal said, the boycott "is destined to fail because the public will not tolerate further medical McCarthyism. Once again, anti-abortion forces are allowing politics to interfere with medicine" (Feminist Majority Foundation 1994). To counter the antiabortion claim that U.S. companies were deterred by boycott threats, Wyden identified at least three companies interested in marketing RU 486 in the country. In a 1992 letter to Sakiz, Wyden enclosed letters of interest from Gynex, Cabot Medical Corporation, and Adeza Biomedical Corporation (Wyden 1990a).

The manufacturers' response to the long-awaited boycott announcement made it clear that the boycott threat had been nothing more than a symbolic excuse for inaction and that now even the boycott's power as a symbolic strategy had evaporated. The boycott was derided as irrelevant by Roussel Uclaf and Hoechst officials. In response to the June antiabortion boycott announcement, Euvrard stated, "Obviously we are not pleased, but we don't believe that the boycott against Roussel Uclaf will work." Added Euvrard, "We are a pharmaceutical company and I sincerely believe that American doctors prescribe drugs according to criteria which are rational, and not emotional. I don't believe for one minute that American doctors' professionalism would allow them not to prescribe a drug that they know will help a sick patient" (AFP-Extel News Limited 1994). Andrea Stine of Hoechst Celanese told Gannett News Services, "We're an industrial company, so we do not sell consumer products. I don't know how a consumer would tell" (Gannett News Service 1994, A3).

Threats of an economic boycott against Roussel Uclaf and Hoechst AG were a key strategy in the antiabortion movement's symbolic arsenal. Initially, with the help of the manufacturers, antiabortion forces convinced most segments of the U.S. public that boycott threats were real and that these threats were a key factor in preventing distribution of RU 486. Whether the manufacturers actually viewed the threats as viable or whether they simply used them as a cover for inaction did not really matter. The manufacturers identified boycott threats as effective, and so they were. When antiabortion forces finally launched a boycott, it was then in the interest of Hoechst AG and Roussel Uclaf to downplay the strategy's efficacy. In the end, the manufacturers had the power to render the symbolic boycott strategy irrelevant.

Abortion rights supporters, with the encouragement of allies within Roussel Uclaf, mounted their own symbolic counteroffensive to the anti–RU 486 boycott threat. By demonstrating public and scientific support, identifying U.S. distributors, and threatening to develop products to compete with RU 486, advocates provided Hoechst and Roussel with a symbolic excuse for U.S. introduction of the compound.

The Symbolic Ban: The FDA's Import Alert on RU 486

The FDA's import alert on RU 486 was the Bush administration's direct contribution to antiabortion symbolic strategies to keep the drug off the formal agenda. On June 6, 1989, FDA Commissioner Frank Young, in response to pressure from antiabortion members of Congress (Hyde et al. 1989; Helms 1989), issued an import alert on RU 486, banning its importation for personal use. A year earlier, the FDA had relaxed its rules to accommodate the importation of medical treatments related to AIDS and other serious diseases. The FDA had the discretion to ban unapproved drugs that represented direct or indirect risks, promotion for the purposes of mail shipment, or health fraud (FDA 1989b). The FDA used this discretion to issue an import alert, which stated:

> Questions have been raised about a new abortifacient product RU 486 or Mifepristone (Import Bulletin 66-B13 9/26/88) and whether the agency should use its discretion, pursuant to the Pilot Guidance for Release of Mail Importations (7/20/88), or otherwise, to allow its importation for personal use. FDA has concluded that unapproved products of this kind would be inappropriate for release under the personal importation policy. The intended use of such drugs could pose a risk to the safety of the user. (FDA 1989a).

Preventing individual women from bringing personal supplies of RU 486 into the country was not the real purpose of the alert, however. A congressional subcommittee memorandum investigating the import alert concluded: "There seems to be no scientific or procedural safety issue providing foundation for this FDA action, and no record of attempts to bring the drug into this country. However, the timing of the import alert did coincide with pressure then being brought upon the agency by Congressional abortion opponents" (U.S. House 1990, 7). As the FDA conceded in congressional hearings, no black market existed. Nor was any black market likely, given the tight control on European RU 486 supplies (Chesemore 1990, 37). The alert also had nothing to do with the safety or risk of RU 486. The FDA and leading scientists testified that no scientific evaluation of RU 486 data had occurred before the enactment of the import alert.

Instead, the import alert's primary value was symbolic. Antiabortion forces used the alert to convey to RU 486 manufacturers that the political climate in the United States was hostile to RU 486. As Wyden stated in a hearing on the FDA alert, "The anti-abortion forces have successfully lobbied the Reagan-Bush Administrations to impose and maintain the alert in order to send a message to the drug's manufacturers and that message is very clear: Don't try applying for a general drug approval for RU 486 in the United States. You won't get a fair shake" (Wyden 1990b, 2). In meetings with advocates, Hoechst AG officials repeatedly identified the import alert as an obstacle to introduction.

Another symbolic goal of the import alert was to cast doubt on the drug's safety and efficacy. In a letter reassuring Senator Helms that personal importation of RU 486 would not be allowed, FDA Commissioner Young claimed that RU 486 "could present an unreasonable safety risk." Young maintained, "The intended use of this drug makes it likely it would be used without benefit of supervision of a physician and indiscriminate or unsupervised use could be hazardous to the patient's health. For example, side effects of the drug which include uterine bleeding, severe nausea, vomiting and weakness which might require prompt medical intervention could occur" (Young 1989). Antiabortion organizations were able to use the alert as evidence of the alleged danger that RU 486 posed to both "unborn babies" and women.

The import alert, however, was effectively transformed from a symbolic antiabortion strategy to a symbolic tool for abortion rights groups. Congressional hearings in 1990, 1991, and 1992 exposed that the alert had been politically motivated and produced evidence from leading scientists that the import alert had hindered research on nonabortion uses of RU 486, such as in the treatment of Cushing's syndrome, breast cancer, and meningioma. Freedom of scientific inquiry and access to medical advances for a wide range of diseases displaced the safety issues around RU 486 that antiabortion forces had sought to raise with the alert. In testimony before Congress, Smeal (1991) said, "If we permit these forces to stop the pursuit of knowledge, the United States will not be a first rate country in terms of health care, scientific research, or human rights."

In addition, RU 486 supporters used the import alert to further galvanize support and activity. The Feminist Majority Foundation succeeded in having resolutions introduced and passed at most major scientific and medical associations calling the alert "neither scientifically nor medically necessary" and warning that the alert "may cause confusion, delays, and obstacles for scientists seeking the drug for research purposes" (Endocrine Society Council 1991).

A direct legal challenge to the alert generated massive publicity about RU 486 and portrayed the FDA as an agency motivated by politics rather than science. ARM recruited Leona Benten, a pregnant social worker, to bring a dosage of RU 486 into the United States from England. U.S. Customs seized it from Benten upon her return to the United States (Lader 1995). In his decision ordering the drug's return to Benten, a federal district court judge said of the FDA import alert: "This was a lawsuit waiting to happen." Judge Sifton, in relating the ban's history, said, "it appears much more likely . . . that the decision to ban the drug was not from any bonafide concern for the safety of users of the drug, but on political considerations having no place in FDA decisions on health and safety" (Sifton 1992). Although Sifton's judgment to return the RU 486 to Benten was overturned on appeal, abortion rights advocates won the public-relations war over the import alert.

The symbolic power of the import alert was made clear by the fact that one of the first executive orders issued by President Clinton after his inauguration asked Secretary of Health and Human Services (HHS) Donna Shalala to determine whether RU 486 should be excluded from the personal importation exemption. If RU 486 met the criteria to allow importation for personal use, Shalala was instructed to take steps to rescind the import alert. Clinton also directed HHS to review how the department could "promote the testing, licensing, and manufacture of RU 486 or other anti-progestins in the United States" (Clinton 1993). The executive order was intended as a signal to RU 486 manufacturers that the political climate on abortion in the United States had shifted with the 1992 election.

Whether or not the actual alert was repealed became insignificant. The fact that the import alert remains on the books today, drawing little attention from supporters, foes, or manufacturers, underscores the symbolic rather than the resource basis of the alert and the fluidity of symbolic strategies. The message that the Clinton administration supported RU 486 reached Roussel Uclaf and Hoechst AG, which soon thereafter began serious negotiations with the Population Council to bring RU 486 to the United States.

Fearing the Worst: The Symbolism of Violence

Violence was not a strategy of last resort for opponents. Threats of violence—implied and direct—were made against manufacturers throughout the drive to prevent the introduction of RU 486 in the United States. Bomb threats against Roussel Uclaf were made in the fall of 1988 in response to the company's initial plans to market it in France (Palca 1989). In fact, French health minister Claude Evin attributed Roussel Uclaf's decision to remove RU 486 from the market in France to threats of violence against the families of company officials as well as boycott threats. Evin explained, "Their wives and children were threatened through anonymous letters. This is totally inadmissible and utterly cowardly" (Henry 1988, 4A). The early threats of violence in France were taken particularly seriously, because they occurred in the context of a series of arson attacks by religious groups on Paris theaters showing the film *The Last Temptation of Christ* (Graham 1988, 2). In the United States, the context of intense violence at abortion clinics was of particular concern to Hoechst AG, because of its large number of U.S. facilities.

The entry into the fray of antiabortion groups associated with violence and harassment at clinics represented an implied threat of violence. On June 18, 1993, Operation Rescue held a demonstration at the French embassy to protest RU 486 in Washington, D.C., as Roussel Uclaf's stockholders met in Paris. Demonstrations at other French consulates and embassies and Hoechst subsidiary plants were sponsored by the Pro Life Action League, Rescue America, and Advocates for Life Ministries. The *Life Advocate,* which serves as a mouthpiece for the extremist, violent wing of the antiabortion movement, reported on the protests (deParrie 1993, 12).

The more militant wing of the antiabortion movement also targeted physicians and facilities participating in clinical trials in 1994 and 1995, which were held in preparation for submission of the Population Council's new drug application to the FDA. In December 1994, Operation Rescue protested clinical trials at the Burlington, Vermont, Planned Parenthood clinic (Toten 1994, 1A). Advocates for Life picketed Oregon Health Sciences University, the trial site (deParrie 1993, 12), and the homes of Oregon researchers ("RU 486 Testing Begins" 1995, 18). In 1994, a clinic worker was murdered by an antiabortion extremist at a Planned Parenthood trial site in Brookline, Massachusetts, but no evidence was found linking the shooting to the RU 486 trials.

Antiabortion violence also backfired as a symbolic strategy to keep RU 486 off the FDA's agenda. Abortion rights supporters recast the very antiabortion violence that was meant to deter manufacturers from making RU 486 available as a reason for marketing the compound in the United States. Advocates argued that its availability would diminish clinic violence by decentralizing the provision of abortion services. The media and policy makers also took up the theme of RU 486 as a solution to clinic violence. As the Portland *Oregonian* stated in a 1994 editorial, if it becomes available in the United States, "a lot of the reason for noisy anti-abortion demonstrations, violence, and mayhem outside of abortion clinics will disappear.... Today's clinics doing surgical abortions have been natural targets for demonstrators, but RU 486 can be administered in the privacy of any doctor's office with no one the wiser" ("A Breakthrough on RU-486" 1994).

The participation of militant antiabortion groups in anti–RU 486 demonstrations strengthened the symbolic potency of threats of violence. The decision to transfer RU 486 patent rights to the Population Council, however, was made in the midst of one of the most violent periods of the antiabortion movement. This fact suggests that the threats of violence carried little weight once Roussel Uclaf had convinced Hoechst AG to allow U.S. introduction. Moreover, this climate intensified calls for the immediate introduction of RU 486 in the United States as a way to avert violent antiabortion tactics.

TRANSLATING SYMBOLISM: HOW RU 486 GOT ON THE AGENDA

Despite the vigorous symbolic campaign waged by antiabortion forces, an application to market RU 486 in the United States was submitted for FDA approval in March 1996. Agenda access was delayed for eight years rather than denied. Roussel Uclaf's decision to transfer patent rights to the Population Council in May 1994 made clear the role of symbolic strategies in the contest.

The formal announcement of the transfer of patent rights took place on May 16, 1994, prior to a scheduled hearing before the same congressional sub-committee that had held hearings on the FDA's import alert on RU 486. Shalala, Wyden, FDA Commissioner Kessler, and representatives from the Population Council and Roussel Uclaf announced the agreement in front of an audience of media representatives and abortion rights leaders. Of significance, in the back of the room—invisible to the media—were Sakiz and Euvrard, who had success-fully shepherded RU 486 onto the FDA's agenda through eight years of internal and external barriers.

In public, Roussel Uclaf fully credited the Clinton administration with cre-ating the conditions under which the transfer of patent rights could occur. Roussel Uclaf's brief statement said that its decision had been made "in response to on-going requests by President Clinton and Secretary Shalala" to make RU 486 available in the United States (Roussel Uclaf 1994). In testimony prepared for a hearing that day, Roussel Uclaf's attorney, Lester Hyman, explained:

> Literally hundreds of thousands of letters have been sent to our client de-manding in the strongest terms either that the pill comes in or the pill stays out. Add to all of these the fact that, in the previous Administration, the situ-ation was precisely the opposite of what it is today. Then President Bush spoke stridently against any procedure that would result in early pregnancy termination. In the face of the opposition of the U.S. Government, Roussel Uclaf decided not to bring mifepristone to the United States. It was only when President Clinton changed the governmental policy and specifically asked Roussel to make the procedure available here that it, out of respect for the President of the United States, agreed to make every effort to comply with his request. (Roussel Uclaf 1994)

The power of the presidency that finally brought RU 486 to the United States also was largely symbolic. The Clinton administration took no action against Roussel Uclaf, nor did it have the power to do so. However, Clinton's election and the subsequent involvement of his administration in RU 486 negotiations were interpreted by Hoechst AG and Roussel Uclaf as representing a shift in the cli-mate toward abortion rights and RU 486. Before Clinton even took office, Kessler made overtures to Roussel Uclaf. In a December 14 letter to Sakiz, Kessler "all but invited" Roussel Uclaf to apply for FDA approval based on French data. To an extent, Kessler's overtures to Roussel Uclaf also represented a symbolic ges-ture to the Clinton administration; Kessler, a Bush appointee, was seeking reap-pointment as FDA commissioner ("Kessler and Clinton" 1993, A14). In a De-cember 1992 letter to Wyden, Carol Scheman (1992) of the FDA said that the agency would consider accepting foreign data and estimated an expedited six-month schedule for approval. President Clinton's executive order gave Shalala the authority she needed to convey to RU 486 manufacturers that their future relationship with the U.S. government was on the line with RU 486. She even set a deadline of May 15, 1994, for the conclusion of stalled negotiations between the Population Council and Roussel Uclaf (Kessler 1994).

More privately, RU 486 supporters were told of the significance of their symbolic strategies to the decision to transfer patent rights. Letters, petitions, and calls from advocates to Hoechst AG and Roussel Uclaf consistently counterbalanced antiabortion demands. Sakiz (1994) wrote to Smeal following the announcement that RU 486 would be coming to the United States: "Although I have been personally involved in the project and followed each step of its development, I would like to say that it is mainly your own determination and that of all the Feminist Majority Foundation's members and other pro-choice supporters that largely contributed to this successful issue." The Clinton administration tipped the scale in favor of RU 486 distribution by giving its allies within Roussel Uclaf the symbolic ammunition they needed to convince Hoechst AG that it was politically and economically expedient to transfer patent rights to the controversial product.

CONCLUSION

This case study of how abortion opponents kept RU 486 off the FDA's agenda for eight years delineates some of the factors necessary to explain how resources—symbolic and real—gain political currency. Cobb and Ross in chapter 1 are correct in observing that resources alone do not determine whether or not an issue achieves agenda access. Antiabortion forces ultimately failed in keeping RU 486 off the agenda, despite the significant resources of the Catholic Church and, for that matter, Hoechst AG. In addition, when the resources of the Clinton administration were added to the support of medical, feminist, and congressional allies and the public, the resources of RU 486 supporters were comparable to those of opponents, making it hard to call the outcome based on resource differentials alone.

The boycott threat, FDA import alert, and threats of clinic violence were strategies that rested on symbolism rather than on the exercise of resources. Similarly, symbolic strategies, not the exercise of abortion rights resources, gave RU 486 supporters the edge they needed. The only resources that mattered in the contest were those in the hands of Roussel Uclaf and Hoechst AG. They had the power to determine the significance of symbolic strategies and to convert the symbolic strategies of contestants into agenda denial or agenda access.

The fact that Hoechst AG and Roussel Uclaf were in many respects boycott-proof was irrelevant. Antiabortion forces created the perception that a boycott could be waged. By not publicly refuting the boycott claims until a boycott was announced in 1994, manufacturers gave that strategy credibility. The boycott thus created a cover for inaction on the part of the manufacturers.

Similarly, the import alert, with the exception of the confiscation of Leona

Benten's RU 486 supply in 1992, had no practical effect. Tight controls within those countries in which it was available made importation into the United States all but impossible. However, the manufacturers perceived the import alert as the Bush administration had intended it: as a proxy for the U.S. political climate. The alert thus became another credible excuse for inaction and another roadblock advocates had to overcome. The decision to transfer U.S. patent rights to the Population Council, even though the import alert remains on the books, attests to the fluidity of symbolic power.

Threats of violence were yet another case in which the symbolic agency of a strategy outweighed its substantive possibilities. In the context of antiabortion violence in the United States, threats of violence did not even need to be direct; the mere involvement of militant groups in the conflict was enough to imply that violence was a strategic option for antiabortion forces. Threats of violence provided another excuse for refusing to introduce RU 486 in the United States. At the same time, RU 486 became a strategy in itself for defusing antiabortion violence.

In each case, antiabortion symbolic strategies unraveled as abortion rights supporters, including the Clinton administration, successfully launched their own symbolic initiatives to counter opposition. Pro–RU 486 petitions, polls, state resolutions, and scientific and medical association endorsements also carried only the symbolic import that the manufacturers attached to them. Visible supportive campaigns neutralized the effects of the sustained anti–RU 486 effort in the eyes of its manufacturers.

The actions of the Clinton administration that ultimately won Roussel Uclaf's decision to transfer U.S. patent rights were also symbolic. In December 1992, following the election, the FDA's Kessler made largely symbolic overtures to the manufacturers, urging submission of an application for approval. President Clinton's 1993 executive order was equally symbolic. He urged the Department of Health and Human Services to explore ways to make RU 486 available and to investigate the validity of the import alert. Manufacturers took the president's action as the signal they needed to demonstrate that the U.S. position on abortion had changed. The Clinton administration's request for RU 486 carried with it the prospect that by continuing to withhold the drug from the U.S. market, Roussel Uclaf and Hoechst AG risked alienating the U.S. government. This combination of largely symbolic factors convinced the company that the United States now met the criteria for RU 486 introduction. In the end, allies within Roussel Uclaf were able and, most importantly, willing to translate these symbolic indices of support into agenda access.

Whether or not antiabortion forces made good on their threats did not matter as much as how manufacturers interpreted, translated, and used the information. The influence of symbolic strategies rested on how they were interpreted and the responses they elicited. The mediators thus were as important as the strategies themselves. Symbolic strategies, however, did play a critical role in the contest. Withholding RU 486 from the United States would have been far more difficult for Hoechst AG in the absence of antiabortion strategies. Similarly, Roussel Uclaf would probably not have been able to maneuver U.S. introduction without pro–RU 486 efforts.

The RU 486 case attests to the fundamental vulnerability of symbolic strategies to symbolic reprisal and symbolic mediation. Symbolic strategies by their very nature are illusory and necessarily short term. Their success is contingent on interpretation and social construction by those in positions of power. These strategies—particularly in the absence of concrete resource advantages—are subject to the whims of their intended target. In this case, the manufacturers initially accorded credibility to the symbolic strategies of opponents. However, antiabortion symbolic strategies were eventually more than matched by those of supporters, who in 1992 were joined by the symbolic actions of an administration committed to bringing RU 486 into the country. The symbolic mediators then switched their interpretation. As was seen in this case, once Roussel Uclaf and Hoechst AG rejected the symbolic claims of the antiabortion movement, the movement was rendered powerless.

The case of RU 486 also holds lessons about the influence of costs on strategy selection. First, costs in the symbolic realm are a particularly murky issue. Boycott threats, the FDA import alert, and threats of violence all would be identified as high-cost strategies in Cobb and Ross's scheme. However, the cost of a strategy is not always constant over time from the perspective of the organization initiating the strategy or the intended target. The boycott threat initially involved little cost to the NRLC; theoretically, the potential costs were heavier for RU 486 manufacturers. The cost of the boycott strategy to antiabortion organizations became higher as the time to move from threat to action neared, and the movement's credibility was on the line. This was the point at which the boycott strategy failed. By the time the boycott was actually announced, Roussel Uclaf was able to state publicly that the efficacy of the strategy was dubious at best and that since the transfer of patent rights was complete, it was no longer the appropriate target. With the change in context, the costs incurred by Roussel Uclaf in relation to the boycott were now very low.

Second, the RU 486 case suggests that the same movement, or even the same organization, often engages in multiple strategies simultaneously. Antiabortion organizations did not select increasingly high-cost strategies, as Cobb and Ross might predict. Instead, the boycott threats, FDA import alert, and threats of violence were employed throughout the campaign to prevent FDA consideration. The concurrent use of different levels of strategies by different organizations is often strategic, with more moderate groups distancing themselves from more radical tactics. The NRLC rejected an offer to join the RCR Fund in 1988 in its threats of economic reprisal against Hoechst and declined participation in protests led by Operation Rescue and other antiabortion organizations associated with clinic harassment and violent strategies. This disassociation had its advantages. More moderate groups reaped the benefits of extremist strategies without assuming any of the costs.

Whether cost-based or not, the selection and execution of symbolic strategies by the antiabortion movement were only part of the agenda denial story. Blue smoke and mirrors alone were not enough to keep RU 486 off the FDA's agenda. The conversion of symbolism into political currency depended on the actions of officials at Hoechst AG and Roussel Uclaf as symbolic mediators. RU 486 was ultimately placed on the agenda because supporters within Roussel Uclaf had the power to translate the 1992 election and public pressure campaigns to license RU 486 from symbolism into action.

POSTSCRIPT

On April 8, 1997, Hoechst AG announced the transfer of worldwide (excluding the U.S.) patent rights on RU 486 without remuneration to Dr. Edouard Sakiz, the former CEO of Roussel Uclaf who oversaw the drug's development and guided the transfer of U.S. patent rights to the Population Council in 1994. The company's official news release said only that the patent transfer would enable Hoechst "to focus its research, development, and marketing efforts on those areas that represent the best opportunities to support the company's growth." In numerous media interviews, however, Hoechst also stated that the $3.5 million annual profit from RU 486 did not merit risking $1.63 billion U.S. business interests to the abortion controversy. This announcement came just a week after antiabortion organizations had launched a boycott of Hoechst's new allergy medication, Allegra, although the agreement with Dr. Sakiz had been underway for more than a month.

By in part attributing the company's decision to relinguish RU 486 to antiabortion boycott threats, Hoechst AG handed abortion foes a symbolic victory. But this victory was indeed hollow. In the ultimate act of symbolic mediation, Hoechst hid behind the antiabortion boycott threat as it transferred patent rights to Dr. Sakiz, whose new company, Exelgyne, will now move forward with distribution and development of RU 486.

REFERENCES

The abortion pill. 1989. *Philadelphia Inquirer,* October 4.

AFP-Extel News Limited. 1994. Roussel Uclaf dismisses planned U.S. anti-abortion groups' boycott. June 2.

Andrusko, D. 1990. RU 486: A way of skirting the abortion controversy. In *Omen of the future? The abortion pill RU 486,* edited by R. Glasow and J. Wilkie. Washington, DC: National Right to Life Committee.

———. 1991. The distortion factor. *National Right to Life News,* January 8, pp. 4, 19, 22.

———. 1994. NRLC convention '94 message: "Stop Clinton health care rationing plan, boycott RU 486, win in November." *National Right to Life News,* July 12, p. 13.

Baulieu, E. 1989. Contragestion and other clinical applications of RU 486, an anti-progesterone at the receptor. *Science,* September 22, pp. 1351–7.

———. 1991. Testimony before the Small Business Subcommittee on Regulation, Business Opportunities, and Energy, Small Business Committee, House of Representatives. December 5.

A breakthrough on RU-486. 1994. *Oregonian,* May 23, p. B6.

Burnett, A. 1993. RU 486: A new era in the abortion battle. *Life Advocate* (August): 2.

Chalker, R., and C. Downer. 1992. *A woman's book of choices: Abortion, menstrual extraction, and RU 486.* New York: Four Walls Eight Windows.

Chapman, F. 1989. The politics of the abortion pill. *Washington Post Magazine,* October 3, pp. 13–4.

Chesemore, R. 1990. Testimony before the Small Business Subcommittee on Regulation, Business Opportunities, and Energy, Small Business Committee, House of Representatives. November 19.

Clinton, W. 1993. Memorandum for the secretary of health and human services, subject: Importation of RU 486. January 22.

Concerned Women for America. 1994. CWA joins coalition to boycott RU 486. News statement. July 7.

Corporate Campaign Inc. 1992. *Breaking the blockade: A strategy for bringing RU 486 to the United States,* March.

CWA pro-family groups boycott major drug companies. 1996. *PR Newswire,* February 20.

deParrie, P. 1993. Worldwide demonstrations expose killer drug—RU 486. *Life Advocate* (August): 12.

DiConsiglio, J. 1993. Pop Council wins RU 486 rights, but abortion pill still years from release. *Family Planning World* (May/June): 1.

Donaldson, M., L. Dorfinger, S. Brown, and L. Benet. 1993. *Clinical applications of mifepristone (RU 486) and other anti-progestins.* Washington, DC: National Academy Press.

Eaton, S. 1990. Boycott of French wines uncorked by abortion opponents. *St. Louis Sun,* April 16.

Endocrine Society Council. 1991. Resolution on RU 486 and freedom of scientific inquiry. June 18.

Feminist Majority Foundation. 1992. Feminist Majority Foundation demonstrates against operation rescue. News release. June 18.

———. 1994. Feminist Majority Foundation condemns anti-abortion "politically correct prescriptions." News release. July 7.

Food and Drug Administration. 1989a. Automatic detention of abortifacient drugs. June 6.

———. 1989b. Regulatory procedures manual. December 11.

Franz, W. 1994. Letter to Robert Guerson, head of Health Policy Pharmaceutical Division, Hoechst AG. May 27.

Fraser, L. 1988. Pill politics. *Mother Jones* (June): 33.

Gannett News Service. 1994. RU 486 company faces boycott. *Marin Independent Journal,* June 2, p. A3.

Glasow, R. 1988. Abortion pill advocates map new strategy to win U.S. approval of RU 486. *National Right to Life News,* June 1, p. 6.

——. 1991. French court decision exposes abortion pill companies' credibility gap. *National Right to Life News,* May 7, p. 8.

——. 1993a. Coast to coast protests against RU 486. *National Right to Life News,* July 14, p. 6.

——. 1993b. Drug company drops plans to market RU 486. *National Right to Life News,* August 11, p. 4.

Glasow, R., and J. Wilkie, eds. 1990. *Omen of the future? The Abortion pill RU 486.* Washington, DC: National Right to Life Committee.

Graham, G. 1988. Paris orders reversal of abortion pill ban. *Financial Times,* October 29, p.2.

Greenhouse, S. 1989a. Fears confine abortion pill to France. *New York Times,* March 26, p. 18.

1989b. A new pill, a fierce battle. *New York Times Magazine,* February 12, pp. 23–5.

Helms, J. 1989. Letter to FDA Commissioner Frank Young. February 23.

Henry, D. 1988. Production of abortion pill ordered. *Baltimore Sun,* October 29, p. 4A.

Hoechst AG. 1991. Drug induced termination of pregnancy with mifepristone (RU 486). Memo prepared by the Health Policy Department of the Pharmaceuticals Division, October.

Howlett, D. 1990. Pressure keeps abortion pill off U.S. market. *USA Today,* April 26, p. 6A.

Hyde, H., et al. 1989. Letter to FDA Commissioner Frank Young. May 5.

Hyman, L. 1994. Testimony before the Small Business Subcommittee on Regulation, Business Opportunities, and Technology, Small Business Committee, House of Representatives. May 16.

Johnson, D. 1988. Title 10 bills bog down under pro-life attacks. *National Right to Life News,* May 5, p. 5.

Kaiser Family Foundation. 1995. *National survey of obstetricians and gynecologists on contraception and unplanned pregnancy.*

Kessler, D. 1994. Testimony before the Small Business Subcommittee on Regulation, Business Opportunities, and Technology, Small Business Committee, House of Representatives. May 16.

Kessler and Clinton. 1993. *Wall Street Journal,* January 12, p. A14.

Lader, L. 1991. *RU 486.* New York: Addison Wesley.

——. 1995. *A private matter: RU 486 and the abortion crisis.* New York: Prometheus Books.

Mathews, J. 1990. NOW leaders threaten boycott over abortion. *Washington Post,* July 1, p. A22.

Melich, T. 1996. *The Republican war against women.* New York: Bantam.

Moral Majority. 1989. News release. March 22.

National Right to Life Committee. 1993. RU 486: The abortion pill. Tape from the National Right to Life Convention, Milwaukee.

——. 1994. Statement of Wanda Franz. July 7, p. 2.

Newman, B. 1993. Among those wary of abortion pill is maker's parent firm. *Wall Street Journal,* February 22, p. 1.

Palca, J. 1989. The pill of choice? *Science,* September 22, pp. 1319–23.

Pogash, C. 1991. Does the abortion pill have a future in America. *San Francisco Examiner Image,* April 14, pp. 10–5.

Robins Carbide Reynolds Fund. 1988. Declaration to Hoechst AG.

Roussel Uclaf. 1994. Press release. May 16.

Rovner, J. 1990. RU 486: Tiny pill with big impact. *Congressional Quarterly,* February 24, p. 598.

RU 486 testing begins—and so does pro-life response. 1995 *Life Advocate* . (January): 18.

Sakiz, E. 1994. Letter to Eleanor Smeal. May 30.

Scheman, C. 1992. Letter to Rep. Ron Wyden. December 15.

Sifton, C. 1992. Leona Benten against David Kessler memorandum decision and order. U.S. District Court, Eastern District of New York, CV-92-3161 (CPS).

Simons, M. 1988. A medical outcry greets suspension of abortion pill. *New York Times,* October 28, pp. A1, A8.

Smeal, E. 1991. Testimony before the Small Business Subcommittee on Regulation, Business Opportunities, and Energy, Small Business Committee, House of Representatives. December 5.

Stone, D. 1988. *Policy paradox and political reason.* Boston: Scott, Foresman.

Tempest, R. 1988. France orders company to distribute abortion pill. *Los Angeles Times,* October 29, p. 1.

———. 1990. Pill: RU 486 maker has declined to apply for marketing in the U.S. *Los Angeles Times,* August 11, p. A18.

Toten, S. 1994. Opponents come face to face. *Burlington Free Press,* December 4.

Townsend, L. 1991. Vatican condemns RU 486. *National Right to Life News,* May 7, p. 15.

U.S. House. 1990. Small Business Subcommittee on Regulation, Business Opportunities, and Energy. Memorandum on efficacy and safety of French abortifacient RU 486. November 1.

———. 1991. Small Business Subcommittee on Regulation, Business Opportunities, and Energy. Memorandum on federal import restriction of the drug RU 486 has hampered life-saving research into dread disease. November 27.

Wilkie, J. 1991. We met with the abortion pill people. *National Right to Life News,* January 8, p. 5.

Wyden, R. 1990a. Letter to Dr. Edouard Sakiz. December 2.

———. 1990b. Opening statement of Rep. Ron Wyden. The effect of the federal ban of RU 486 on medical research, new drug development, and pharmaceutical manufacturers. Hearing, Subcommittee on Regulation, Business Opportunities, and Energy, Small Business Committee, House of Representatives. November 19, pp. 2–3.

Young, F. 1989. Letter to Sen. Jesse Helms.

Zald, M. N., and B. Unseem. 1987. Movement and countermovement interaction: Mobilization, tactics, and state involvement. In *Social movements in an organizational society,* edited by M. N. Zald and J. P. McCarthy. New Brunswick, NJ: Transaction Publishers.

PART IV
Public Health Issues

7

Symbolic Politics and Health Care Reform in the 1940s and 1990s

Robert B. Hackey

Efforts to enact a comprehensive national health insurance system in the United States have commanded attention from policy makers and the public on numerous occasions during the postwar period. In recent decades, optimistic reformers frequently declared that sweeping reform was "inevitable" or "imminent" because of a growing "crisis" in the nation's health care system. Despite strong public support for more extensive federal involvement in financing health care and endorsements from prominent public officials, however, no national health insurance proposal has been passed by Congress in the postwar era. American exceptionalism in social policy has traditionally been viewed as either a consequence of intense interest-group opposition (e.g., the American Medical Association) or a by-product of divided government and the diffusion of policy-making authority (Morone 1995; Steinmo and Watts 1995). A variety of institutional explanations have been offered to account for the absence of national health insurance in the United States, including the relative weakness of the U.S. labor movement and the lack of a viable socialist party (Starr 1982), the inability of congressional supporters to forge a mutually acceptable compromise in the face of partisan and ideological divisions (Brady and Buckley 1995; White 1995), and targeted campaign contributions and public-relations campaigns on the part of well-financed industry groups (Center for Public Integrity 1995, 1996; Navarro 1995; Watzman and Woodall 1995; Podhorzer 1995).

The failure of Congress to pass national health insurance can also be viewed as a case of symbolic politics in which the definition of political issues played a crucial role in the demise of reform. This chapter explores the strategies and tactics used by opponents of national health insurance in the 1940s and 1990s to deny reformers access to the legislative agenda. In effect, opponents sought to ensure that reform efforts received symbolic, not substantive, consideration by undermining the legitimacy of the nation's "health care crisis" and attacking proposed solutions as unworkable, unaffordable, and un-American.

Since the 1930s, public opinion polls have reported that a majority of Americans favor a larger federal role in the health care system to guarantee access to essential services and to control costs (Erskine 1975; Jacobs, Shapiro, and Schulman 1993). Although public concern over health care reform has remained strong over the past several decades, policy makers' attention to the issue has waxed and waned. In particular, congressional attention to *comprehensive* health care reform has been sporadic, despite the fact that both the House and the Senate frequently held hearings, considered amendments, and passed legislation that affected the operation of ongoing programs (e.g., Medicare and Medicaid). Indeed, despite broad-based public support for health care reform since 1945, opponents managed to prevent Congress from seriously considering national health insurance proposals for much of the postwar period. Proposals for comprehensive reform of the U.S. health care system were conspicuously absent from the formal policy agenda in Congress during the 1950s, 1960s, and 1980s, despite growing concerns among the public and policy makers about medical costs and access to health care.

Timing is particularly important for groups seeking to keep issues off the legislative agenda, for a successful delaying action can prevent a bill from being heard until the agenda is full or new issues have appeared that cannot be postponed (e.g., the budget). If issue opponents succeed in their efforts to raise doubts about the need for, or the consequences of, a particular bill, it may be impossible to schedule committee hearings or formal votes on an issue. Furthermore, bills that do not receive serious consideration before the end of a legislative session must be reintroduced into the legislative hopper (possibly with new co-sponsors and/or committee assignments) in the next Congress (Kingdon 1984). In practice, the distinction between agenda denial and issue containment is one of timing; once a bill has been debated or voted on in Congress, it has achieved formal agenda status.

Groups seeking to keep comprehensive health care reform off the congressional policy agenda utilized several distinct strategies each time the issue surfaced as a topic of serious consideration. Although reformers believed that a "policy window" (Kingdon 1984) had opened on several occasions, opponents used symbolic appeals to decision makers, relevant interest groups, and the mass public to redefine the focus of policy debates and undermine support for reform. The content of specific reform proposals changed markedly over five decades, but the symbolic strategies employed by opponents of reform did not. The failure of national health care reform proposals, therefore, affords an opportunity to examine the strategies and tactics of "non–decision making" in Congress on a highly visible issue with considerable support among the mass public (Jacobs, Shapiro, and Schulman 1993). The tactics employed by health providers, insurers, businesses, and other conservative opponents differed little in style or substance from the 1940s to the 1990s. Opponents simultaneously sought to deny the legitimacy of the issue and invoked well-worn symbolic appeals to undermine support for proposals that threatened to destabilize the status quo (Bachrach and Baratz 1970, 45).

Political discourse about health care reform was substantially divorced from the content of specific legislative proposals during each reform era. The public remains especially vulnerable to symbolic appeals on issues of health care reform, for the complexity of many reform proposals makes it difficult for many policy makers, let alone the general public, to engage in "rational" debate over the merits of alternative proposals sought by policy wonks (Skocpol 1993). As Kathleen Hall Jamieson noted, health care reform debates in the 1990s were conducted in "an insider language, virtually incomprehensible to people" (Clymer 1994). Numerous national surveys in the 1990s painted a portrait of an electorate that supported reform in the abstract but remained both confused and cross-pressured about the means to achieve it. The public's knowledge of key issues in health care reform proposals remained low after more than two years of intense media coverage of the issue, and it actually declined in some areas (Yankelovich 1995). Furthermore, complaints about the quality of public discourse ignore the fact that policy problems are socially constructed, not objectively defined. As Edelman (1987, 15) notes, social problems often have "a diversity of meanings . . . stemming from the range of concerns of different groups, each eager to pursue courses of action and call them solutions."

THE RHETORIC OF REACTION IN THE 1940s AND 1990s

National health insurance has received serious consideration (e.g., formal committee hearings or votes) in Congress on several occasions. Legislation to create a universal health insurance system in the United States first appeared on the congressional agenda in 1916 (Numbers 1982); proposals for national health insurance have been introduced in every Congress since the 1940s. The Truman administration's support for a universal program of hospital insurance for all Americans led the American Medical Association (AMA) to underwrite an unprecedented "national education campaign" against "compulsion" and "socialized medicine" in the 1940s (Kelley 1956). The failure of comprehensive reform efforts led social reformers to narrow their proposals to address the needs of the nation's most vulnerable and "deserving" citizens in the 1950s and 1960s—the elderly. Less than five years after the passage of Medicare and Medicaid, several proposals to create a comprehensive national health insurance system were introduced in Congress by both Democrats and Republicans during the early 1970s. The Carter administration also made national health insurance a major legislative priority from 1977 to 1979, in an effort to control spiraling health care costs.

National health insurance disappeared from the formal agenda of Congress in 1981 with the arrival of the Reagan administration in Washington, but by the end of the decade, it had returned as a major policy issue that attracted bipartisan interest in Congress. Health care reform was once again the subject of intense discussions in the U.S. Senate in the early 1990s (Peterson 1993), as legislators weighed the merits of "pay or play" approaches for increasing access to health care. By 1993, the debate over national health insurance became the nation's most contentious and visible domestic policy issue. In each era, however, reformers failed to build support within Congress to sustain the momentum generated by the media and the mass public. Each time health care reform has emerged on the public agenda and ultimately gained a position on the congressional agenda, it has been an integral part of a Democratic electoral strategy to appeal to anxious working- and middle-class voters. As an electoral issue, the appeal of national health insurance to voters is undisputed, but to date, reformers have yet to persuade policy makers in Congress and the attentive public (Cobb and Elder 1982) that reform can be achieved in a manner consistent with American values.

The U.S. experience with comprehensive health care reform suggests that agenda denial and issue containment strategies must be seen as a seamless continuum, for opponents' initial definition of the problem and their critiques of proposed solutions have the potential to reframe the questions and issues considered by decision makers later in the policy process. The analysis presented in this chapter is confined to the pre-decision-making phase of the policy process; each of the symbolic strategies discussed herein was initiated prior to formal votes or committee hearings on specific policy proposals. Even failed agenda denial strategies are salient, because they set the stage for subsequent efforts at issue containment. Health care reform proposals frequently reached the formal agenda based on policy makers' view that an issue of such public importance deserved a fair hearing. However, similar themes and strategies were used by opponents of national health care reform as a means of issue containment once the issue was under active consideration by decision makers.

The analysis presented in this chapter focuses on two of these reform episodes in which health care reform dominated domestic policy discussions. In both eras, Democratic presidents enthusiastically endorsed reform and made the enactment of national health insurance a cornerstone of their domestic agendas. Polls suggest that public opinion in both eras was also supportive of reform. In the mid-1940s, opponents succeeded in defining "socialized medicine" as a dangerous proposal that was inconsistent with basic American beliefs in liberty, free markets, and voluntary solutions to public problems. Similar themes reappeared during the debate over the Clinton health care plan in 1993, as third-party insurers, small businesses, and other groups opposed to comprehensive reform contended that the administration's remedies were unwarranted, intrusive, and ultimately counterproductive.

The symbolic strategies used in each era to discredit health care reform proposals are drawn from a comprehensive review of stories on health care policy and medical care that appeared in the *New York Times* before the initiation of formal committee hearings in the 79th and 103d Congresses. Other quotations were obtained from sources that served as a forum for opponents' attacks on reform proposals in each period (e.g., the *Journal of the American Medical Association*). This chapter does not purport to present a comprehensive history of political rhetoric against national health insurance, but instead seeks to uncover enduring patterns and themes that characterized debates over reform in each decade.

Although proposals to create a national health insurance system had been introduced in Congress during the war years by Representative John Dingell and Senators Robert Wagner and James Murray (all Democrats), health care reform aroused little interest until 1945. In May 1945, companion bills were introduced by Dingell, Murray, and Wagner in both the House (H.R. 3293) and the Senate (S. 1050) to create a national "sickness insurance" program. Later in the year, President Truman identified national health care reform as one of his principal legislative priorities in a postwar message to the members of the 79th Congress. Following the earlier Wagner-Murray-Dingell proposals, the Truman plan outlined a five-point program that would allocate funds to construct new hospitals and other health care facilities, expand public and maternal health services through state grants, and improve funding for medical education and research.

The most controversial proposal in both plans, however, was the creation of a national health insurance program to provide "prepaid personal health service benefits," including hospitalization, physicians' office visits, and dental services, to most Americans. Both the president's program and the Wagner-Murray-Dingell bills promised to preserve individuals' ability to choose their doctors or health providers; similarly, participation in the new system would remain optional for doctors and hospitals. On the same day that President Truman issued his postwar message to Congress, Dingell and his cosponsors in the Senate introduced a new, more streamlined version of their earlier proposal entitled the National Health Act of 1945 (H. R. 4730, S. 1606). No hearings were held on either version of the bill during 1945, but hearings on S. 1606 began before the Senate Finance Committee in April 1946. Despite two months of heated debate over "compulsory" health insurance, neither version of the Wagner-Murray-Dingell bill emerged from committee during the 79th Congress.

A similar debate over national health insurance faced Congress nearly five decades later. The Clinton administration's health care reform proposals first gained public agenda status during the 1992 presidential campaign. Actual legislative proposals did not gain formal agenda status until after the president's address to Congress in late September 1993. Earlier in the year, various congressional committees had held numerous hearings at which academic experts, health care providers, insurers, and other interested parties outlined the scope of the problems facing the U.S. health care system and suggested possible solutions. At this point, however, the Clinton administration's health care reform plan was not formally on the agenda of the 103d Congress. Fact-finding hearings, which discuss a problem in general terms, reinforce the importance of an issue on the public agenda but differ considerably from focused hearings, which debate the merits of specific proposals. Preliminary hearings on the issues outlined in the president's address began in late September and continued throughout the fall, as Hillary Rodham Clinton and other senior administration officials testified before five separate committees that claimed jurisdiction over health care reform. The final version of the Clinton plan, entitled the Health Security Act, was submitted to Congress on October 27, 1993, and formally introduced in the House as H. R. 3600 and in the Senate as S. 1757 on November 20. Neither bill was reported out of committee in 1993.

AGENDA DENIAL STRATEGIES

Groups seeking to preserve the status quo may respond to new challengers "at any point along the process of issue emergence" (Gaventa 1980). Low-cost strategies seek to deny the legitimacy of the claimants' position by refusing to recognize the problem or minimizing its importance. Opponents of national health insurance, however, have most frequently turned to medium-cost strategies that either attack the legitimacy of the initiating group or raise concerns about the impact of proposed reforms. In particular, opponents have relied on fear-based appeals in an effort to deny supporters of national health insurance access to the congressional agenda. Furthermore, the themes established during the process of agenda denial provided the basis for subsequent issue containment efforts once the issue reached the formal agenda (Hackey 1995).

As Hirschman (1990) notes, the popularity of many progressive reforms such as national health insurance often precludes a direct attack on the goal itself (e.g., providing quality health care for all). Instead, opponents are likely to endorse the idea of reform but insist that existing proposals are flawed or ill conceived or will have dire consequences. Regardless of the specific content or goals of individual policy proposals, opponents of reform consistently returned to several distinct themes in their efforts to redefine and undermine support for reform proposals. Proposals for reform have been attacked on the grounds that they are unworkable, unaffordable, or inconsistent with basic American values. These arguments closely paralleled the theses of perversity, futility, and jeopardy described by Hirschman (1990) in his review of "reactionary" rhetoric: "According to the perversity thesis, any purposive action to improve some features of the political, social, or economic order only serves to exacerbate the condition one wishes to remedy. The futility thesis holds that any attempts at social transformation will be unavailing, that they will simply fail to 'make a dent.' Finally, the jeopardy thesis argues that the cost of the proposed change or reform is too high as it endangers some previous, precious accomplishment" (Hirschman 1990, 7).

A familiar cycle emerged during each reform period, as advocates called attention to the shortcomings of the nation's health care system and sought access to the formal agenda in Congress. In each era, reform proposals drew praise and endorsements from both the public and key decision makers; with a groundswell of popular support, reform was hailed as "inevitable" by both public officials and pundits. Over time, however, the terms of debate in each era shifted in response to opponents' arguments that national health care reform would inexorably lead to an expansion of "big government" and that the unintended consequences of reform would be "worse than the disease." In the end, "ownership" of the problem (Rochefort and Cobb 1994) shifted from reformers to issue opponents each time national health insurance emerged on the public agenda.

THE POLITICS OF FEAR

The ideologically charged and intensely partisan context of health care reform debates in both the 1940s and the 1990s provided a hospitable environment for the creation of symbolic enemies. Through the creation of symbolic enemies, opponents presented reformers or their proposals as threats to basic, deep-seated American values and institutions. Two principal paths were followed by opponents of national health insurance in the postwar period: attacking the legitimacy of reform proposals, and questioning the consequences of reforms if enacted. Both rely on the creation of symbolic enemies to mobilize public opposition to national health insurance. As Edelman (1987) notes, the creation of political enemies is a useful strategy, for it implies that a group is dangerous or that its proposals threaten important traditions and values. Many groups that are demonized by their opponents have done "no harm at all, though the attribution of harm served a purpose for their antagonists" (Edelman 1987, 80). Opponents contend that national health insurance is inconsistent with many of the higher-order symbols of the political community (Elder and Cobb 1983), such as liberty, freedom, and the "American way." A system of "compulsory" insurance, in this view, would lead to a socialized economy or, at a minimum, establish a precedent for massive government intervention in other areas of American life. Playing on the public's fear of "big government," opponents branded national health insurance proposals as "un-American" solutions that would rob citizens of their freedom, erode the quality of medical care, increase taxes on individuals and businesses, and disrupt the doctor-patient relationship.

Big Government and "Socialized Medicine" in the 1940s

As Stone and Marmor (1990, 255) note, "[i]n a society that is deeply distrustful of public power and hesitant about redistribution, health services cannot be easily legitimized by claims about the essentialness of health, the requirement of

equal treatment, or the obligations of a community to its members." Soon after
the introduction of the Wagner-Murray-Dingell bill in the 79th Congress, the
American Medical Association evoked the higher-order symbols of the political
community in its efforts to undermine support for the legislation. In a joint resolution endorsed by its board of trustees and the Council on Medical Service and
Public Relations, the AMA declared that "the Constitution of the United States,
the Bill of Rights, and the 'American Way of Life' are diametrically opposed to
regimentation or any form of totalitarianism. According to available evidence in
surveys, most of the American people are not interested in testing in the United
States experiments in medical care which have already failed in regimented countries" (quoted in Bauer 1945, 945).

The AMA's opposition to "socialized medicine" is well known, but the belief
that national health insurance was inconsistent with basic American values in
each reform era was widely shared. Dr. Harold Low, president of the Association
of American Physicians and Surgeons, declared that the bill would be "an entering wedge for the accomplishment of a completely socialized economy for this
nation" ("Federal Health Plan" 1946, 9). The AMA had made this point in 1945,
when its board of trustees proclaimed that "[n]otwithstanding Senator Wagner's
claim that this bill [S. 1050, the Wagner-Murray-Dingell bill of 1945] is not socialized medicine, it is just that. It is paternalistic and inevitably will lead to national
socialism." In addition, opponents charged that any scheme of universal, state-
sponsored health insurance would undermine traditional values. Compulsion, in
short, was "un-American" (Bauer 1945, 948). Physicians in New York regarded
the Wagner-Murray-Dingell plan as a measure "contrary to our national spirit
and traditions of self-government" that would "obliterate local community initiative and responsibility in matters of health and medical care, promote the cen-
tralization of power . . . and create a gigantic self-perpetuating bureaucratic machine that will inevitably become the master rather than the servant of the
people" ("Physicians Divided" 1946, 18).

The politics of agenda denial in the 1950s built on the themes developed in
the previous decade; Representative John Davis Lodge of Massachusetts set the
tone for debates over reform in the 1950s when he characterized "any state or
Federal plan of socialized medicine" as a "repulsive suggestion" that was "contrary to American ideas of privacy and decency" ("State Medicine Opposed"
1950, 24). Even modest proposals, such as the Eisenhower administration's "rein-
surance" plan to encourage the growth of private insurance companies, were assailed as a "foot in the door" to a federal takeover of the medical profession. A
lack of confidence in the public sector provided numerous opportunities for opponents of health care reform to raise doubts about the reformers' ability to
fulfill their promises. In 1945, Senator Leverett Saltonstall of Massachusetts cau-
tioned his colleagues to be wary of asking the government to "make promises
that it cannot live up to" ("Federal Health Plan" 1946). From this perspective,
proponents of national health care reform are well intentioned but naive about

the ability of the federal bureaucracy to administer a system of universal health insurance.

Fears of Big Government in the 1990s

Images of massive government bureaucracies became one of the primary weapons wielded by opponents of health care reform in the 1990s. Despite the collapse of communism in Europe and the former Soviet Union during the late 1980s, attacks on "socialized medicine" continued unabated. Michael Novak charged that "[h]owever he may be denying it, Clinton proposes socializing medical care. . . . Instead of being true to the American tradition, Dr. Clinton prescribes European-style statism at the very moment when Europeans are turning away from it" (1993, 192). Critics conjured up images of a national health insurance system that would require "such a preposterous Rube Goldberg construction that the great Rube himself wouldn't have had the nerve to put it in the comic strips" (Baker 1993, A27). The end result, according to conservative opponents, would "create more centralized government control. Government bureaucrats will decide what services you receive. Government bureaucrats will decide how much you will pay. Government bureaucrats will decide what services your doctor can provide. . . . This is socialism! And, like the social welfare programs of the 1960s, once socialized health care is in place, we will never go back to a market based system" (Glavin 1993, 4).

Furthermore, opponents questioned the capacity of federal agencies to implement a massive new government program in an efficient manner. Corporate leaders frequently contended that despite their good intentions, public officials were simply not up to the task. As General Electric chief executive officer Jack Welch warned, "If you believe regional purchasing alliances in 50 states can weed out $200 billion in waste, go visit your local motor vehicle department. It's absolutely foolhardy" (Dowd 1993, 128). In a similar vein, Ross Perot questioned the capacity of the federal government to manage a system as complex as that proposed by the Clinton administration's Health Security Act. "We have a system that needs dramatic improvement. But just turning it over to the federal government, with its history of mediocrity and failure in managing social programs and its total lack of discipline on spending . . . this is an airplane with no wing" ("Perot Criticizes Clinton Proposal" 1994, A12).

A faceless, monolithic government bureaucracy became the principal symbolic enemy in the debate over health care reform in the 1990s. As Senator Robert Dole warned, "we will have a crisis if we take the President's medicine—a massive overdose of government control. . . . Sen. Arlen Spector has prepared a chart of what the health care bureaucracy would look like under the President's plan, and I'd like to show you this chart. It's a great, big chart. It contains 207 boxes. It would take a long time to fully explain it, and frankly, I have difficulty understanding it myself" (Dole 1994, A15). In short, opponents in the 1990s assailed the Clinton plan as a threat to existing values or institutions or linked it to distasteful symbols (e.g., socialism) that had strong resonance with the mass public. In short, opponents presented an ideologically consistent explanation for why Americans should oppose reform that was tied to deeply held political beliefs in U.S. political culture.

Fears of Substandard Medicine in the 1940s

Government intervention in the health care system was also assailed on the grounds that national health insurance would drive a wedge between doctors and their patients. Rules, regulations, and red tape would replace sound medical practice as government sought to control costs and standardize procedures. In addition, opponents claimed that a federally financed health insurance system would place doctors in a straitjacket by defining the scope and content of medical practice. Republican Senator Robert Taft of Ohio argued that under the Truman administration's reform proposals, "practically all doctors would become in effect employees of the government which pays them and not to their patients who do not. You know better than I whether that would improve medical service, make better doctors, and stimulate progress in medicine" ("Taft Hits Truman" 1946, 26). In addition to its effects on the autonomy of health providers, opponents argued that any national health insurance system would lead to a proliferation of "assembly-line" clinics, create queues for specialists and surgical procedures, and dramatically slow progress in technology, pharmaceuticals, and medical education. Physicians predicted that under the Truman administration's health care proposals to Congress, "a poor type of medical care is encouraged— quantity without regard to quality. Inefficiency, red tape, and political medicine will result" (Bauer 1945, 948). These themes reappeared later in 1945, when Republican Senator Saltonstall of Massachusetts warned that any improvements to the nation's health care system must guard against "the loss of initiative that goes with private medicine" ("Saltonstall Asks" 1945, 37). In a similar vein, the president of the New York Academy of Medicine warned that "any scheme of national compulsory medical insurance at this time would lead to most unfortunate results affecting the health of the public and the science as well as the practice of medicine" ("Medical Academy" 1946, 24).

Finally, opponents of national health insurance repeatedly warned that universal health insurance funded by the federal government would prevent individuals from choosing health providers or insurers. Each proposal represented a "slippery slope" that would inexorably lead to a loss of personal freedom and the end of a patient's right to self-determination. The AMA's Medical Program for the American People argued that national health insurance would ultimately limit individuals' free choice of provider. "While free choice of physician is provided for in the bill, this is a 'come on,' as it means free choice of the physician who will take part in the scheme" (Bauer 1945, 948). In addition, the AMA raised fears of impersonal bureaucrats interfering with the doctor-patient relationship. National health insurance, in this view, introduced a third party (i.e., government) "between the doctor and the patient, and the doctor is responsible to that third party" (Bauer 1945, 948).

Threats to the Quality of Medical Care in the 1990s

The specter of federal bureaucrats dictating standards of medical practice to hapless doctors reappeared in the 1990s. Fears of government interference in the practice of medicine were heightened by the central role of managed care in several of the reform proposals under consideration by the 103d Congress. Since health maintenance organizations and other managed care providers had a financial incentive to cut costs, opponents of reform argued that "managed competition holds the potential of severely disrupting the traditional doctor-patient relationship. . . . [T]he Clinton administration apparently believes that physicians should be responsible to insurers rather than their patients. This means that the patient's choice of a physician will be limited to give the insurer increased bargaining power with the doctor" (Glavin 1993, 2).

Concerns about the impact of reform on the quality of care were particularly evident during the debate over the Clinton administration's Health Security Act. Conservative economist Thomas Sowell (1993, 140) invoked the jeopardy thesis to critique the Democratic proposals for universal health insurance coverage in 1993 when he asked, "Should we destroy the world's finest medical care, in hopes of helping to rescue the irresponsible?" Furthermore, critics warned, "the one common characteristic of socialized health care systems is a shortage of health care services" (Glavin 1993, 2). Opponents of the Clinton plan warned voters that the president's vision of "managed competition" would remove the ability of doctors and patients to choose the care that was most appropriate for their personal circumstances. As Senator Dole argued:

> The President's idea is to put a mountain of bureaucrats between you and your doctor. For example, if you are a family member and want to receive care from a specialist or clinic outside of your own state—let's say you live in Kansas and want to go to Minnesota—then you probably can't do it without asking for approval. And under his plan, information about your health and your treatment can be sent to a national data bank without your approval. And that's a compromise of privacy none of us should accept. (Dole 1994, A15)

In a widely cited article in *The New Republic,* Elizabeth McCaughey (1994) warned that passage of the Clinton plan would lead to de facto government control over the practice of medicine. In particular, McCaughey (1994, 21) argued that patients would "have to settle for one of the low budget health plans selected by the government. The law will prevent you from going outside the system to buy basic health coverage you think is better, even after you pay the mandatory premium. The bill guarantees you a package of medical services, but you can't have them unless they are deemed 'necessary' and 'appropriate.' That decision will be made by government, not by you and your doctor." Similar themes were echoed by opponents of the Clinton plan during congressional debates over the Health Security Act throughout the spring and summer of 1994. Fearful images of care rationed by faceless bureaucrats, physicians stripped of their professional autonomy, and the forced enrollment of millions of Americans in bargain-basement health plans that compromised their privacy were designed to persuade voters and members of Congress that national health insurance was inconsistent with the values that Americans had come to expect from their health care system. In short, national health insurance threatened the very survival of the system it purported to fix.

CONCLUSION

Symbols, metaphors, and "causal stories" (Stone 1989) are particularly potent in health care policy making because of the complexity of the legislative proposals and the low levels of information held by the mass public. In the wake of the Clinton plan's demise, Brown and Marmor (1994, 193) complained that "the debate about potential remedies for these problems have [sic] satisfied almost no one. Labels and symbols of proposals, not realistic standards for their assessment, have dominated the discussion." Symbolic politics is inevitable in discussions of health care reform, however, for "symbols are the currency of the communication process. They represent the focal objects of political attitudes and opinions and serve to define the procedural and substantive concerns of government" (Elder and Cobb 1983, 9). The problem for frustrated reformers is not that debates over health care reform were framed in symbolic terms or that opponents frequently resorted to rhetorical bombasts. Instead, throughout the postwar period, opponents of reform proved to be more adept in designing symbolic appeals than those who sought to remake the health care system.

The success of opponents in undermining proposals for national health care reform reflects the nature of their symbolic appeals. Proponents of reform made extensive use of more specific situational symbols to present their case to the public (e.g., managed competition, single-payer plans), whereas opponents relied on broad themes using higher-order symbols and regime norms (e.g., choice, freedom, the American way). The demise of the Clinton administration's Health Security Act illustrates the different paths followed by each group. The administration built a technically sophisticated but inaccessible case about the merits of various alternatives for controlling costs and improving access to quality health care. While voters were deluged with detailed accounts of how health insurance purchasing cooperatives ("alliances") would work by administration officials, academic experts, and members of Congress, opponents presented a deceptively simple argument that attacked the Clinton plan for limiting individuals' freedom to choose their doctors. Furthermore, each of the strategies outlined above was closely linked to deep-seated values in U.S. political culture. Americans' preference for private solutions to public problems (McConnell 1966) and an enduring suspicion of government in general and bureaucracy in particular (Morone 1990a) are not new, but rather are recurring themes in U.S. political discourse.

Symbolic attacks on national health insurance are particularly effective because they link opposition to various reform proposals to widely held beliefs in democracy, liberty, and other symbols of the political community. As Elder and Cobb (1983, 39–40) observed, higher-order symbols such as "freedom of choice," "big government," and "the American way" may be applied to more contexts and evoke a more intense response from targeted audiences than more specific situational symbols. Opponents of national health insurance have consistently played on the public's fear of intrusive government by employing symbolic rhetoric designed to arouse fear about the consequences of reform. Reformers, in contrast, have been less successful in linking their appeals to higher-order symbols. Since the higher-order symbols employed by opponents typically command greater affect than lower-order symbols, strategies that rely on higher-order symbols prevail over those using lower-order ones when the two conflict (Elder and Cobb 1983, 39–40).

Although the Clinton administration's initial emphasis on "health security" in 1993 appealed to uninsured and underinsured Americans, opponents succeeded in raising doubts among millions of voters who were satisfied with their existing private insurance plans. In addition, reformers were unable to reclaim ownership of the problem after opponents defined health care reform in terms of big government, higher taxes, and lost choices (see Fallows 1995). The consistency of opponents' rhetoric over the past fifty years is instructive, for despite the technical merits of various reform proposals, each was rejected by policy makers or the public as an unwarranted assertion of government control. In retrospect, Skocpol's (1993, 547) warning was prophetic: "If reformers in the 1990s fail to paint an appealing picture of government sponsored reform, conservatives will ... win yet another round in the overly protracted struggle to bring affordable and accessible health care to all Americans."

The frustration expressed by social reformers in the 1990s lends credence to George Lakoff's (1995, 178) claim that "liberals do not understand the form of metaphorical thought that unifies and makes sense of the full range of conservative values." In short, conservatives have won the metaphorical wars waged over national health insurance during the twentieth century by resorting to an arsenal of well-tested strategies. Americans' attitudes toward government have vacillated between a fear of state power and a yearning for participatory democracy for more than two hundred years (Morone 1990a). By linking their opposition to national health insurance to Americans' traditional distrust of public authority and concentrated power, physicians, businesses, and other groups seeking to preserve the status quo succeeded in defining the terms of political debate in both the 1940s and the 1990s. By appealing to the strengths within communities at the state, local, and national levels, opponents claimed that government intervention was either an unnecessary intrusion (e.g., denial) or a threat to the prevailing professional, social, and economic order.

Symbolic politics also defined the process of issue containment during each era in which national health insurance appeared on the congressional agenda (Hackey 1995). The dual strategies of denial and fear were complemented by assurances that comprehensive reforms were not needed because voluntary efforts by private groups could address the system's shortcomings without the heavy hand of government. This strategy of tokenism expanded on the themes established during the process of agenda denial. In this view, the growth of private insurance would ultimately increase access to health care without jeopardizing the quality of care, individuals' free choice of providers, or physicians' autonomy. After more than two years of intense public debate over health care reform, Republican National Committee chairman Haley Barbour contended that "we don't have to have a government run health care program to do health care reform" (Toner 1994, 24).

Opponents of comprehensive reform also portrayed private solutions to the public's health care problems as a uniquely American approach that built on the virtues of private citizens and organizations. As the American Medical Association declared in 1949, "the voluntary way is the American way—and the people will resolve this problem, in a very short number of years, under the voluntary systems now available to them" ("AMA Statement" 1949, 8). In the 1940s, opponents touted the promise of voluntary health insurers, particularly Blue Cross plans, as a means of expanding coverage without coercion. By the 1990s, opponents turned to the power of free markets, as evidenced by the growth of managed care, as a means of controlling costs and increasing the quality of health care services. In each era, government intervention was portrayed not only as unnecessary but also as a threat to the substantial progress that had been achieved by the private sector.

In the face of strong support from the mass public and key decision makers for government-sponsored health insurance, critics first managed to raise doubts about the existence of a problem that required government action. Second, opponents successfully defined comprehensive reform as "compulsory medicine" that threatened the quality of health care and Americans' choices of and personal relationships with health care providers. The power of the rhetorical broadsides hurled against national health insurance drew on well-established conservative themes in U.S. political culture. As Lakoff (1995, 209) observed, "conservatives have carefully coined terms and images and repeated them until they have entered the popular lexicon." The lesson for would-be health care reformers from both the 1940s and 1990s is clear: The definition of policy problems and options remains central to the resolution of political conflicts. A fundamental overhaul of the U.S. health care system will continue to be an illusory goal unless reformers are able to reclaim the language and images that are the currency of policy debates.

NOTE

Previous versions of this chapter were presented to the annual meeting of the New England Political Science Association in Springfield, Massachusetts, on May 3–4, 1996, and the 67th annual meeting of the Southern Political Science Association in Tampa, Florida, on November 1–4, 1995. I am indebted to Roger Cobb and Marc Ross for their perceptive comments and patience during the preparation of this manuscript. This chapter would not have been possible without the efforts of Brian King and Christine Phillips, whose many hours of photocopying and tracking down materials in the library provided the raw material for the analysis presented here.

REFERENCES

AMA assails health plan of Truman as "scourge." 1946. *New York Times,* April 25, pp. 1, 8.

AMA statement on Truman health plan. 1949. *New York Times,* April 25, p. 8.

Bachrach, P., and M. Baratz. 1970. *Power and poverty.* New York: Oxford University Press.

Baker, R. 1993. Hazardous to health. *New York Times,* December 8, p. A27.

Bauer, L. 1945. Medical care for the American people. *Journal of the American Medical Association* 129:945–9.

Baumgartner, F., and B. Jones. 1991. Agenda dynamics and policy subsystems. *Journal of Politics* 53:1044–74.

Brady, D., and K. Buckley. 1995. Health care reform in the 103rd Congress: A predictable failure. *Journal of Health Politics, Policy, and Law* 20:447–55.

Brown, L., and T. Marmor. 1994. The Clinton plan's administrative structure: The reach and the grasp. *Journal of Health Politics, Policy, and Law* 19:193–9.

Center for Public Integrity. 1995. Well healed: Inside lobbying for health care reform, part I. *International Journal of Health Services* 25:411–453.

———. 1996. Well healed: Inside lobbying for health care reform, part III. *International Journal of Health Services* 26:19–46.

Clymer, A. 1994. Hype about health. *New York Times,* February 5, p. 8.

Cobb, R. W., and C. D. Elder 1983. *Participation in American politics,* 2d ed. Baltimore: Johns Hopkins University Press.

Dole, R. 1994. Excerpts from the Republicans' response to the president's message. *New York Times,* January 26, p. A15.

Dowd, A. 1993. Companies hate the health plan. *Fortune,* November 29, pp. 122–8.

Edelman, M. 1987. *Constructing the political spectacle.* Chicago: University of Chicago Press.

Elder, C., and R. Cobb. 1983. *The political uses of symbols.* New York: Longman.

Erskine, H. 1975. The polls: Health insurance. *Public Opinion Quarterly* 39:128–43.

Fallows, J. 1995. A triumph of misinformation. *Atlantic Monthly* (January): 26–37.

Federal health plan splits medical units. 1946. *New York Times,* April 19, p. 9.

Gaventa, J. 1980. *Power and powerlessness.* Urbana: University of Illinois Press.

Glavin, M. 1993. Health care and a free society. *Imprimis* 22(11): 1–4.

Hackey, R. 1995. The rise and demise of health care reform, 1945–95. Paper presented to the 67th annual meeting of the Southern Political Science Association, Tampa, FL, November 1–4.

Hirschman, A. 1990. *The rhetoric of reaction.* Cambridge, MA: Belknap.

Jacobs, L. 1993. Health reform impasse: The politics of American ambivalence towards government. *Journal of Health Politics, Policy, and Law* 18:629–56.

Jacobs, L., R. Shapiro, and E. Schulman. 1993. Poll trends: Medical care in the United States—an update. *Public Opinion Quarterly* 57:394–427.

Kelley, S. 1956. *Professional public relations and political power.* Baltimore: Johns Hopkins University Press.

Kingdon, J. 1984. *Agendas, alternatives, and public policies.* Glenview, IL: Scott, Foresman.

Lakoff, G. 1995. Metaphor, morality, and politics, or why conservatives have left liberals in the dust. *Social Research* 62:177–213.

Loomis, B. 1995. *Time and politics.* Lawrence: University Press of Kansas.

Marmor, T. 1995. A summer of discontent: Press coverage of murder and medical care reform. *Journal of Health Politics, Policy, and Law* 20:495–502.

McCaughey, E. 1994. No exit. *New Republic,* February 7, pp. 21–5.

McConnell, G. 1966. *Private power and American democracy.* New York: Knopf.

Medical academy sifts Truman plan. 1946. *New York Times,* January 4, p. 24.

Morone, J. A. 1990a. *The democratic wish.* New York: Basic Books.

———. 1990b. Epilogue: Tales of trouble. *Journal of Health Politics, Policy, and Law* 15:435–9.

———. 1995. Nativism, hollow corporations, and managed competition: Why the Clinton health care reform failed. *Journal of Health Politics, Policy, and Law* 20:391–8.

Navarro, V. 1995. The politics of health care reform in the United States, 1992–1994: A historical review. *International Journal of Health Services* 25:185–201.

Novak, M. 1993. It hurts too much. *Forbes,* November 8, p. 192.

Numbers, R. 1982. The specter of socialized medicine: American physicians and compulsory health insurance. In *Compulsory health insurance,* edited by R. Numbers. Westport, CT: Greenwood.

Perot criticizes Clinton proposal. 1994. *New York Times,* January 24, p. A12.

Peterson, M. 1993. Momentum toward health care reform in the U.S. Senate. *Journal of Health Politics, Policy, and Law* 17:553–74.

Physicians divided over health law. 1946. *New York Times,* April 23, p. 18.

Podhorzer, M. 1995. Unhealthy money: Health reform and the 1994 elections. *International Journal of Health Services* 23:393–401.

Poen, M. 1979. *Harry S. Truman versus the medical lobby.* Columbia: University of Missouri Press.

Rochefort, D., and R. Cobb, eds. 1994. *The politics of problem definition.* Lawrence: University Press of Kansas.

Saltonstall asks health aid study. 1945. *New York Times,* November 22, p. 37.

Skocpol, T. 1993. Is the time finally ripe? Health insurance reforms in the 1990s. *Journal of Health Politics, Policy, and Law* 18:531–50.

"Socialized medicine" opposed by Kefauver. 1951. *New York Times,* September 14, p. 19.

Sowell, T. 1993. Memo to policy reformers. *Forbes,* June 21, p. 140.

Starr, P. 1982. *The social transformation of American medicine.* New York: Basic Books.

State medicine opposed. 1950. *New York Times,* July 2, p. 24.

Steinmo, S., and J. Watts, 1995. It's the institutions, stupid! Why comprehensive health care reform always fails in America. *Journal of Health Politics, Policy, and Law* 20:329–72.

Stone, D. 1989. *Policy paradox and political reason.* Boston: Little, Brown.

Stone, D., and T. Marmor. 1990. Introduction. *Journal of Health Politics, Policy, and Law* 15:253–7.

Taft hits Truman over health bill. 1946. *New York Times,* October 8, p. 26.

Toner, R. 1993. Clinton facing reality of health-care reform. *New York Times,* May 21, p. A14.

———. 1994. GOP on health care: Seeking a second opinion. *New York Times,* March 4, p. 24.

Watzman, N., and P. Woodall. 1995. Managed health care companies' lobbying frenzy. *International Journal of Health Services* 25:403–10.

West, D., D. Heith, and C. Goodwin. 1996. Harry and Louise go to Washington: Political advertising and health care reform. *Journal of Health Politics, Policy, and Law* 21:35–68.

White, J. 1995. The horses and the jumps: Comments on the health care reform steeplechase. *Journal of Health Politics, Policy, and Law* 20:373–84.

Yankelovich, D. 1995. The public and the Clinton health care plan. *Brookings Review* (summer): 37–41.

8

Agenda Denial
and Water Access
in Texas Colonias

Cynthia M. Lopez and Michael R. Reich

All along the U.S.-Mexico border exists a series of unregulated human settlements, called colonias, without potable water access.[1] On the U.S. side of the border, the majority of colonias are in Texas. In recent years, colonia water access (CWA) has appeared and disappeared as an issue on the congressional and state legislative agendas. We analyze the problem's presence and absence as an issue on these formal agendas from 1988 to 1995, as a way of examining agenda denial processes while the problem worsened and the local political structure remained relatively stable.

This chapter focuses on the strategies used by the opponents of colonia water access at the local level. Our analysis shows that opponents consistently used low- and medium-cost strategies to challenge the legitimacy of colonia residents and encouraged negative stereotypes of those needing water to undermine the legitimacy of demands for government action. At times, opponents demonstrated symbolic concern about the problem, withdrew their resistance, and supported CWA proposals favorable to their own interests. These symbolic actions served to limit support for CWA as potential supporters perceived that the problem was being resolved or improving. These symbolic and cultural strategies fostered a negative social construction of colonia residents and increased the residents' sense of powerlessness and quiescence. These strategies were applied in a political environment characterized by sharp power disparities between CWA proponents and opponents, and the strategies deepened these disparities.

This study of colonia water access as a public issue and as an issue on the formal agenda relies on information from public health statistics, news reports, and direct interviews. Our analysis demonstrates the importance of CWA as a public health problem and its consistent status as a public issue. We then describe the opponents, their views, and their use of symbolic and cultural strategies to limit agenda access and contain the CWA issue on the legislative agenda. The concluding section is a discussion of agenda access, water access, and power disparities, suggesting that agenda access is a necessary condition to obtaining water access and that agenda access is conditioned by power relationships.

Some aspects of the water access problem were on the federal congressional agenda during 1988–1989 and 1994 but were not present during other years under study. At the state level, the period of greatest legislative consideration of CWA and other colonia issues was in 1991. Although there was some governmental activity at the state and federal levels, this chapter explains why local decision makers sometimes neglected this issue and why, when they considered it, the solutions developed were partial and symbolic. As Crenson (1971, vii) notes, "The analysis of non-decisions and non-issues seems to require that the analyst provide an explanation for things that do not happen, and some political scientists have argued that there is simply no reasoned and reliable way to construct such explanations."

Complicating the analysis of nonissues is the fact that for every issue there are infinite alternative problems that have not achieved placement on a formal agenda (Crenson 1971, 26). These are "potential public issues" that exceed "the capabilities of decision-making institutions to process them" (Cobb, Ross, and Ross 1976, 126). In effect, any researcher studying a nonissue selects it from a multitude of potentially important problems and demonstrates what he or she, not the decision makers, considers important. However, a researcher who ignores nonissues and focuses only on issues in which overt political action has occurred also holds an implicit hypothesis that the nonissue did not reach issue status because of lack of concern over the problem; in fact, other reasons for nonissue status may exist (Crenson 1971, 26–7).

In this chapter, we examine the uneven agenda status of a social problem that steadily increased in severity over a six-year period as measured by the number of colonias and residents. We seek to explain the observed changes in agenda status. Finally, we explain the lack of congruence between agenda status and problem severity by analyzing the characteristics and strategies of those who opposed the issue's access to the congressional and state legislative agendas.

METHODS

In this study we focus on El Paso County colonias for the following reasons: colonias, dwellings, and residents are highly concentrated in El Paso County; the majority of colonia residents without water access live in the county; data are readily available; and the county has more than a twenty-year history of colonia presence. The local government is that of El Paso County.

Data for the analysis were collected from published and unpublished documents and from semistructured interviews with twenty-seven individuals. We reviewed congressional and state legislative records and testimony, agency reports, and news articles to identify community and political leaders and key organizational positions for interviews.[2] We also identified key positions in the local government, state legislature, civil service, business and financial institutions, local environmental groups, nonprofit organizations, and religious groups. The interviews examined CWA as a public issue and its status as an issue on formal agendas over time, and they explored the symbolic and cultural language and images associated with the issue. Opponents were identified from news reports, legislative records, and interviews. Data derived from an epidemiological survey of colonia residents were also used in our analysis (Lopez 1995) to assess the colonia residents' perceptions of themselves and of the problem of water access.

THE PROBLEM OF COLONIA WATER ACCESS

Inadequate access to clean water by colonia residents is a well-recognized public health problem in Texas. In 1987–1988, staff from the Texas Department of Health and Human Services (TDHHS) conducted a comprehensive and representative survey of colonia residents from select border counties.[3] They identified 932 colonias in Texas, with 537, or 55 percent, in El Paso County. They estimated the number of colonia residents to be 140,000, or 49 percent, in El Paso County (TDHHS 1988, 1–4).[4] The remainder of colonias and colonia residents were located in the U.S.-Mexico border counties of Willacy, Hidalgo, and Cameron and in the Lower Rio Grande Valley (TDHHS 1988, 1–3).

Some federal and state monies became available in the late 1980s to extend water and sewer lines in those counties that adopted model subdivision rules.[5] Despite these new monies, a 1995 reconnaissance survey of water and wastewater needs conducted by the Texas Water Development Board (TWDB) indicated that the number of colonias had grown since its 1992 survey. The 1995 update identified 1,436 colonia areas in Texas with a population of 339,041 people in twenty-three counties (TWDB 1995, 8). In El Paso County alone, there had been an increase of 22 percent in the number of colonia dwellings since 1992 (TWDB 1995, 17). Part of the increase was due to an improvement in TWDB survey methods and a change in the definition of colonia since 1992. However, by checking tax and utility connection records, TWDB staff confirmed that the growth was real (and not just a reporting artifact) and that most growth occurred in the number of colonia households in existing colonias rather than by the establishment of new colonias.

The profile of an "average" colonia resident is one that is typical of disadvantaged groups: poor and of a minority group. The 1988 TDHHS survey concluded that the majority of El Paso colonia residents were born in the United States (68 percent), of Hispanic descent (96 percent), poor (average annual household income, $11,497), and young (average age, twenty-six); many did not have health insurance (57 percent), and most claimed to own their homes (84 percent)

(TDHHS 1988). Colonia residents build homes on land purchased from local developers, usually subdivided from unproductive farmland, through contract for deed or executory contract (Rodriguez 1995a, 1995b). These contracts typically allow for sellers to take advantage of colonia residents "by charging usurious rates of interest as well as allowing unbridled discretion to evict" (*Vernon's* 1995, 4895). According to these contracts, ownership is not transferred to the buyer until the contract is paid in full.

Even if colonia growth were checked, water availability would still be limited in the border region (TWDB 1992, 3). In El Paso County, demand for water has increased over the past ten years due to population growth and industrial expansion. The aquifer that supplies the majority of El Paso's drinking water, the Hueco Bolson, is expected to be depleted by 2025 (Williams 1996, 1A). To meet drinking water needs in the near future, El Paso County will have to rely increasingly on Rio Grande surface water. Currently, over 50 percent of El Paso City's drinking water is derived from the river (Bath, Tanski, and Villarreal 1994).

River water quality is already compromised, particularly downstream, near El Paso County floodplain colonias.[6] Untreated waste contaminates the river, its drainage basin, and floodplain wells. Many colonias are located in river floodplains, and residents depend on shallow wells for water (Lopez 1995).[7] In a waterquality survey conducted since 1994, hundreds of water samples from the river near floodplain colonias and from wells of residents contained coliform bacteria (Lopez 1996; Lopez and Byrne 1996). Colonia residents who live in the Rio Grande floodplains report that they frequently come into contact with these contaminated waters. Of the Texas colonia residents interviewed for this study, 6 percent report fishing and swimming in the river, and 66 percent report washing and bathing with untreated well water (Lopez 1996). These residents have three private options for avoiding exposure to water contamination. First, they can pay for a professionally constructed and "certified" well and septic system, and second, they can purchase potable water. Few residents can afford these options, however, because professionally constructed wells and bottled water are expensive. A third option, the self-construction of wells, often does not avoid contamination, because the water is usually not adequately treated and can be contaminated with human waste from leaky septic systems in close proximity (U.S. House 1988, 1–2).

These problems have contributed to an increase in waterborne diseases, such as hepatitis A and dysentery, among colonia residents. One study conducted in an El Paso County floodplain colonia, San Elizario, indicated that by age thirty-five, 85 to 90 percent of San Elizario residents have been infected with hepatitis A (Sawyer et al. 1989, 2–5). In El Paso County, the hepatitis A infection rate "has been on occasion five times" the U.S. average (Nickey 1994, 5). Even cholera, absent from this hemisphere for a century, is reemerging along the border (Nickey 1994, 5). The city-county health department director, Dr. L. N. Nickey, estimated that a dozen cholera cases had been reported near the Texas-Mexico border in 1993, including three in Ciudad Juarez.[8] The reemergence of cholera is probably associated with increasing water contamination. In public testimony, Nickey stated: "There is no question in the minds of public health officials in the border region that years of neglect of providing border residents with clean, safe drinking water and adequate sewage treatment has set the stage for a possible disaster" · (Nickey 1994, 6).

The media also portray colonias and lack of water access as a major border problem. For example, a report by *60 Minutes* described colonia conditions as "third world" and compared them to conditions in places such as Calcutta, Rwanda, Bosnia, and Bangladesh (CBS 1995). Such media reports contribute to the public perception that a serious colonia water access problem exists in Texas.

Colonia Water Access as a Public Issue

Colonia water access is recognized as a significant public issue in Texas, and we measure public concern for the issue in terms of the number of news articles on the topic and through direct questions in the semistructured interviews. Since 1991, reporters for two El Paso newspapers have identified colonias and water access as a problem and have covered the problem approximately two to three times a month. Colonia water access was covered more often than other border environmental and social problems (see Figure 8.1). For example, since 1991, the local press wrote stories on air pollution approximately twice a month, and immigration stories appeared less than once a month.

Respondents overwhelmingly identified CWA as an issue of public importance. Eighty-nine percent listed CWA as one of the top five border problems since 1990. Of the respondents in regular contact with the public, the majority (88 percent) stated that the public was aware of the CWA problem. Eighty-nine percent of all respondents expressed the opinion that CWA should now have a place on the state legislative and/or congressional agenda.

Most respondents believed the problem to be complex, requiring federal funding and incentives to encourage state action to achieve resolution. They suggested that formal agenda status at the national level was required. However, interest in colonia water access is much weaker at the national level than at the local level. A review of the *Wall Street Journal* ProQuest listings indicates that the national press has only occasionally covered colonias and their water access. Between 1985 and 1995, the colonia problem was covered a maximum of four times a year. In contrast, the national press covered issues such as air pollution and immigration more frequently during the same period—a minimum of thirty-two and seventy-nine times a month, respectively—suggesting that the colonia problem is not a significant public issue on the national level.

Colonia Water Access on the Formal Agenda

In the period under study, both Congress and the Texas state legislature considered and passed some legislation concerning the CWA problem. In this sense,

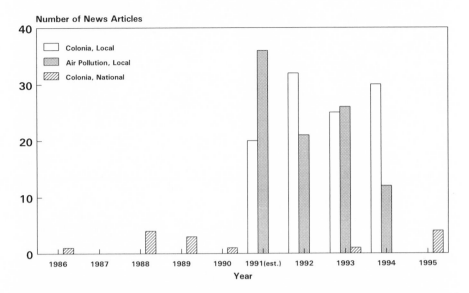

Number of News Articles

Figure 8.1. Coverage of Colonia Water Access by the Local and National Press (Comparison with Air Pollution Issue).

CWA did achieve congressional formal agenda status. In 1988, for example, there was some funding for water and sewage projects in the colonias. However, the content of the legislation and the meager resources allocated were in no way sufficient to address the issue. Furthermore, although supporters strongly argued that federal and state funds were needed to provide adequate water supplies, the actual implementers of a policy would be the local authorities in El Paso, who, as we argue below, have consistently denied the seriousness of the problem and have continually favored local developers rather than colonia residents.

Colonia water access as a distinct issue first appeared on the U.S. congressional agenda in March 1988, although the CWA problem had existed since the 1960s. In that month, the Committee of Public Works and Transportation held hearings in El Paso and Brownsville, Texas, to discuss colonias, receive testimony, learn more about the problem, and learn about state and local efforts to alleviate the problem (U.S. House 1988, 1–2). During the hearings, individuals representing local and state interests testified about the lack of access to water and other services in the colonias.

At the state level, the legislature considered twelve bills (including two sets of companion bills) and two resolutions affecting colonias between 1989 and 1995, and six passed into law. Three of the six laws enacted, and the two resolutions, provided or requested loan and/or grant monies for the construction of water and sewage infrastructure. The remaining three laws instituted new water and wastewater regulations affecting colonia developers. None of the bills or resolutions directly addressed the El Paso County water distribution system.

Effects of Legislation

The congressional and state legislative activity resulted in limited funding to provide colonia water access primarily through three programs: the Farmers Home Administration Program (FmHA), community development block grants administered by the state, and state funding through the Economically Distressed Areas Program (EDAP). Multiple problems have limited the impact of these programs. Some colonias that do not have water access may remain ineligible due to EDAP criteria. Water lines to the colonia may be provided, but direct connections to colonia homes are not. There may be restrictions on constructing water and wastewater infrastructure in the floodplains, where many colonias are located. These funds require reauthorization, which creates funding instability. Some colonia residents find the application criteria complex and unclear, particularly for loan monies (Negron 1996, A1).

Most important, the financial assistance to develop colonia water and wastewater infrastructure is less than a third of what is needed to bring water access to all border colonias. In 1992, TWDB staff estimated that approximately $700 million was needed to provide water and wastewater infrastructure to the Texas border colonias identified (TWDB 1992, 5). This estimate did not include costs for connection fees, indoor plumbing, or water rights. In 1995, TWDB estimated that $205.4 million had funded ongoing colonia construction projects (TWDB 1995). More funding is needed to provide water access to existing colonias, and the "target" is moving, since colonias continue to grow at a faster rate than funding or connections can be provided.

Last, these programs do not consider whether water is available for use. It is possible that infrastructure to provide municipal water service may be developed but prove useless, because residents cannot afford hookups or the water itself will be unavailable. "The cost estimates for water needs do not include the acquisition of water or water rights. . . . These costs could have a significant impact on individual projects where water availability is limited" (TWDB 1992, 2).

THE OPPONENTS AND THE ADVOCATES

In Texas, no one explicitly expresses opposition to people having access to water. Water access is generally perceived as a basic right: water provides life; lack of it kills. Yet many oppose measures necessary to end colonia proliferation or to provide water access to existing colonias. Respondents identified funding, land use and subdivision regulations, adequate enforcement authority for local regulatory agencies, and increases in the affordable housing stock as measures necessary to ensure colonia water access.

Interview respondents suggested that these opponents are more likely to influence the political agenda, whereas colonia residents are less influential. When

interview respondents were asked if they thought that colonia residents were politically powerful—defined as "able to get CWA on the political agenda"—the
majority (93 percent) responded negatively. The reasons cited included that they
don't vote, aren't registered to vote, are unaware, don't know how to manipulate
the political system, are uneducated, are not rich, have no resources, are illiterate,
lack time, and have no one to fight for them. The few who believed that colonia
residents were powerful cited their numbers, suggesting that colonia residents
could be powerful if they mobilized some collective action. Most El Paso County
floodplains colonia residents believe that their lack of resources contributes to
their lack of potable water access (Lopez 1995, 1996). For example, residents cite
their lack of time, money, or other resources to access alternative water sources,
such as driving into the city to get water.

When asked if those opposed to CWA measures were more politically powerful than colonia residents, the majority (93 percent) of respondents said yes.
The resources available to opponents included wealth, education, influence, time,
control of El Paso water resources, and knowledge of how to access the system.
A small proportion (7 percent) of respondents believed that the opponents were
not as politically powerful, citing the fact that colonia residents outnumber the
opponents.

The analysis identified three main opponents to measures designed to facili-
tate colonia water access: developers, the Public Service Board (PSB), and El
Paso City taxpayers and ratepayers.

Developers

The most consistent opponents over time were developers, including advocates for the construction and real estate industries. In general, Texas developers
and developers from other states with colonias, such as New Mexico, have lobbied
against measures that would restrict their ability to develop land. Most developers, particularly those specializing in colonia developments, are opposed to local
and/or state land use restrictions, including regulations that require the provision
of water and sewage infrastructure. They publicly argue that "more subdivision
rules will make their industry unprofitable" (Herrick 1987, A1).

However, colonia developers are not necessarily opposed to grant monies
that provide cheaper water and sewage infrastructure to colonia residents. In fact,
some developers with lots remaining for sale may benefit from the provision of
water lines to their colonias through federal and/or state grant programs. Once
water lines are provided, all lots within the colonia have access to water, making
lots for sale more valuable. In fact, these federal and state monies can subsidize
and "reward" colonia developers at taxpayer expense (Earle 1996).

As a result, the position of developers on increasing the affordable housing
stock, as a measure to prevent colonia development, is mixed. Some colonia developers argue that they are providing the affordable housing that border resi-

dents need and want (CBS 1995). One interview respondent, a banker connected to developer interests, stated that the banking community strongly supports the financing of affordable housing. Despite this support in principle, 39 percent of El Paso County applicants, most of them Hispanic, were unable to obtain home loans in 1991 (Bath, Tanski, and Villarreal 1994, 19).

The limited availability of good-quality water in El Paso County, and along the U.S.-Mexico border in general, constrains development. Developers of affordable housing projects with water presumably compete for this scarce resource against developers who require water for more lucrative investments. This competition over limited water could divide developers if water connections were required of all developments. The more powerful developers of El Paso County would be competing against those who provide housing to poor colonia residents. Given the importance of water to El Paso developers, their involvement in water-related issues and their participation in entities such as the PSB are predictable.

Public Service Board

The second most frequently mentioned opponent to water access for the colonias is the five-member El Paso City Public Service Board, which manages the city water utility. In the 1950s, Mayor Fred Hervey reorganized the PSB to increase its autonomy and to encourage operations similar to a private corporation for the purpose of easing the financing of new water projects (Brock 1988a–e; Bath, Tanski, and Villarreal 1994, 24). Only one PSB member is a publicly elected official, the mayor of the city of El Paso, who serves only during his mayoral term (Brock 1988a–e; Bath, Tanski, and Villarreal 1994, 24). Members other than the mayor serve for four-year terms, with a two-term limit. In the event of a PSB vacancy, the City Council must approve nominees proposed by the mayor and the existing PSB chair (Brock 1988a). The majority of appointed members have represented developer interests, and most elected city officials are sympathetic to developer interests.

The PSB is "considered the most powerful of all appointed boards in the city" (Moore 1995, B1). The PSB has been accused of working "to satisfy real estate interests" (Bath, Tanski, and Villarreal 1994, 25) and of representing individual interests; it has also been criticized for acting as a monopoly ("Mayors, Critics Call for Changes" 1988, A7). The PSB monopolizes El Paso's drinking water supply through its control of city water rights, approval of subdivision connections, funds for the exploration of new water sources and the maintenance of existing sources, and hiring of management for the city water utility. No other entity controls as much groundwater in the county. The only other significant public water agency in the region able to affect CWA is the Lower Valley Water District Authority (LVWDA) serving southeast El Paso, where many colonias are located. The legislature, with local voter approval, created the LVWDA in 1985 to serve customers from southeast El Paso County (Macias 1994), outside the city limits of El Paso. The LVWDA has little control over treated water supplies. It has rights only to Rio Grande surface waters and does not have funds to explore, develop, maintain, or treat its water sources. To get treated drinking water, the LVWDA had to negotiate with the PSB and agree to have its untreated river water diverted to PSB plants in exchange for treated drinking water. In these ways, the PSB effectively constrains the activities of the LVWDA.

The PSB is also El Paso's largest landowner, holding 37,453 acres in the county in 1970 (Bath, Tanski, and Villarreal 1994, 24) and currently owning over 50,000 acres in El Paso and neighboring counties (Negron 1993, A1; Hernandez 1993, B1). The PSB has been accused of molding "its municipal water management and distribution policies to fit its role as El Paso County's biggest land speculator" (Brock 1988e, A1). The rationale for these land purchases was to obtain additional groundwater rights and to protect the city's future water supply (Brock 1988e, A1; Bath, Tanski, and Villarreal 1994, 24). The PSB has sold much of this land to developers, in a process that does not encourage the highest bidding, while retaining the water rights (Brock 1988c, A6). Despite this uncompetitive process of selling the city's land assets, the PSB has been "regarded as one of the soundest public utilities in the nation" (Bath, Tanski, and Villarreal 1994, 25).

Until 1991, the PSB had a policy of not extending water lines outside city limits, citing its primary responsibility to guarantee water provision for city residents. However, when an influential individual or area of El Paso County wanted service, board members either circumvented their own policy by supporting annexation or provided the connections outright (Brock 1988a, A6; 1988d, A8). Most areas annexed after 1960 were in west and northeast El Paso, where PSB land ownership is concentrated (see Figure 8.2). A review of current city limits and annexations, pre- and post-1960, demonstrates a seeming avoidance of areas with colonias in the east, southeast, and northwest (colonia areas are represented by points on the map). However, even annexation will not guarantee water service, as the PSB requires that customers pay a share of hookup costs. For example, some poor areas of Ysleta had not yet received water connections several years after annexation. Although the PSB publicly rescinded its policy of not extending water lines outside city limits in 1991, most interview respondents still considered PSB an opponent of CWA measures. To date, few colonias appear to have benefited from the policy change (Kolenc 1992, B1; "Water Agency OK's PSB Control" 1992, B1).

City Taxpayers and Water Customers

The third most frequently mentioned CWA opponents were city and state taxpayers and city ratepayers or water customers who already had water access. According to respondents and local news reports, these opponents do not want to pay for CWA. They fear that providing CWA will increase their own taxes and/or water rates. The PSB argues that annexation of poor areas with colonias that do

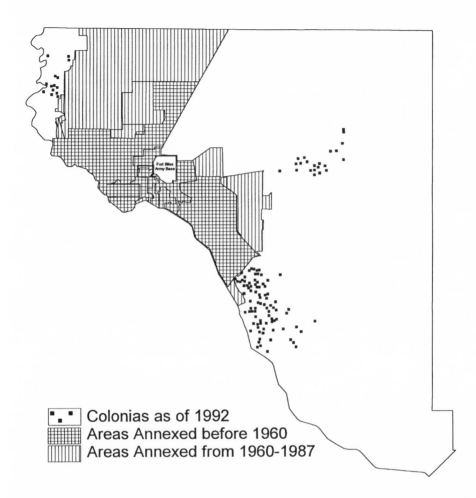

Figure 8.2. Comparison of Annexed Areas with Colonia Locations in El Paso County (Annexations as of 1987 and Colonia Locations as of 1992). Map by Michael Gorjanc, May 1996.

not have water, such as the case of Ysleta, strains the financial resources of the city of El Paso. This fear of rate and/or tax increases contributes to a more general resentment of colonia residents by taxpayers and water customers.

Other CWA Opponents

Interview respondents identified other CWA opponents, although with less frequency. They included federal taxpayers who oppose subsidies for border infrastructure; the city of El Paso and several prior mayors; Texas citizens concerned about government spending, subsidies, welfare, and regulatory activities; some county commissioners and the Association of Counties, which want to avoid angering constituents; some private-sector attorneys working for developers or the PSB; anti–North American Free Trade Agreement (NAFTA) activists who believe that funding infrastructure facilitates NAFTA; and other utilities that do not want their authority and control over resources questioned.

CWA Advocates

Although this chapter focuses on opponent strategies to deny or contain the CWA issue, a brief mention of CWA advocates is needed. The analysis identified the following pre-1993 advocates for colonia water access: colonia residents; grassroots organizations such as the El Paso Interreligious Sponsoring Organization (EPISO) and Valley Interfaith; Texas state legislators Rosson, Montford, Ciffranini, and Vowell; U.S. Representative Coleman; health care professionals; former governor Richards and lieutenant governor Hobby; the Texas Water Development Board; the city of Socorro; the County Commissioner's Office; and the county attorney. After 1993, Vowell, Richards, and Hobby were no longer in office to support CWA, but an additional supporter mentioned was the attorney general's office.

Advocates have attempted to organize a marginalized and disenfranchised community where the existing organizational infrastructure is weak. In addition, the advocates of CWA have limited organizational infrastructure and political resources. A thorough review and analysis of advocate positions and actions are presented by Bath and coauthors (1994).

LOW-COST STRATEGIES

Our analysis finds evidence that opponents to colonia water access in Texas used four low-cost strategies to oppose consideration of the issue. Through these strategies, opponents defined the problem as a nonissue not needing government attention.

Declare It a Nonproblem. The CWA problem has been called a nonproblem by at least one developer. In an interview broadcast nationally on *60 Minutes,* developer Deborah Kastrin argued that "there are other systems for delivery of water besides the tap water," such as "buying water" or "trucking it" into the colonias (CBS 1995). In effect, she suggested that developing subdivisions without water access is not a problem, because residents have "other means of getting the water." There were high-cost consequences to the user of this low-cost, nonproblem strategy, including adverse effects on the Kastrin family's reputation

(Kastrin 1995, A11) and on the political career of their friend, Representative Ronald Coleman.

Define It as a Basic Right. The same developer used the argument that people have a basic right to buy land, if that's how they want to spend their money: "Are we going to start telling people what they can and cannot buy?" (CBS 1995). The developer argued that colonia residents are exercising their free will and have a right to purchase and build on any land they choose, even if the property does not have a municipal water connection. This strategy embodies the idea of "let the buyer beware" and implies that government has no obligation to provide any basic services, such as access to water. By preventing or hindering buyers from purchasing land that a developer has for sale, or by regulating land use and/or the sales transaction, the government intrudes on the individual rights and freedoms of both the buyer and the seller. Kastrin argued that buyers understand that the purchase is for land without water and are willing to accept the lack of a water connection. In short, the buyers know what they are getting into. This sentiment was expressed by some interview respondents as their own opinions or those of their clients or constituents.

Advocates respond to this in several ways. First, many colonia residents purchase lots with the (mis)understanding that they will eventually receive water because of deceptive sales tactics. The poor need affordable housing, and alternatives to colonias are limited; hence, there is no choice. Other water services are unlikely to be used; a poor person who cannot purchase a home with water service is unlikely to be able to afford a weekly delivery service and storage tank. Poor water storage practices, as well as water availability, contribute to illness. Other forms of water delivery, if not used or if the water is poorly stored, will continue to contribute to the public health hazard of colonias.

Declare the Problem to Be a Solution. Colonias are portrayed as a solution to another problem—the lack of affordable housing. Colonia developers, in this view, are simply supplying goods to meet the demand for affordable housing. Without colonias, El Paso would suffer from an increase in the homeless population. If developers were forced to provide water access, and the PSB or the LVWDA charged for the access, the costs of lots would increase to buyers. Lots for homes would become prohibitively expensive, and "affordable" housing could no longer be provided. Restricting colonia development or imposing regulations on developers is presented as restricting the supply of affordable housing. This argument implies that colonias prevent these people from becoming homeless and that developers are, in effect, providing a public service.

Refuse to Discuss the Problem. Another low-cost strategy is to refuse to participate in debates, forums, discussions, or interviews about the CWA problem; this is another way to ignore the problem or call it a nonproblem. For example, the current mayor of the city of El Paso refused to be interviewed on the CWA topic for this research study and has refused interviews for other articles (Skolnick 1996). Many politicians and agency staff from the city combine this strategy with a medium-cost strategy: the "outside my jurisdiction" argument, in which the problem is acknowledged but the venue is disputed. It has been argued that the colonia problem is a county problem, not a city problem. This argument places the burden of proof that the problem deserves city attention on issue advocates.

MEDIUM-COST STRATEGIES

Medium-cost strategies involve attacking the initiator and the initiator's position or taking symbolic action to placate the initiator. CWA opponents used medium-cost strategies for the purposes of agenda denial and agenda containment. Here, the opponent acknowledges that the problem exists and commits additional resources (such as time, expertise, and money, or apparent changes in behavior) to prevent supporters' proposals from gaining active government consideration. Sometimes low- and medium-cost strategies overlap and are used simultaneously. For example, a medium-cost strategy such as restricting access to information assumes at least a private acknowledgment of the problem, but this strategy may be combined with a public avowal that the problem does not exist.

Declare the Problem to Be Outside One's Jurisdiction. A medium-cost strategy with relatively low resource use for preventing agenda access is to claim that the problem is outside of one's jurisdiction. The PSB in particular has used this strategy—for example, by arguing until 1991 that its primary mission was to provide water to El Paso City residents and to ensure the city's future water supply. As most colonias were located outside the city's boundaries, providing colonias with water was not a PSB responsibility; it was outside its jurisdiction. However, as the primary municipal drinking water supplier in the region until 1985, the PSB had the ability to place colonias and CWA under its jurisdiction. The city doubled in size from annexation practices that were supported by the PSB and seemingly orchestrated to avoid colonia regions; thus, the PSB's actions belie its arguments. When rich and/or powerful interests wanted water access outside the city's boundaries, the constraints of PSB jurisdiction evaporated, and water access received immediate approval and implementation.

Restrict Access to Information. Opponents such as developers and the PSB can restrict access to information to deter colonia residents from seeking agenda status for their issue and to restrict the efforts of CWA advocates. For example, individual colonia developers have been accused of providing purchase information verbally, rather than in written contract form, to potential buyers. The PSB has also restricted information access by limiting the number of monthly meetings open to the public. Without information or access to a forum where they can obtain information, colonia residents and advocates may be unable to identify actions or procedures detrimental to their interests. The denial of information also creates costs for advocates. If advocates must expend resources to obtain information, those resources cannot be used elsewhere.

Provide Misinformation. Some opponents to CWA measures have provided misinformation about water access. For example, individual buyers of colonia lots have complained that developers promised during purchase negotiations that water lines and hookups would be installed eventually. Many residents have waited years with the expectation that they would be receiving water service soon. This strategy has delayed the recognition by colonia residents that their private trouble is a public issue and has obstructed collective efforts by colonia residents to recognize their individual water problems as a public problem.

Define It as a Private Trouble. Two interview respondents, representing developer and PSB interests, argued that CWA does not belong on the formal agenda because the problem should be resolved privately between colonia developers and residents, without government intrusion. This rationale is consistent with Cobb and Ross's argument in chapter 2 that the issue is not a legitimate public concern and ought to be resolved privately. This argument also implies that government, if involved, will be ineffective and will probably worsen the problem. Defining a problem as a private trouble and not a public issue can effectively deny agenda access and deny redress to victims of social injustice (Reich 1991).

Carry Out a Symbolic Policy Change. The PSB's action in 1991 to rescind its "no water outside the city" policy coincided with the year of greatest state activity on the water access issue, as measured by bills and resolutions passed. This represented a symbolic action to combat public criticism and avoid legislative proposals that would affect PSB operations. Rescinding this policy after many years reflected a significant public change in PSB policy but resulted in little change in PSB behavior. The PSB has not actively taken the lead in projects to provide water access to the colonias. Rescinding the policy represented symbolic action, because it provided minimal redress to colonia residents. The policy change provided the appearance of substantive change and suggested that no intervention was needed by city politicians or the state (for example, to review PSB policies and procedures).

Make Funding Available but Not Spendable. Funds to construct water and wastewater infrastructure in colonias have become available through various loan and grant programs, as a result of placing the CWA issue on past congressional and state legislative agendas. But these loan monies are unlikely to be accessed by poor colonia residents, and eligibility criteria for grants exclude some colonias. According to EPISO, a colonia advocacy organization, $2 million in federal monies for low-interest loans administered through the Rio Grande Council of Governments has not been spent after three years, even though $117,000 in administration fees has been paid from these funds (Negron 1996, A1).

Support a Policy That Benefits Oneself. Of the state legislation directly affecting colonias, eight proposals (six bills and two resolutions) passed between 1988 and 1995. Of these six laws and two resolutions, five were related to the provision of tax monies for grant and loan programs, three affected land use, and none impacted water distribution. The laws and resolutions for grants and loans resulted in increasing funds for infrastructure but did not adversely affect developers or the PSB—and may even have benefited them. Land owned by developers becomes more valuable with new water connections supplied from loans and grants. Under these programs, the PSB does not incur the costs of water connections.

Support Regulations with Loopholes. Existing legislation concerning land sales and subdivisions have loopholes that allow continued colonia development. Model subdivision rules exempted properties that had been subdivided before the rules were enacted (Valdez 1993, A1). Developers anticipated the changes and subdivided many lots prior to enactment. For this reason, "grandfathered" subdivisions have contributed to much of the recent growth in colonias (TWDB 1995). Recent legislation, House Bill 1001, removed the county's authority to regulate all land subdivisions and also exempted owners of small tracts of land (one-half to ten acres) from regulation (Rodriguez 1995a, 1995b). It is estimated that seventy-five to a hundred of these subdivisions occur each year in El Paso County alone (Rodriguez 1995a, 1995b). In the aggregate, and over the long term, the county attorney's office estimated that the legislation "will have the same negative effect as having no regulation at all" and may actually contribute to colonia growth (Rodriguez 1995a, 1995b).

Attack the Issue Initiator. One of the most effective medium-cost strategies used by opponents is to attack the legitimacy of colonia residents. Evidence of this strategy comes from a number of interview respondents who had regular contact with the public. When asked to describe the average El Pasoan's perception of the average colonia resident, the predominant description was undocumented, illegal, and a Mexican immigrant. This perception contrasts with data demonstrating that the majority of colonia residents are U.S. born (68 percent) (TDHHS 1988) or residing legally. The second most common descriptors were "poor" and "low-income," characteristics more reflective of the data. Some respondents reported that their clients or constituents had negative perceptions of colonia residents, describing them as free riders, unwilling to pay taxes, unreasonable, greedy, sponging off society, demanding, and unwilling to work. When asked about general pejorative references to colonia residents that respondents had heard of or read about, the following responses were received: illegals, wetbacks, dirty, free riders, ignorant, unreasonable, have low standards, greedy, outsiders, prolific (reproducers), disease carriers, rats or vermin, opportunists, "should have known better," and "should go back to Mexico if they don't like it here."

These pejorative references and remarks reflect a negative social perception that is broadly accepted by some Texans, that undermines the legitimacy of colonia residents, and that contributes to the denial of the legitimacy of demands for water access. The statements made in interviews represent a negative social construction of colonia residents that contributes to denying CWA agenda access (Schneider and Ingram 1993).

CONCLUSION

This analysis of agenda access and water access in Texas colonias illustrates several broader points about the politics of water along the U.S.-Mexico border. First, without real agenda access, obtaining adequate water supplies is not possible for marginalized colonia communities. Second, the case illustrates the battle over the social construction of colonia residents—a battle that opponents of colonia water access seem to be winning—which creates obstacles to agenda access for the CWA issue. Third, the strategies for agenda denial that CWA opponents adopted reflect the power disparities in the border region and contribute to reinforcing them.

Opponents used both low- and medium-cost strategies in their efforts to deny agenda access by refusing to recognize the existence of the problem and the legitimacy of colonia residents. Low-cost strategies, however, were not entirely successful in keeping the CWA problem off the agenda. However, these strategies did have other effects. For example, both low- and medium-cost strategies served to weaken issue advocates by forcing them to expend resources to provide evidence that the problem was serious and growing.

When low-cost strategies failed to keep CWA off the formal agenda, opponents used medium-cost strategies to contain the CWA issue. For example, opponents supported "solutions" that provided only symbolic or minimal resolution to the problems of water access but provided some real benefits to the opponents. The medium-cost strategy of taking symbolic action, such as changing the policy of no water connections outside city limits, was associated with a public perception that the CWA problem had been resolved. This perception served to diffuse support for colonia residents and their advocates. About half of the interview respondents (52 percent) perceived that the CWA problem had changed since 1994, and of these, 64 percent believed that the problem had changed for the better, in spite of evidence to the contrary.[9]

Opponents did not explicitly reject the provision of potable water to colonias, but they did oppose any measures that would directly and adversely affect their interests. The policies that would not harm developers and the PSB included state and federal government provision of loans and grants to finance water infrastructure. These policies are precisely the types of proposals that were on congressional and state agendas between 1988 and 1995, and those most easily passed. In short, when the issue reached the formal agenda, the issue was defined in ways to limit water access and cost to CWA opponents (indeed, to create benefits for the opponents).

This case suggests that access to the state and federal formal agendas was a necessary condition to obtaining limited water access for some colonias. Without intermittent agenda access and legislative successes between 1988 and 1995, grants and loans to develop limited water and sewage infrastructure would not have been made available. However, intermittent access to the federal and state formal agendas resulted in only partial resolution of the CWA problem. The lack of more complete resolution at the local level resulted not only from the strategies adopted by opponents but also from the social construction of the issue and power disparities, as discussed below.

This case demonstrates the importance of low- and medium-cost strategies that foster and encourage a negative social perception of issue initiators. The pejorative references and terms used by some interview respondents reflect opponents' tendency to use a strategy of cultural characterizations, stereotypes, and negative popular images to portray colonia residents as undeserving "deviants." As shown in other cases of pubic policy debates, deviants are less likely to receive government assistance, because policies to assist deviants are not viewed favorably by politicians or the public (Schneider and Ingram 1993).

Ironically, advocates of colonia water access used similar characterizations and images to portray residents as victims or "dependents." Advocates used the image of colonia residents as immigrants to argue that, as immigrants, they were only trying to pursue the American Dream and were hardworking contributors to society (CBS 1995). The residents became the victims of "unscrupulous" developers who took advantage of residents' inexperience, "making millions off the backs of hardworking immigrants" (CBS 1995). Victims are perceived sympathetically by the public and are more likely to benefit from government policies and action (Schneider and Ingram 1993).

These two social constructions are two faces of the same coin—one as negative deviant, and one as positive victim. There exists a tension between these two different constructions, and a battle ensues for dominance in the public consciousness.[10] In the current social and political climate, which is unfavorable to immigrants and their issues, advocates may be unintentionally contributing to the negative social construction; allying colonia issues with immigrant issues may be a counterproductive advocacy strategy for residents. With a social construction of colonia residents as victims, legislative action is likely to take the form of charity rather than protection of colonia residents' right to water.

Low- and medium-cost strategies that foster a negative social construction of colonia residents both reflect and reinforce power disparities between opponents and residents. These strategies tend to enhance a sense of powerlessness among colonia residents. The powerful not only can influence agenda setting and issue formation but also can shape the perceptions of "reality" by the powerless, through their ability to shape beliefs, culture, language, and symbols (Lukes 1974). To control beliefs and political symbols is to control "a vital link between the individual and the larger social order" (Elder and Cobb 1983, xiii). The establishment of a deep sense of powerlessness within the individual "may manifest itself as extensive fatalism, self-deprecation, or undue apathy about one's situation" (Gaventa 1980, 17). Through such manipulations, the powerful can rationalize and legitimize power and resource inequities. Incomplete resolution of the CWA problem and intermittent agenda status reflect the success of powerful elites in exercising their control over the powerless, as well as the limits of this power.

Our analysis indicates that the power of opponents is associated with a lack of power among colonia residents and a tendency for colonia residents to blame themselves for their situation. The majority of colonia residents are poor and young and have a limited formal education. Most residents lack resources, are unable to access the political system, and, according to interview respondents, are not considered politically powerful. The survey showed that colonia residents are likely to blame themselves for not having water, citing their own poverty and lack of time as reasons for their inability to obtain potable water (Lopez 1995). Opponents, in contrast, have ample resources such as time, wealth, knowledge, and influence, and they are generally considered powerful.

This case demonstrates how both agenda access and water access are connected to the distribution of power. The relative powerlessness of colonia residents and the negative social construction that portrays them as deviants would lead one to expect difficulties in resolving the problem of water access. Under normal conditions, colonia residents have limited ability to obtain access to the agenda and influence decision making. In situations of significant disparity, one would usually expect "quiescence" (Gaventa 1980). The appearance of colonia water access on the congressional and state legislative agendas, albeit erratically, may be explained by the strategies used by advocates and by an expansion in the scope of conflict (Schattschneider 1960). But ironically, the limited expansion of water access depended on the strategies of the opponents, particularly their efforts to contain the CWA issue through symbolic actions.

NOTES

1. The Texas Department of Health and Human Services defines colonias as "rural and unincorporated subdivisions of U.S. cities located along the Texas-Mexico international boundary . . . characterized by sub-standard housing, inadequate plumbing and sewage disposal systems, and inadequate access to clean water . . . highly concentrated pov-

erty pockets that are physically and legally isolated from neighboring cities" (TDHHS 1988, 1–3).

2. To create an indicator of leadership stability, we used documents from the mid to late 1980s. Among local, state, and federally elected officials identified from 1988–1989 records, approximately 30 percent lost an election before 1995. Of the remainder, the majority continued in their positions. Less than 20 percent retired or voluntarily changed leadership positions. Among agency staff identified, 65 percent remained in their positions over the seven-year period of interest. Regional leaders are overwhelmingly from the Democratic Party; since 1988, for every Republican vote cast, there were three to five Democratic votes cast. Of the 20 to 30 percent of the registered voters who cast a ballot, 4 to 8 percent cast votes for Republican candidates ("Interview with Robert Moore" 1996).

3. In this study, TDHHS staff conducted twelve hundred face-to-face interviews in the preferred language of respondents. Participants were randomly selected from colonias located in the Lower Rio Grande Valley or El Paso County.

4. Any estimate of the number of colonia residents is likely to be an underestimate. There are logistical problems to tracking and counting people living in unmarked homes in unregulated, swiftly changing communities where homes may house several families.

5. In 1989, the Texas Water Commission, now part of the Texas Natural Resource Conservation Commission (TNRCC), developed model subdivision rules pursuant to section 13.343 of the Texas Water Code. To qualify for state financial aid to construct water and sewage facilities, counties are now required to adopt these rules (U.S. GAO 1995, 2). El Paso County adopted the model subdivision rules in 1990. However, colonias continued to grow because most lands were platted (surveyed) prior to the rules' adoption.

6. Fifty-five million gallons of raw sewage per day flow from El Paso's Mexican neighbor, Ciudad Juarez (Juarez City). This sewage and "an unknown amount of industrial waste" drain into the river (Nickey 1994, 9).

7. For example, in San Elizario and Campestre, two U.S. floodplain colonias, wells are approximately ten to twenty-five feet deep (Lopez 1995; Lopez and Byrne 1996).

8. The number of cases may be underreported due to a lack of health care access among colonia populations at risk, a lack of follow-up, an endemic diarrhea disease state among residents, and the tendency for nontraditional health care providers not to report cases.

9. They described the positive changes as increased public awareness of CWA, some funding to improve water access, some water connections installed in some colonias, and that the term "colonia" is now in the political lexicon.

10. A battle over the dominant social construction of one agenda denier, the developer, also continues. Advocates, the media, and those who wish to appear as advocates attack and vilify developers. Developers portray themselves as responsible contributors to society, and advocates portray them as unscrupulous predators or "snakes" taking advantage of the immigrant victims (CBS 1995).

REFERENCES

Bath, C. R., J. M. Tanski, and R. E. Villarreal. 1994. The politics of water allocation in El Paso County colonias. *Journal of Borderlands Studies* 9(1): 14–38.

Brock, P. 1988a. Becoming a part of the "old elite." *El Paso Herald-Post,* April 21, p. A6.
———. 1988b. Board members avoid making waves. *El Paso Herald-Post,* April 20, p. A9.
———. 1988c. Board's land profits impressive. *El Paso Herald-Post,* April 21, p. A6.
———. 1988d. Many live on shore of city water. *El Paso Herald-Post,* April 20, p. A8.
———. 1988e. PSB deep in land. *El Paso Herald-Post,* April 19, pp. A1, A6.
———. 1988f. PSB said to need change of tide. *El Paso Herald-Post,* April 21, pp. A1, A7.
CBS News, *60 Minutes.* 1995. The other America. October 8.
Cobb, R., J. K. Ross, and M. H. Ross. 1976. Agenda building as a comparative political process. *American Political Science Review* 70:126–38.
Crenson, M. A. 1971. *The un-politics of air pollution. A study of non-decisionmaking in the cities.* Baltimore: Johns Hopkins University Press.
Earle, D. 1996. The constraints of culture, society and context on colonia community development. Paper presented to the Association of Borderlands Scholars hosted by the Western Social Science Association, 38th annual conference, Reno, N V, April.
Elder, C. D., and R. W. Cobb. 1983. *The political uses of symbols.* New York: Longmans.
Gaventa, J. 1980. *Power and powerlessness, quiescence and rebellion in an Appalachian valley.* Urbana: University of Illinois Press.
Hernandez, R. 1993. Council appoints Houghton to PSB. *El Paso Herald-Post,* December 12, p. B1.
Herrick, T. 1987. Poverty a way of life: "Colonias" to see some improvement. *El Paso Herald-Post,* December 31, p. A1.
Interview with Robert Moore, night city editor, *El Paso Times.* March 1996.
Kastrin, D. 1995. Deborah Kastrin: The Kastrins' side of the story. *El Paso Times,* November 28, p. A11.
Kolenc, V. 1992. PSB guarantees 40-year water tap to colonia. *El Paso Herald-Post,* February 27, p. B1.
Lopez, C. M. 1995. Conflict along the Mexican-American border: Who has access to clean water, who suffers adverse health consequences? Paper presented to the Research Seminar Series, Center for U.S.-Mexican Studies, University of California at San Diego, November.
———. 1996. Water contamination in the Rio Grande/Rio Bravo and related health effects among colonia residents. Paper presented to the Association of Borderlands Scholars hosted by the Western Social Science Association, 38th annual conference, Reno, N V.
Lopez, C. M., and J. Byrne. 1996. Using volunteer water quality data in assessing human health effects of El Paso/Juarez Valley colonia residents. Paper presented to Watershed '96 Conference, June.
Lukes, S. 1974. *Power: A radical view.* London: Macmillan.
Macias, M. 1994. *Report on grant projects.* El Paso: El Paso County Lower Valley Water District Authority.
Mayors, critics call for changes. 1988. *El Paso Herald-Post,* April 21, p. A7.
Moore, R. 1993. City picks PSB member Tuesday. *El Paso Times,* March 6, p. B1.
Negron, S. 1996. $2 million for colonias goes unspent. *El Paso Times,* June 5, p. A1.
Nickey, L. N. 1994. Testimony presented to the U.S. Congress and Texas State Legislature, "U.S.-Mexico Border Health and Environmental Issues," January 15.
Reich, M. R. 1991. *Toxic politics: Responding to chemical disasters.* Ithaca, N Y: Cornell University Press.

Rodriguez, J. R. 1995a. Letter to Senators Rosson and Montford, County Attorney, El Paso, TX, July 27.

——. 1995b. Outline presented to El Paso County Commissioners Court, September 13.

Sawyer, J. A., et al. 1989. Hepatitis A in a border community. *Journal of Environmental Health* 4:2–5.

Schattschneider, E. E. 1960. *The semi-sovereign people: A realist's view of democracy in America.* Hinsdale, IL: Dryden Press.

Schneider, A., and H. Ingram. 1993. Social construction of target populations: Implications for politics and policy. *American Political Science Review* 87:334–47.

Skolnick, A. A. 1996. Letter received from Mayor Larry Francis. *Journal of the American Medical Association News and Perspectives,* March 6.

Texas Department of Health and Human Services, Office of Strategic Management, Research and Development, Strategic Management and Development Division. 1988. *The colonia factbook. A survey of living conditions in rural areas of south and west Texas border counties.* Austin: TDHHS.

Texas Water Development Board, Facility Needs Section, Planning Division. 1992. *Water for Texas, water and wastewater needs of colonias in Texas.* Austin: TWDB.

——. 1995. *Water for Texas, water and wastewater needs of colonias in Texas, executive summary.* Austin: TWDB.

U.S. General Accounting Office. 1995. *Rural development: Problems and progress of colonia subdivisions.* GAO/RCED-91-37. Washington, DC: GAO.

U.S. House. 1988. Inadequate water supply and sewage disposal facilities associated with "colonias" along the United States and Mexican border. Hearing before the Subcommittee on Water Resources of the Committee on Public Works and Transportation, March 11 and 12, El Paso and Brownsville, Texas. Washington, DC: U.S. Government Printing Office.

Valdez, D. W. 1993. Loophole allows more subdivisions. *El Paso Times,* November 13, pp. A1, A2.

Vernon's Texas session law service. 1995. 74th legislature regular session, chaps. 921–1062. Laws approved to June 17. No. 13, chap. 979; HB 1001, 4395–4912.

Water agency OK's PSB control over project. 1992. *El Paso Herald-Post,* March 7, p. B1.

Williams, D. 1996. Water supply. *El Paso Times,* April 27, p. A1.

PART V

Agenda Denial as a Comparative Political Process

9

Why Didn't Waldheim's Past Matter More? A Public Agenda Denial in Austria

John Bendix

Cobb and Elder (1983, 12–3) understand agenda setting in the United States as process whereby an issue proposal receives serious consideration from one of the three branches of government. Elaborate filtering of issues preserves the status quo, making it difficult for many policy issues to attain formal agenda status. Agenda denial describes the process whereby specific issues fail to get onto a formal agenda. The outside initiative model (Cobb, Ross, and Ross 1976) argues that a key route by which a policy issue can reach the formal agenda is through the public agenda. What is on the public agenda in any given culture is shaped by media channels, as well as by symbolic representations; what matters is the manner in which meaning is framed.

The Waldheim case is about the denial of public agenda status in Austria to the issue of Austrian collaboration with German Nazis during World War II. An examination of this case suggests the relevance of the agenda-setting framework beyond the U.S. case. The issue of collaboration emerged in the context of questions about Kurt Waldheim's past that arose during his election campaign to become Austria's president in 1986; his past career and some of the key events in the election campaign are detailed in the next section of this chapter. The presidency in Austria is a largely symbolic office, and Waldheim came to symbolize a widely accepted, if particular, postwar accommodation to and interpretation of the war in that country. The public agenda denial in this case was not about a policy issue failing to reach a formal agenda but rather about the inability of a particular issue to be central in a campaign where many expected it to have a key role. As a result, proposals to place it on the formal agenda that might have involved changes in school curricula or public hearings never received serious attention at all.

Austria's wartime past was made irrelevant during the election campaign only partly due to the low- and medium-cost strategies that Waldheim and his supporters adopted. In addition, there was a public consensus among Austrian political parties that Austria and Austrians had behaved correctly and had been victimized during the war. "The past doesn't interest us," many important Austrian politicians stated in 1986, meaning that uncomfortable aspects of the past were not to be allowed to dominate the election. Yet the desire not to revisit the past was made difficult internally by a few probing journalists and externally by questions from a Jewish organization in New York. Austria's wartime record, Austria's difficult relationship with Jews, the problems that Jewish spokesmen had with one another, and some of the international contexts in which the war was being commemorated and reexamined served as an international backdrop to the Waldheim election.

The key issue for the Austrian public agenda was what the attitude toward the past *ought* to be. Waldheim's election focused attention on the defense of the Austrian status quo or, to put it in other terms, reaffirmed a particular partial collective memory. In the context of fortieth anniversary commemorations of the end of World War II in Europe,[1] as well as increased interest in the Holocaust in the United States, it drew unfavorable attention to Austria's self-image. Although Austrian voters could not be persuaded in large enough numbers that Waldheim's past mattered (despite the efforts of international and domestic critics), Waldheim's election would prove to be a Pyrrhic victory that Austria and Austrians paid for throughout his six-year tenure.

WALDHEIM'S BACKGROUND AND THE ELECTION CONTEXT

Kurt Waldheim made his career after 1945 in Austria's diplomatic service—in various capacities in the Foreign Ministry in Vienna, as well as in the embassies in Paris (as first secretary) and Ottawa (as ambassador). From 1964 to 1968, he was Austria's permanent representative at the United Nations (UN), and in 1971 he was elected secretary-general and was reelected in 1976. His earlier involvement in Austrian politics included a two-year stint as foreign minister (1968–1970) in the conservative People's Party (ÖVP) government and an unsuccessful bid for the Austrian presidency in 1971 (Sully 1989, 294). After Waldheim's defeat in 1981 in his attempt to win a third term as UN secretary-general, he again set his sights on the Austrian presidency, a post that would fall vacant in 1986 (Mitten 1992, 43).

The Austrian president has a variety of roles to play as head of state: representing the nation abroad, receiving the credentials of foreign diplomats, signing treaties, and so forth. In domestic politics, the president signs bills into law, formally summons and dissolves Parliament, appoints or dismisses the government, formally approves candidates for certain posts, and has the power of pardon. In postwar Austria, although presidents had an independent source of legitimacy owing to their direct election (much as in France), in practice, their ability to exercise their powers was sharply constrained by Parliament (unlike in France). Postwar Austrian presidents had been cautious in the use of their powers, in a pattern that enhanced the moral authority of the office when they did intervene (Mitten 1992, 45–6; Sully 1989, 296). The symbolic importance of the president, as embodying the self-image of the nation and as a moral and occasionally politically stabilizing force in domestic politics, is high.

The five presidents Austria had elected since 1945 had all been candidates of the Left-leaning Social Democrats (SPÖ). Waldheim, nominally politically independent, was clearly more sympathetic to the conservative ÖVP party, in opposition since 1983, than to the SPÖ. After an early period of confusion over whether he might run as an independent or even as the bipartisan choice of both ÖVP and SPÖ, in early March 1985 he was endorsed as the ÖVP candidate for president. The SPÖ, weakened after a long period (1971–1983) of parliamentary hegemony by having to rule in coalition (1983–1986) with the small national-liberal Freedom Party (FPÖ), feared that Waldheim's international prominence would cause it to lose the office, and the party scrambled to field Kurt Steyrer, then health minister, as its presidential candidate.

These three strands—diplomacy and Austria's international standing, the symbolic importance of the presidency, and the relative fortunes of Austria's parties—determined the desultory campaign in its first year. The strategy of the campaign's advertising firm, Young and Rubicam, was to stress Waldheim's association with the UN. An early election poster showed Waldheim posed against the backdrop of the World Trade Center towers in Manhattan with the slogan "An Austrian Whom the World Trusts" (Cyrus 1986, 144); Waldheim's own description of his role at the UN was as "chief human rights officer of the Planet Earth" (Rosenbaum 1993, xvii). Because it thought that this left an image of a cool, correct, cosmopolitan bureaucrat, Young and Rubicam also wanted Austrians to "recognize the Austrian in Waldheim and see someone who thinks and feels as they do, someone of whom they can be proud" (Mitten 1992, 47). It was necessary to "make an Austrian out of Waldheim again because he had been working abroad for so long" (Wodak et al. 1990, 62), dictating a populist campaign of pressing the flesh, posters showing Waldheim in an Austrian regional outfit, and a certain distancing from party and issues to make Waldheim more broadly acceptable as the embodiment of Austria. The campaign posters and banners that read "Kurt Waldheim: His Experience for Us All" reflected the effort to knit the international together with the national.

The ad campaign's strategy was revealed in September 1985 by the critical Viennese newsmagazine *Profil,* earning the magazine immediate denunciation from the ÖVP and various newspapers as "defamatory" and "part of a smear campaign" against Waldheim (Wodak et al. 1990, 63). Perhaps made suspicious by the vehemence of the defense, *Profil* pursued questions about whether Waldheim had been a member of a Nazi student group during the war, a question initially raised by a German reporter at a news conference in late 1985. Waldheim's *Im*

Glaspalast der Weltpolitik,[2] an autobiography that appeared that year, had been sparing with details about the war period.

Enterprising Austrian journalists began probing, and by February 1986, Waldheim gave a *Profil* reporter permission to examine his war records. There the reporter found documentary proof that Waldheim had indeed been a member of a Nazi student union, as well as a member of a student cavalry group that was part of the Nazi storm troopers, and—in direct contradiction of Waldheim's own claims (as listed in Heindl 1991, 16–7)—had not been mustered out of the German *Wehrmacht* in 1941. Instead, he had been assigned to Army Group E in Saloniki in early 1942, under General Alexander Löhr, just when the mass deportation of the Jews to the concentration camps was taking place (Mitten 1992, 50). *Profil* published this story in early March, and at nearly the same time, the *New York Times* published its own account, alerted to the revelations by the World Jewish Congress (WJC) in Vienna and New York (Rosenbaum 1993, 1–33). The WJC was given the single most damning piece of evidence: an authenticated photograph showing Lieutenant Kurt Waldheim, in a German *Wehrmacht* uniform, at the airfield near Podgorica (Montenegro) on a day in 1943, contradicting his repeated claims to have been in Vienna at the time and long out of military service.

A blizzard of questions about what had actually happened during the war, as well as about Waldheim's own accounts of the time, ensued. In New York, the WJC launched an investigation, and in the two months following the *Profil* article (on March 3), it issued press releases or held press conferences about Waldheim on average every three days. Much of this investigation was about the location of information (e.g., " 'Missing' file shows Waldheim member of third Nazi organization," press release, March 20), possible cover-ups, and Waldheim's truthfulness (e.g., "Waldheim book gives false account of wartime record," press release, March 17). Previous investigations of Waldheim's past by the U.S. Army and the Yugoslav government immediately after the war, and by the Israeli government and the UN in the 1970s, were revisited. Both the U.S. House and the U.S. Senate became involved. The WJC asked the U.S. Justice Department to consider putting Waldheim on the Watch List for former Nazi war criminals. Major American newsmagazines (*Time, Newsweek, U.S. News & World Report*) picked up these stories, as did major newspapers: by one count, the *New York Times* had published 136 (5 of them lead), the *Chicago Tribune* 83, and the *Washington Post* 81 articles on Waldheim, Austria, and the Nazi era by the end of 1986 (Hirczy 1995, 139).

In Austria, Waldheim received 49.7 percent of the vote in the May 4 election (89.5 percent turnout), missing an absolute majority by only sixteen thousand votes. The loss came in part because minor party presidential candidates (FPÖ and Greens; 6.7 percent total) were able to profit from fears about Chernobyl. The minor candidates withdrew in the second round of voting on June 8, and Waldheim won with 53.9 percent of the vote (87.2 percent turnout). In other words, revelations and questions from abroad only seemed to strengthen Austrian resolve. ÖVP politician Alois Mock had stated in late March that it was a "patriotic duty to support Waldheim," and evidently, many Austrians agreed.

A number of the major players have already been identified: the political parties in Austria, major media in Vienna and New York, the WJC in New York, and Waldheim himself. The ÖVP, especially the statements by Mock and party secretary Michael Graff in defense, was quite prominent; notable figures from the SPÖ, such as ex–prime minister Bruno Kreisky and outgoing president Rudolf Kirschschläger, confined themselves to brief position statements. Newspapers in Austria, especially *Die Presse* and the tabloid *Neue Kronenzeitung,* tended to defend Waldheim; *Profil* was one of the few publications to consistently raise questions. Major newspapers and newsmagazines in the United States and Europe gave the story considerable coverage, though rarely in the shrill voice of the *New York Post* ("Papers Show Waldheim was SS Butcher," March 26 headline) or with the probing of the German newsmagazine *Der Spiegel* ("Austria's Silent Fascism: The Waldheim Case," April 14 cover) (Khol et al. 1987, 160–1). Stories and interviews on state-run Austrian television and radio were numerous and, not surprisingly, emphasized Austrian interpretations over non-Austrian voices (Wodak et al. 1990; Gruber 1991). The WJC's leaders and investigators in New York were key players; the Jewish community in Vienna and its best-known member, Simon Wiesenthal, were in a much more difficult position, for reasons detailed later.

LOW- AND MEDIUM-COST ATTACK STRATEGIES

Waldheim used low- and medium-cost strategies to keep his past out of the election campaign; high-cost strategies would have been at odds with the pattern of Waldheim's career. The only example of a high-cost strategy, and significantly not on Austrian soil, was his threat of legal action against the U.S. government if the Justice Department banned him from entering the United States.

Waldheim's first low-cost strategy, on the day that the first *New York Times* article appeared, was to claim that his latest book intended only to show his UN career, not to detail his war experiences, and that he had never tried to hide anything about his military past. Indeed, he even apologized (on CBS's *60 Minutes*) for having left the impression, in his answer to Representative Solarz of New York in 1980, that he had intentionally omitted information about his war service. Rather, it was out of a "general reluctance to speak in detail about my military service" (Heindl 1991, 18–24). Waldheim also argued that the Austrian state police had exonerated him when he first joined the Foreign Ministry in 1946; Austrian newspapers pointed out that he had been investigated by the CIA, KGB, and Israeli government during his candidacy for the UN as well (Wodak et al. 1990, 65, 67). In short, he argued that no problem existed.

Another relatively low-cost strategy was to claim that the facts had been misconstrued about his membership in Nazi student organizations, that he could not remember the details after so many years, and—at the same time—that others had filled out membership forms without his knowledge or, if he had joined himself, that it had been necessary to survive (Heindl 1991, 27–34). When evidence was presented of the medal he had received from the fascist Croatian government for valor in fighting Titoist partisans in 1942 (in a military action estimated to have cost twelve thousand Yugoslav lives, most of them civilians), Waldheim claimed that such medals had been given out routinely.[3]

In responding to WJC claims that documents showed that he had been a staff officer at a time and place in the Balkans where massacres or interrogations had occurred, Waldheim denied any direct involvement: "at the date of these atrocities, I was not in the area" (Heindl 1991, 51). As for his role in deporting Jews from Saloniki, Waldheim stated in early April, "I was definitely not aware that they had taken place" (Heindl 1991, 63). The strategy seemed to be to admit to nothing about his actions until irrefutable evidence was presented; the significance of the evidence was then downplayed, or it was suggested that the nature of the situation had not been understood (what Cobb and Ross describe as anti-patterning in chapter 2). However, the strategy was not costless to Waldheim, since contradictory or evasive constructions hurt his credibility and encouraged those pressing for further information.

The medium-cost strategy of discrediting opponents and their issues took on several forms. By far the most important in Austria was to regard questions as a continuation of the "witch-hunt" and "defamation campaign" begun with the *Profil* story on Young and Rubicam. Waldheim himself would call it the "greatest slander campaign in the [Austrian] Republic since 1945" (Wistrich 1992, 256–7). The idea of the campaign against Waldheim would strongly influence Austrian media coverage.

Rather than responding to the accusations, this strategy focuses on the motivations of accusers' attempts to discredit Waldheim (Khol et al. 1987). In the view of prominent ÖVP politicians, the most likely candidate for this strategy was the SPÖ (Mitten 1992, 55; Gruber et al. 1992), which "by providing damning documents and information to those abroad would damage Waldheim's international reputation, his major advantage over Steyrer" (Wodak et al. 1990, 104). In the context of Austrian party politics, where it looked as though the SPÖ was about to lose the dominant position it had held for fifteen years, an accusation about the tricks it was using to stay in power might seem plausible to jaded voters. There was little interest in independently verifying or evaluating the evidence during the election campaign.

The specter of an international conspiracy to slander Waldheim had a variety of advantages for Waldheim's defenders. First, it focused attention on who was behind the accusations, deflecting any interest in whether the accusations were accurate. Second, every new revelation and question could be cast as yet another part of the "slander campaign," not to be taken seriously. Third, it permitted generalizations about the opposition: it was not the *New York Times* or the

New York Post but "the East Coast media"; it was not just individual journalists or an organization in New York but critics "from abroad" who were to blame. Having (undifferentiated) foreign opponents was useful, because the participants in the conspiracy could be extended at will as the story developed. Critics from abroad were a convenient foil in a nationalistic election for the symbolic head of state; they allowed Austrians to express righteous indignation about outsiders interfering in domestic affairs, thereby increasing the emotional temperature of the election.

Even if the puppet master supposedly was the SPÖ, the messenger and major actor in the revelations about Waldheim was the WJC.[4] In the course of the election, its efforts were greeted with hostility in the Austrian media—a media nearly unanimously of the opinion that the WJC had accused Waldheim of being a war criminal but had been unable to prove it (Wodak et al. 1990, 69).[5] These were "disgraceful attacks of that dishonorable lot (*ehrlose Gesellen*) from the World Jewish Congress" (Mitten 1992, 119, 228), coming from "the little whippersnapper General-Secretary Singer . . . and the private association with the bombastic name World Jewish Congress" (Gruber 1991, 200). Waldheim himself dismissively referred to "those people" and "these groups" in New York, to "Mr. Singer and the rest of them" (Wodak et al. 1990, 187). As for the WJC's motivations, some Austrian journalists opined that these Jews were motivated out of hatred and rage or were psychically damaged as a result of the war; Singer was angry, a journalist argued, because his father had had to clean Vienna's streets with a toothbrush (Mitten 1992, 232). Waldheim's explanations were more political: the WJC wanted revenge for what it saw as his pro–Palestine Liberation Organization (PLO) politics while he was at the UN (e.g., allowing Arafat to speak at the UN; the 1975 resolution calling Zionism a form of racism [Rosenbaum 1993, 6]), and the WJC was attacking Austria because it had not paid reparations to Israel (Heindl 1991, 125). In a compilation of the terms that were used, Wodak wrote that the "men of the WJC" were characterized as "dishonorable, outrageous, malicious, despicable, unbridled habitual slanderers, defamers, mafiosi who attacked others in a dishonorable, unserious and hate-filled manner; they dirtied others, took the law into their own hands and engaged in character assassination" (1990, 188). From all this came a defiant new election poster showing only the text "We Austrians Will Elect Whom *We* Want!! Now More Than Ever, Waldheim" (Khol et al. 1987, 160).

This medium-cost strategy of focusing on those behind the accusations was a familiar tactic in Austrian politics and well within the party polemics of the day. Yet in an election campaign stressing Waldheim's suitability to represent all of Austria, it was unwise to attack the SPÖ (or other parties) domestically, even if they were suspected of dirty tricks: it could cost votes in a close election. It cost much less to attack a small group far away that enjoyed low legitimacy and visibility in Austria and to frame the issue as the defense of Austria's honor from slanderers abroad. The attacks on the leaders of the WJC by name were clearly intended to make Austrian voters doubt the ethics and honesty of those who were raising questions about Waldheim.

AUSTRIA DURING THE WAR AND THEREAFTER

The perception that Waldheim was being hounded was rapidly reinterpreted as attacks on the Austrian nation and Austrians in general. The progression of campaign slogans from "An Austrian Whom the World Trusts" or "His Experience for Us All" (e.g., an individual's international standing and how it will help Austria) to the defiant "We Austrians Will Elect Whom *We* Want!!" (e.g., domestic decision making independent of outside opinion) makes this switch to a "we" discourse clear. "*We* behaved decently," Waldheim said before the second round of elections, defending the behavior of those Austrians who had acted as he had during the war (Wodak et al. 1990, 191). The question is, how did Austrians act during the war, and how did they subsequently process the experiences?

Austrian Responses to Nazi Annexation

In what has come to be known as the *Anschluss,* Austria was annexed by Germany in 1938. After the war it was fashionable—particularly within Austria—to characterize that country as the "first victim of Nazi aggression" (Pauley 1989, 34). However, Austrian-born Adolf Hitler had learned his hatred of Jews and his German nationalism in Linz and Vienna, and the Austrian Nazi Party antedated the German Nazi Party by sixteen years (Pauley 1989, 52). When the *Anschluss* came, it was enthusiastically welcomed, particularly in Vienna, where the largest concentration of Austria's Jews lived. In 1938, Jews were attacked in Vienna's streets, robbed of their homes and possessions, and forced to scrub walls and streets with lye or hydrochloric acid in "orgies of violence" that were so extreme that even Hitler was taken aback: both the SS and the German Foreign Office tried to stop such "wild Aryanization." There was "heartfelt approval and deep-seated satisfaction with the final removal of the Jews" to the concentration camps (Bukey 1989, 156, 160).[6] As Austrian historian Gerhard Botz pointed out, the expropriation of Jewish businesses and apartments also served instrumental purposes in resolving an acute housing shortage in 1938 and in rapidly relieving economic pressures by reducing unemployment by 60 percent in a single year: "The Jew must go—and his cash stays here!" the Nazi newspaper *Völkische Beobachter* trumpeted on April 26, 1938 (Wistrich 1992, 208, 215; Bukey 1989, 155).

It was the experience of economic hardship, of the welcome relief brought by the *Anschluss,* and of a generation of young men going off to war and a quarter of them not surviving that Waldheim represented. He had been, Waldheim said, "a proper soldier, who like hundreds of thousands of others was forced to do service in the German Army" ("Wir Österreicher" 1986, 152). Left out of this were those with mixed motivations: to judge by the large number of party members and the joy shown at the *Anschluss,* quite a few Austrians were enthusiastic about being part of the new German Empire and getting rid of the Jews. Some who joined may have seen the wisdom, for their own self-preservation, in becoming members of relatively innocuous parts of the Nazi edifice such as the Nazi Student Union. To separate those who joined out of conviction from those who joined out of opportunism would prove too difficult for the Austrian government after the war, however.

Those who served during the war faced a particular problem. When Waldheim said "I didn't do anything different than hundreds of thousands of other Austrians, namely do my duty as a soldier," he reflected the troubled split between a constructed half-memory validating the disagreeableness of forced duty in the German Army and a collective half-suppression of the pleasurable intensity of a duty seen as honorable (Ziegler and Kannonier-Finster 1993, 242–4).

The Partial Postwar Reckoning with the Past

The immediate postwar government in Austria chose to view the country as the first victim of Nazi aggression and occupation. Austria's fortunes had been tied to a defeated empire, so the "liberation" in 1945 was from the German embrace. The new Austrian government wanted to stress independence and to distance Austria as much as possible from Germany in the process. In this it was met halfway by the Allies, whose main concern was to fight German, not Austrian, militarism and National Socialism. Some of the first state doctrines formulated by the postwar Austrian government argued that Austria was not legally implicated but instead victimized. The new social tone, at least in Vienna, stressed Austrian innocence: people had been fellow travelers (*Mitläufer*) rather than convinced Nazis, and widespread resistance to Nazism had been offered (a considerable exaggeration) (Kaindl-Widhalm 1990, 36–8; Luza 1984).

Right after the war, Austrians engaged in a policy of denazification, which began with the immediate dismissal of 100,000 civil servants from their jobs by the new Austrian government. Although these administrators were not prosecuted, investigations began; the very scale of the action angered many former Nazi Party members, since they felt that they were all being tarred as guilty, regardless of what they had done. Protests were sufficiently intense that in less than a year, a new law separated those deemed complicitous (perhaps 10 percent) from those deemed "less incriminated," and few prosecutions were ever carried out.

The distinction was made early on between the vast majority of *Mitläufer* (like Waldheim), who claimed to have gone along, and the tiny minority of active, "true" Nazis. Excuses were even made by the parties for the helplessness of the *Mitläufer* as victims of the economic crisis, Nazi propaganda, and the behavior of the Great Powers. Passivity seemed almost a virtue after the war: those who had cooperated with the Nazis were used to going along and would accept the new democratic institutions—and, given time, would learn democratic values (Kaindl-Widhalm 1990, 38).

In Austria, as in Germany, the Allies worked hard to institute a competitive political system that became widely viewed as democratic. At the same time, there were dirty secrets in Austrian postwar politics concerning how *both* the SPÖ and the ÖVP worked to attract former Nazis; both courted the right-wing FPÖ, which had many former Nazis as members. Faced with the choice, the two major parties chose to integrate rather than isolate former Nazis, the price of which has been "a foggy relationship towards Nazism in their political practice" (Pelinka 1989, 247, 255), meaning toleration of attitudes and individuals that might have been spurned in other countries, particularly by the political Left. As early as 1946, the Socialists called for an end to the denazification persecution and for integration and forgiveness after a certain period of reflection by those who had gone astray. That Social Democrats could find a modus vivendi with countrymen whose former persuasion they had little sympathy with can be seen in the first SPÖ cabinet of the Kreisky government (1970), with its four former Nazi Party members (Knight 1992, 291; Herzstein 1988, 250).[7] Though one can argue that this was only a tactic—incorporating members of the opposition to defuse their power—some critics have put it down to an Austrian propensity to accommodate to nearly anything, much the way the *London Sunday Times* characterized Waldheim in November 1985 as demonstrating how one could bend over backwards and forwards at the same time (Sully 1989, 298). Likewise, on the Right, beginning in 1945, the ÖVP called for an "unqualified amnesty for all those who were forced to go along and become Nazi Party members though they never agreed with Nazi ideas." As a result, former Nazis had the bewildering experience of first feeling as though they were being collectively condemned and persecuted and then being courted for their votes; neither experience encouraged a reevaluation of their actions in the war (Meissl et al. 1986, 99).

In short, the standard construction was that what had happened in the war was not Austria's or Austrians' fault or responsibility. Instead, they had been victimized by the German *Anschluss,* men had been conscripted to fight Hitler's war, party members had joined out of expediency rather than conviction, and Austrians had offered resistance. The exoneration of nearly all former Nazi Party members, and the manner in which they were welcomed into the new political parties, suggested that the war was a closed chapter of a dreadful book. What the questions about Waldheim brought home—although quite a few Austrian historians had valiantly been trying to argue so since the early 1970s—was that anti-Jewish prejudice and Nazi ideology were also Austrian products and that large numbers of Austrians had been party members, including many high in the Third Reich. The Allied Occupation had been as much about liberation as it had been about checking resurgent fascist tendencies. Many Austrians had willingly victimized Jews and others and had voluntarily joined the party or happily gone off to fight in the Nazi cause; very few had resisted. Austrian Nazis were not absolved of their crimes or actions but were integrated in political life for fear of the political, social, and economic consequences if they were not. The past was suppressed, not processed, and few of those Austrians who mattered remained politically unimplicated.

The remarkable part is that it took forty years for the standard version to finally be questioned. Austria had done a good job of portraying itself as a land of culture and Alpine beauty, the inheritor of the greatness of the Austro-Hungarian Empire. A 1967 U.S. survey asked about people's first association with "Austria"; the results indicated that, at least in the United States, Austria was a "5M country—mountains, music, Mozart, Metternich, Maria Theresa" (Bunzl 1995, 36f). Austrians, as German Chancellor Adenauer put it, understood perfectly how to deal with their past after 1945: they made everyone believe that Beethoven was an Austrian, but Hitler was a German (Botz 1994, 92).

So, in symbolic (and party) terms, what Waldheim was defending was that the Austrian postwar consensus to bury the past was still appropriate. Outsiders might be concerned about guilt or innocence in committing war crimes, but what mattered was the reconciliation and accommodation with those who had participated in the war, as well as the implicit exoneration in the absence of widespread prosecution. A 1976 poll found that 85 percent of the population agreed that former war criminals had paid enough for their crimes and should be released from prison; in early 1985, 57 percent opposed further discussions of war crimes (Kaindl-Widhalm 1990, 105, 205; Meissl et al. 1986, 98). A shining sign of Austrian mastery of its past was the thirteen-year presence (1970–1983) of Bruno Kreisky (an assimilated Jew) as prime minister. And now, of all things, the postwar consensus was being violated, and by Jews.

THE JEWISH DIMENSION IN THE CONTROVERSY

Not dealing with the past in Austria also meant not dealing with what had happened to Jews in Austria. Or rather, the Jews in Austria who had been persecuted by Austrians were equated with those Austrians who claimed to be victims of the Germans. The unwillingness to restore appropriated Jewish property after the war was based in part on an argument that it would violate constitutional equal treatment doctrines to do so, for "one race [would] receive special privileges." In terms of restitution, Jewish victims were in effect being equated with their persecutors (Wistrich 1992, 222–3). This attitude was supported by 69 percent of the population polled in 1986, who agreed with the statement "it is Germany's, not Austria's, responsibility to pay reparations to Jews and their descendants" (Meissl et al. 1986, 98). And if Jews had been victims, it was their own fault. In a 1982 poll, 57 percent agreed in part (and 22 percent fully) with the statement "it is not coincidence that the Jews have been so often persecuted in the past; at least in part they are also responsible for this persecution" (Bunzl and Marin 1983, 246).

A large percentage of the Austrian population harbors resentment, prejudice, and misconceptions about Jews, at least as measured by opinion polls. Over half of those polled in 1980 believed that Jews still constituted 10 percent of the population (750,000 people), though in fact they constituted only 0.001 percent (8,000 people). With this exaggeration came distaste: 63 percent (1986) stated, "I would not live next to a Jew"; 59 percent (1987) stated, "it is fine if Jews are run down in Austrian newspapers"; and 60 percent (1986) agreed that "all Jews should move to Israel" (Pauley 1992, 305–6).[8]

Despite what such results suggest about hostile Austrian attitudes, explicit discriminatory action was made illegal after 1945; it is even unclear whether agreeing with polling statements implies an intent to discriminate. In fact, in Austrian political discourse, although prejudice clearly exists, "the open expression of more vulgar anti-Jewish prejudice is . . . stigmatized" (Mitten 1992, 40). So post-war Austria, where few Jews still lived, exhibited the oddity of an "anti-Semitism without Jews" and even an "anti-Semitism without anti-Semites," because few would openly admit to their prejudices (Bunzl and Marin 1983, 171; Marin 1987). All the more reason, therefore, that Austrian discourse was oblique and in code, filled with self-referential disclaimers, or used what Gordon Allport (1954) called "re-fencing" devices (e.g., "some of my best friends are Jews") to acknowledge exceptions to the rule of prejudice.

The Complex Roles of Jewish Organizations and Leaders

Many Austrians shared the views of political leaders, which became overt after a *Profil* interview with the heads of the WJC (Singer and Steinberg) was published in late March. In it they said, "the next six years will be no bed of roses if Waldheim is elected . . . Jewish and non-Jewish organizations all over the world will prepare a proper reception for Waldheim in whichever country he travels to. . . . The Austrians must bear the consequences . . . [of having] a former Nazi and liar [as] Austria's representative. Everyone with an Austrian passport will be traveling with this cloud of uncertainty" (Mitten 1992, 216–7). Such statements incensed the Austrian press, which saw them as threats on the part of Jews everywhere to turn on Austria—reinforcing the old anti-Semitic prejudice of a Jewish world conspiracy. Even more surprising, Austria's best-known Jews, Nazi hunter Simon Wiesenthal and former prime minister Bruno Kreisky, accused the WJC of "reviving anti-Semitism," of "disgusting meddling" and "colossal vileness" afterward (Mitten 1992, 220; Wodak et al. 1990, 111–5).

The WJC, in turn, was "convinced that the [Austrian] electorate would find the 40-year cover-up of those experiences intolerable in a candidate for the presidency" (Rosenbaum 1993, 89). The WJC thus assumed that Austrian politics worked like post-Watergate U.S. politics and that news of the cover-up would lead the Austrian electorate to reject Waldheim (Cohen and Rosenzweig 1987, 147). Yet the WJC had previous reason to be affronted by the Austrian government. It was upset over the Austrian government's role in welcoming back a Nazi prisoner from Italy one day and welcoming WJC delegates to their international conference the next day.

The WJC had several dilemmas. It wanted the truth from Waldheim and justice for the persecuted (especially Jews), even if it took a Watergate-style set of revelations. It also wanted support, if possible, from the Austrian Jewish community. Wiesenthal, no less than the WJC, wanted truth and justice (Wiesenthal 1996), but not at the cost of delegitimizing postwar political arrangements in Austria. In effect, a number of his statements defended Waldheim, and after the election he said, "Waldheim is a false symbol of the Nazis" (Palumbo 1988, 154). To some in Austria, Wiesenthal, in his guise as moral guide, was "one of the few who found the right words for National Socialism" (Jancsy and Schmiederer 1996, 47), but to those who wished to say that the past didn't interest them, he was a potentially dangerous nuisance. At the same time, to have a prominent Jewish figure in Vienna defend Waldheim was helpful to the ÖVP, and the party widely publicized Wiesenthal's exonerating statements. Wiesenthal's politics may have come from his marginalization by the communist- and socialist-dominated Jewish community organization (*Kultusgemeinde*) in Vienna immediately after the war, but whatever the cause, he was both strongly anti-SPÖ and wary of certain Jewish organizations, including the WJC (at one point, for example, questioning whether the WJC understood the organization of the *Wehrmacht*). The WJC worried that the more it probed, the greater the danger of backlash to Austrian Jews, so it wanted Wiesenthal's support or the support of the *Kultusgemeinde*. To the WJC, it didn't matter whether Waldheim was the right or wrong *symbol* of Nazism: Waldheim's postwar career, it declared, was "an intolerable affront to human decency" (Rosenbaum 1993, 472). Even if the WJC was "not in the Nazi-hunting business," according to its president, Bronfman, it wanted support for the stance that "the word 'silence' had to be banished from the Jewish lexicon" (Rosenbaum 1993, 57).

So Austrian Jewish leaders and the WJC not only mistrusted each other, they also misread or misunderstood each other's differing political cultures. WJC leaders thought that scandalous revelations about a politician would obviously affect the behavior of Austrian voters; Wiesenthal and Kreisky functioned in an environment in which scandals only reified preexisting electoral preferences.[9]

There's No Business Like the Shoah Business?
Transnational Symbolic Contexts in the 1980s

Beyond the difficulties of Austrian views of Jews and the difficulties that Jewish organizations and leaders had with one another, there was a transnational context for what the Germans call *Vergangenheitsbewältigung*—the coming to terms with (or mastering of) the wartime past. In both Europe and the United States, the memorializing, commemorating, and "museumifying" of the recent past had become part of the public agenda.

Mid-1984 had seen a contretemps over whether German Chancellor Helmut Kohl should attend the fortieth anniversary of D day in Normandy: was it appropriate for the major political representative of the vanquished enemy to attend a memorial for and of the victors? Late 1984 saw the beginning of a controversy over where President Reagan would commemorate the fortieth anniversary of Victory in Europe day: Chancellor Kohl suggested that he visit both a German military cemetery and the Dachau concentration camp site in mid-1985. Reagan declined doing the latter with the Waldheimian comment, "I want to put that history behind me," only to raise new problems in press conferences. He would not visit a concentration camp (so as not to reevoke German guilt) but instead, "in a spirit of reconciliation," would visit the military cemetery at Bitburg. It then turned out that Bitburg contained the graves of forty-nine SS men. Reversing himself, Reagan then announced that he would visit a concentration camp site (Bergen-Belsen) but continued to defend his visit to Bitburg by saying that the dead German soldiers "were victims of Nazism, just as surely as the victims in the concentration camps" (Hartman 1986, xiii–xv). If one sees this as symbolic discourse, then at least some in the international community seemed to be saying that Austrian-style defenses—that everyone was a victim, not just the Jews—were justifiable.

Reconciliation was one thing, remembrance another, many American Jews said in protesting Bitburg. By doing so, they were riding the crest of making the Holocaust into a "quasi-religious element of their identity" (Bunzl 1995, 49). The reason to latch onto this symbol had much to do with the passing of the generation of Holocaust survivors, but it also came as a by-product of the rise of ethnic militancy among various racial and nationality groups in the United States, the increasing importance of political lobbying in public life, and the professional prominence of many Jewish refugees and their descendants in postwar America.

In the late 1970s, these tendencies came together officially not only in the creation of the Office of Special Investigations in the Justice Department—its task to find Nazis living in the United States and prosecute or deport them for their deeds—but also in President Carter's creation of a presidential commission to decide how to commemorate the Holocaust—the origin of the Holocaust Museum that was later built in Washington, D.C. By 1993, the boom in American Holocaust remembrance had led to the creation of "34 Holocaust archives, 25 Holocaust research centers, 20 Holocaust Museums, 12 Holocaust monuments, 5 Holocaust libraries, 3 specialized journals and the creation of 'Holocaust Studies' at numerous universities" (Bunzl 1995, 50). Whether what was being transmitted was a universal moral message or "never again" lessons of particular resonance to Jews, the practical result of this boom was to create academic and political platforms that aggregated and concentrated "Jewish interests."

Financial and commercial considerations were not far behind. In 1978, the TV miniseries *Holocaust* was first aired, to be followed by many others (including Claude Lanzmann's nine-hour documentary *Shoah,* shown on German TV and in the United States during 1986), and numerous prominent Hollywood figures were recruited to help in fund-raising for various remembrance projects. The symbol of the Holocaust was sufficiently potent by the 1980s that it came to re-place Israel (or Zionism) as a rallying issue and identifier for Jews in the United States. Indeed, as a way to raise money for Holocaust museums and institutions such as the Simon Wiesenthal Center in Los Angeles, the joke began to circulate that there was no business like the *Shoah* business—pretty grim humor, since *Shoah* means catastrophe or disaster (Bunzl 1995, 52).[10] However, at the very least, this background helps explain why it was both literally and figuratively the business of organizations like the WJC in the United States to be involved in Holocaust questions.

CONCLUSION

In their various ways, during the 1980s, countries that had been combatants were putting the issue of how to deal with World War II on their public agendas, from the "historian's controversy" in Germany (Maier 1988) to the ongoing trial in France of the "butcher of Lyons," Klaus Barbie (Kramer 1988), and the build-ing of Holocaust museums and memorials in the United States (Bunzl 1995). At the same time, Austria was conspicuously keeping it off the public agenda. Its paradoxical attitude was neatly summarized by the claim, "we are all innocent perpetrators" (Wodak et al. 1990, 9). In that, Austria could look to the partial absolution offered by German Chancellor Kohl's remark about the "grace of late birth" of Germans born during and after the war, to President Reagan's Bitburg statement that "we do not believe in collective guilt," and to Waldheim's own as-sertion that "we Austrians are a decent people."

In Austria, journalists and party spokespeople—and even prominent Jews— in effect defended their postwar accommodations with Austrian collaborators. The issue was denied public agenda access during Waldheim's election cam-paign, as well as throughout much of 1987, to outside (and a few Austrian) critics. "People were angry, defensive, and defiant," Austrian political scientist Anton Pelinka wrote, in a "response to the international reactions [that] might be called unreasonable" (Harms et al. 1990, 64). After the first round of elections in May 1986, according to *Der Spiegel,* 60 percent of the population was convinced that the reputation of the country had not been damaged in the previous months. Ac-cusations against Waldheim were interpreted as accusations against Austria, turning the election decision into a matter of patriotic duty, the defense of na-tional honor, and an assertion that an independent, sovereign actor should be self-determining.

The issue in Austria was not about Waldheim's personal culpability—"for Austrians, the Catholic Waldheim had never looked much like a Nazi war criminal" (Sully 1989, 300)—but about collective memory and collective forgetting. "Here in Austria," literary figure Josef Haslinger wrote soon after the election, "forgetting is staged, by the state and by the media. Forgetting is not the detritus of an action, but rather a national, long-term therapy, a way of life practiced for decades" (Haslinger 1987, 99). The defense strategies that Waldheim and his supporters adopted in this election were symbolic (defending the Austrian national sense of self), and the attack strategies were also symbolic (the "campaign" against Waldheim, the "media justice" meted out, and so forth).

In the key terms of remembrance and reconciliation used at Bitburg, and in a notable speech by German President Richard von Weizsäcker on May 8, 1985, in which he said, among other things, that "there were many ways of not burdening one's conscience, of shunning responsibility, of looking away, keeping mum," Austrians were denying remembrance (of collaboration) and responsibility (for victims). Reconciliation had been with the half a million Austrian *Mitläufer,* not with the victims of Nazism. Issues perceived as being in Jewish interests (reparations, return of property, prosecution of Nazis) were clearly *not* on the Austrian public agenda and were either actively or passively denied. It took the "case of a 'typical' Austrian *Mitläufer* with its 'typical' suppression and denial of the Nazi years to hit the sore spot of many Austrians. The disjuncture between official version and collective memory became obvious, because how could one—following the thesis of victimization—see it as doing one's duty to be forced to fight a war on the side of the occupier?" (Uhl 1992, 86). Waldheim was significant precisely because he was neither particularly bad nor particularly good but fit the average behavior of the average Austrian: "that was why it was so painful—and coming from abroad in addition—to have a mirror held up to the ugly features of the average Austrian" (Pelinka 1990, 45).

The Waldheim affair, as a symbol of Austrian failure to come clean, served to "pull the cork out of the bottle in which the spirit of the Austrian past was lodged" (Uhl 1992, 16). This led to a more painful and open discussion in 1988 on the occasion of the fiftieth anniversary of the *Anschluss* (Wodak et al. 1994), including how Waldheim's generation had been "incapable of making free choices" (Haslinger 1987, 29). What had been angrily treated as a threat (the WJC leaders' statement that it would be "no bed of roses" for Austria) became a reality as one democratic government after another declared President Waldheim persona non grata, following the U.S. Justice Department's decision to bar Waldheim from entering the United States in 1987.

Austria forged a national consensus immediately after the war in part by papering over its deep political cleavages through the grand coalition government, by ignoring ex-Nazis through their incorporation, and by contrasting the " 'good' victimized Austrian . . . to the 'bad' German" (Markovits and Rabinbach 1986, 409)—helped, it must be added, by Allied Occupation policies. Austria developed a reputation for political stability, economic success, and East-West diplomacy during the cold war, creating a positive international image that Austrian politicians were happy to sell to Austrian voters. Yet by the mid-1980s, political hegemony (in coalition or not) was proving more difficult, economic success was threatened, and the episodic disruption to the sense of national self (Peter, Reder-Frischenschläger, and adulterated wine scandals) was weakening the self-image as an "island of the blessed."

Now a symbolic referendum was being held on the country's future, as symbolized by the presidency, which asked what bargains had been struck in the past to create the modern Austria. The WJC wanted to frame the case as "Waldheim has not been truthful about his past"; Austrian voters should not trust him and should not have him as a national symbol, given his Nazi connections—a stance driven by a particular U.S. cultural and political framework in which the WJC functioned. The ÖVP and Austrian press, by contrast, wanted to frame the case as "this is a base campaign against Austria"; Austrians should close ranks against calumnies from abroad and from Jews, and voters should trust Waldheim all the more *because* he was being attacked. If "the majority of Austrians voted for self-deception" (Markovits and Rabinbach 1986, 411), their denying public agenda access to the issue of wartime collaboration epitomized Austrian accommodation to circumstances.

NOTES

1. The fortieth anniversary per se was not special; rather, "there is a strong case for recalling, periodically, soberly and somberly, the war that ended in 1945. That case does not rest on pride or nostalgia; nor on the obligation to honor the victims of war. Primarily, it rests on the duty to prevent obliteration of the past" (*The Economist,* January 19, 1985).

2. Literally, *In the Glass Palace of World Politics,* referring to UN headquarters in New York, though with overtones of "those who sit in glass houses. . . . " The English edition is called *In the Eye of the Storm: A Memoir.*

3. Mitten (1992, 127) claims that Waldheim was the 916th recipient, suggesting that his defense was a reasonable one, but avoiding the moral questions of receiving any commendation from the brutal Ustashi government and claiming to have been nowhere near the place at the time.

4. The WJC is an umbrella organization, founded in the 1930s, to provide aid to Jews, but after the war, it served more as a forum. The "Global Plenary Assembly," for example, held in Israel every five years, allows "hundreds of delegates" representing the "Jewish communities of dozens of nations" to meet (Rosenbaum 1993, 1). As an organization, it is thus a little like the UN, and like the UN, the office that matters most is the one in New York.

5. Although the WJC accused Waldheim of lying, being part of the Nazi war machine, having been in places where atrocities occurred, and having been culpable in the terms defined by the Nuremberg Trials, it was careful not to actually accuse him of having

committed war crimes. Mitten gives the WJC the benefit of the doubt: "whatever one may justifiably criticize about the WJC's research . . . be it the hyperbolic choice of words, the incomplete research, their insistent and exaggerated self-assurance or the bias of many of their assumptions . . . the substance of the allegations they made against Waldheim remain broadly confirmed, and where mistaken, nonetheless intelligible" (1992, 133).

6. Austria had 191,000 Jews in 1934, of whom 92 percent lived in Vienna, making the fate of Vienna's Jews near-synonymous with the fate of Jews throughout the country (Botz in Wistrich 1992, 199).

7. Herzstein (1988, 250) notes that this "somewhat unholy alliance" was defended by Kreisky "with the argument that by bringing extremists into the Austrian political mainstream, he was preventing the potentially dangerous alienation of a sizeable segment of the population," but he forgets that this was the same argument used in the late 1940s to justify quickly admitting former Nazi Party members back into public life.

8. The results are significant comparatively as well. Sizable but considerably smaller groups of Germans (48 and 44 percent, respectively) answered that they would not live next to a Jew and that all Jews should move to Israel; the levels of agreement among U.S. respondents (9 and 13 percent, respectively) were tiny by comparison. Some Austrians averred even stronger antipathies: 25 percent (1987) agreed that "it is fine if politicians make anti-Semitic remarks for political advantage," and 8 to 15 percent (1987–1989) agreed that "Austria would be better off without Jews."

9. I am indebted to Matti Bunzl for this elegant formulation.

10. The "awkward and obsessive" Jewish insistence on victimhood, even as it serves as a "central legitimation," also creates a variety of problems for Germans and Jews, especially if it reaches the point of making "a fetish of Auschwitz" (Maier 1988, 164–8).

REFERENCES

Allport, G. W. 1954. *The nature of prejudice.* Cambridge: Addison-Wesley.

Botz, G. 1994. Verdrängung, Pflichterfüllung, Geschichtsklitterung: Probleme des "typischen Österreichers" mit der NS-Vergangenheit. In *Kontroversen um Österreichs Zeitgeschichte,* edited by G. Botz and G. Sprengnagel. Frankfurt: Campus.

Bukey, E. 1989. Popular opinion in Vienna after the Anschluss. In *Conquering the past: Austrian Nazism yesterday and today,* edited by F. Parkinson. Detroit: Wayne State University Press.

Bunzl, J. 1995. Österreichpolitik und öffentliche Meinung in den USA. In *The sound of Austria: Österreichpolitik und öffentliche Meinung in den USA,* edited by J. Bunzl et al. Wien: Braumüller.

Bunzl, J., and B. Marin. 1983. *Antisemitismus in Österreich.* Innsbruck: Inn-Verlag.

Cobb, R. W., and C. D. Elder. 1983. *Participation in American politics: The dynamics of agenda-building.* Baltimore: Johns Hopkins University Press.

Cobb, R. W., J.-K. Ross, and M. H. Ross. 1976. Agenda setting as a comparative political process. *American Political Science Review* 71:126–38.

Cohen, B., and L. Rosenzweig. 1987. *Waldheim.* New York: Adama Books.

Cyrus, I. 1986. Dr. Kurt Österreicher und seine Waldheimer. *Der Spiegel,* April 14, pp. 144–5.

Gruber, H. 1991. *Antisemitismus im Mediendiskurs: Die Affäre "Waldheim" in der Tagespresse.* Wiesbaden: Deutscher Universität Verlag.

Gruber, K., et al. 1992. *Wir über Waldheim—Urteil der Mitbürger.* Wien: Böhlau.

Harms, K., et al. 1990. *Coping with the past: Germany and Austria After 1945.* Madison: University of Wisconsin Press.

Hartman, G. 1986. *Bitburg in moral and political perspective.* Bloomington: Indiana University Press.

Haslinger, J. 1987. *Politik der Gefühle.* Frankfurt: Luchterhand.

Heindl, B. 1991. *"Wir Österreicher sind ein Anständiges Volk"—Kurt Waldheim.* Linz: agis/sandkorn

Herzstein, R. 1988. *Waldheim: The missing years.* New York: William Morrow.

Hirczy, W. 1995. Waldheim in den USA. In *The sound of Austria: Österreichpolitik und öffentliche Meinung in den USA,* edited by J. Bunzl et al. Wien: Braumüller.

Jancsy, I., and E. Schmiederer. 1996. Österreich ist nicht mehr Waldheims Land (Interview with Elan Steinberg). *Profil,* February 26, pp. 44–7.

Kaindl-Widhalm, B. 1990. *Demokraten wider Willen? Autoritäre Tendenzen und Antisemitismus in der 2. Republik.* Wien: Verlag für Gesellschaftskritik.

Khol, A., et al. 1987. *Die Kampagne: Kurt Waldheim—Opfer oder Täter? Hintergründe und Szenen eines Falles von Medienjustiz.* München: Herbig.

Knight, R. 1992. Haider, the freedom party and the extreme right in Austria. *Parliamentary Affairs* 45(3): 285–99.

Kramer, J. 1988. *Europeans.* New York: Penguin.

Luza, R. 1984. *The resistance in Austria, 1938–1945.* Minneapolis: University of Minnesota Press.

Maier, C. 1988. *The unmasterable past: History, holocaust, and German national identity.* Cambridge: Harvard University Press.

Marin, B. 1987. Antisemitism before and after the Holocaust: The Austrian case. In *Jews, antisemitism and culture in Vienna,* edited by I. Oxaal et al. London: Routledge & Kegan Paul.

Markovits, A., and A. Rabinbach. 1986. Why Waldheim won in Austria. *Dissent* 33:409–11.

Meissl, S., et al. 1986. *Verdrängte Schuld, verfehlte Sühne: Entnazifizierung in Österreich 1945–1955.* Wien: Verlag für Geschichte und Politik.

Mitten, R. 1992. *The politics of antisemitic prejudice: The Waldheim phenomenon in Austria.* Boulder, CO: Westview Press.

Palumbo, M. 1988. *The Waldheim files: Myth and reality.* London: Faber & Faber.

Pauley, B. 1989. The Austrian Nazi Party before 1938. In *Conquering the past: Austrian Nazism yesterday and today,* edited by F. Parkinson. Detroit: Wayne State University Press.

———. 1992. *From prejudice to persecution: A history of Austrian antisemitism.* Chapel Hill: University of North Carolina Press.

Pelinka, A. 1989. SPÖ, ÖVP, and the "Ehemaligen": Isolation or integration. In *Conquering the past: Austrian Nazism yesterday and today,* edited by F. Parkinson. Detroit: Wayne State University Press.

———. 1990. *Zur Österreichischen Identität.* Wien: Ueberreuter.

Rosenbaum, E., with W. Hoffer. 1993. *Betrayal: The untold story of the Kurt Waldheim investigation and cover-up.* New York: St. Martin's Press.

Sully, M. 1989. The Waldheim connection. In *Conquering the past: Austrian Nazism yesterday and today,* edited by F. Parkinson. Detroit: Wayne State University Press.

Uhl, H. 1992. *Zwischen Versöhnung und Verstörung. Eine Kontroverse um Österreichs historische Identität fünfzig Jahre nach dem "Anschluss."* Wien: Böhlau.

Waldheim, K. 1985. Im *Glaspalast der Weltpolitik.* Dusseldorf: Econ Werlag.

Wiesenthal, S. 1996. Die Wahrheit Verteidigen. *Profil,* March 4, p. 87.

Wir Österreicher wählen, wen wir wollen. 1986. *Der Spiegel,* April 14, pp. 138–51.

Wistrich, R. 1992. *Austrians and Jews in the 20th century.* New York: St. Martins Press.

Wodak, R., et al. 1990. *"Wir Sind alle unschuldige Täter": Diskurshistorische Studien zum Nachkriegsantisemitismus.* Frankfurt: Suhrkamp.

———. 1994. *Die Sprachen der Vergangenheit: Öffentliches Gedenken in österreichischen und deutschen Medien.* Frankfurt: Suhrkamp.

Ziegler, M., and W. Kannonier-Finster. 1993. *Österreichisches Gedächnis: Über Erinnern und Vergessen der NS-Vergangenheit.* Wien: Böhlau.

10
Conclusion: Agenda Denial— The Power of Competing Cultural Definitions

Roger W. Cobb and Marc Howard Ross

The U.S. political process provides opportunities for aggrieved individuals and groups to place their demands on the relevant governmental agenda. However, to be taken seriously, new issues must compete with issues already on the too-full institutional dockets for the attention of officials with serious time and resource constraints. This inherent disposition to pass over new issues, along with opponents' strategies to actively resist consideration of proposals for new actions, means that many grievances fail to get serious consideration. Many issues simply die a natural death due to the inability of the initiators to overcome the resistance of the opposing forces and the disinterest of the public.

Yet there are many issues that attract sufficient interest so that opponents cannot simply ignore them and must take some action to keep the issues from gaining serious consideration. Chapter 2 outlined a series of low- to high-cost strategies that public officials and affected groups use to oppose putting an issue on the formal agenda. It was hypothesized that low-cost strategies would be used first, followed by medium-cost and then high-cost strategies. Only if the initiators are able to turn back the various strategic attacks of opponents does the grievance get on the formal agenda and receive serious governmental attention.

Our most unexpected conclusion was the relative infrequency of the use of high-cost strategies involving threats (or violence) to achieve agenda denial. We believe that this is a crucial feature of policy conflicts in the 1990s that is worth highlighting and not just a function of the cases in this volume. Although instances of high-cost violent strategies directed toward oppressed groups such as blacks, women, and gays exist and draw media attention, we suggest that they are not the norm of contemporary U.S. politics. We hypothesize that the cases reflect the range of issues and tactics that occupy most politicians and bureaucrats in agenda disputes—commonly used verbal attacks and symbolic redefinition of disputes that occur between initiators and opponents and are reflected in the key issues of our time: public health, the economy, and ethnic identity.

Another conclusion to highlight is the importance of identity politics in virtually all agenda conflicts. One does not have to examine only dramatic issues such as those involving race, gender, or sexual orientation to see identity at work. Rather, the cases reveal that even SEC regulation and bovine growth hormone approval, which at first glance seem to be technical and unemotional matters, involve identity issues. Every case in the volume involves both identity concerns and substantive interests. Identity concerns are important even in "ordinary" conflicts, and this needs to be better understood. It is also the case, however, that in terms of the centrality of identity issues, the cases in the volume offer a range. At least three of the cases (colonias, RU 486, and Waldheim) are primarily about identity politics; in two of the others (bST, health care), identity issues play a crucial role; and in two (SEC and accounting), identity is present but less central.

This chapter reviews the hypotheses about agenda denial strategies presented in the first two chapters in light of the seven extended cases presented in the subsequent chapters. To do this, we first summarize the characteristics of initiators and opponents in each of the cases (see Table 10.1) and then discuss the emphasis on medium-cost strategies that occurred in these cases, distinguishing between opponents' attack and symbolic placating strategies as alternative routes for achieving agenda denial. We end with some reflections on the power of competing symbolic definitions and their consequences for agenda denial. Our analysis understands agenda conflicts on two levels. The first concerns a governmental decision whether or not to seriously consider a particular grievance. The second is about competing interpretations of political problems and the competing worldviews that underlie them—about how people ought to live, how society ought to act, what should or should not be done by government, how we should treat the environment, and who threatens people's security. The ways in which issue initiators and opponents associate specific issues with these more general worldviews in agenda disputes are of particular concern in this last chapter.

CHARACTERISTICS OF THE ISSUES, INITIATORS, AND OPPONENTS

Issues

With one exception, the issues in the conflicts studied touched on concrete interests (often, but not always, economic) found in everyday life and also concerned social, cultural, and political identities that invoke strong fears and raise issues of recognition and legitimation for many of the key participants. Agenda disputes, like political conflicts more generally, are about both interests and identities (Ross 1993). Most obviously, the specific interests of people's daily lives were found in the cases that raised public health issues. Clearly, without access to clean water and viable health insurance, people will get sick and die. And bST could affect anyone who drinks milk.

The intensity of feelings and the persistence of the protagonists are not just a function of the material interests at stake. These are also related to the identities of actors on all sides who are linked to the outcome of the dispute. In the SEC regulatory cases, the conflict involved legitimation of competing ideas of justice; in the bST conflict, different ideas about how we should relate to nature raised fears on both sides; the RU 486 conflict was another chapter in the long-running abortion controversy and focused on fundamentally different ideas about life and choice in which each side sought validation of its worldview (Ginsberg 1990); national health insurance in the United States raised identity concerns—one side portrayed an overbearing government invading people's daily lives, and the other side portrayed the abandonment of citizens in need of care and nurturance; the dispute over water in El Paso was about the political and social identity of immigrants in the region and whether or not their needs should be addressed by society. Only in the case concerning the public judgment of Kurt Waldheim's past can we say that there were few implications for people's daily lives; this conflict, which attracted worldwide attention, revolved around core identity issues for the key parties both within and outside Austria.

Initiators

What can we say about initiators seeking to place new issues on the agenda from the cases presented in this book? First, these cases are not a random sample of those with issue grievances. They are highly slanted in a particular direction. With one exception, the issue initiators possessed significant political resources that included size; visibility; legitimacy; political experience; and access to decision makers, including actors from both political parties (but primarily Democrats), major pressure groups, the media, and even presidents. The one exception among these cases was that of colonia residents in El Paso, where the initiating group was at a serious resource disadvantage in dealing with opponents.

Second, many of the issues that initiators promoted have been around for some time. There have been recurrent battles to place them on the formal agenda, and some were buried only to be raised in succeeding generations, as in the cases involving SEC regulation of securities and the accounting industry and attempts to achieve national health insurance. The other conflicts, although not going on for decades, involved issues that persisted over an extended period: the bST decision, the approval of RU 486, the access to water, and the issue of Austria's Nazi past.[1]

This leads to a third conclusion. The cases here involved some powerful political actors on both sides. The issue initiators were not inexperienced amateurs,

Table 10.1. Summary of Case Studies and Strategies Used to Oppose Consideration of Issues

Initiators	Opponents	Opponents' Symbolic Strategies	Opponents' Attack Strategies
SEC regulation of securities industry **Public officials:** Sporadic congressional interest **Affected groups:** Sporadic media interest Consumer groups	**Public officials:** SEC officials **Affected groups:** Securities industry	Showcasing: more reporting releases Conducted studies of problem	Issue attack: negative symbols (big government, regulation)
SEC regulation of accounting practices **Public officials:** Sporadic congressional interest (Democrats) **Affected groups:** Consumer groups	**Public officials:** SEC officials **Affected groups:** Accounting profession	Industry-created commissions Denial: issue not a public concern, isolated concerns not a problem	Issue attack: negative symbols (big government, states' rights)
FDA consideration of bST **Public officials:** Politicians from dairy states **Affected groups:** Environmental groups Public-interest groups Small dairy farmers	**Public officials:** FDA officials **Affected groups:** Pharmaceutical industry Veterinary medicine community Biotechnology research community	Conferences: emphasize research, scientific support	Issue attack: negative symbols, question leader's judgments, scare tactics, "modern-day Luddites" Positive symbols: product safety, progress, efficiency, it's found in nature
FDA consideration of RU 486 **Public officials:** Democratic president and members of administration **Affected groups:** Feminist, pro-choice groups	**Public officials:** Bush administration Pro-life members of Congress **Affected groups:** RCR Fund National Right to Life Committee	Threat of boycott Postponement	Group attack: baby killers Issue attack strategies: negative symbol attachment (death pill, pesticide, threat to women's lives)

Table 10.1. continued on next page

Table 10.1. Continued

Initiators	Opponents	Opponents' Symbolic Strategies	Opponents' Attack Strategies
National health insurance **Public officials:** Politicians from both parties (more Democrats than Republicans) **Affected groups:** Labor interests Academics, policy analysts General public	Public officials: Conservative political officials (mainly Republicans) **Affected groups:** Insurance industry Medical organizations (e.g., AMA) Business groups	Tokenism by insurance industry, medical groups	Issue attack: negative symbols (big government, red tape, rules) Patriotism: un-American, right to choose doctors Criticism of details of proposals
Clean water for colonias in El Paso **Public officials:** A few state legislators Governor and lieutenant governor One congressman **Affected groups:** Colonia residents in El Paso area Health care professionals Advocacy organizations, e.g., EPISO	Public officials: El Paso Public Service Board **Affected groups:** Developers City taxpayers and water customers	Showcasing: loopholes in regulations	Group attack: negative stereotypes of immigrants Issue attack: not public problem, jurisdiction issues, spread of false information
Kurt Waldheim's past in presidential election **Public officials:** European leaders Many leaders in all Austrian parties **Affected groups:** World Jewish Congress	Public officials: Kurt Waldheim **Affected groups:** Austrian press Austrian political parties	Create commission of historians to review case Appeal to patriotism	Group attack: attack World Jewish Congress for interfering in domestic politics, charge personal vendetta Issue attack: false information, dispute facts of the case

and most were able to get officeholders from the state, local, or national level to endorse their claims. Although the number of public officials supporting new proposals was smaller than the number of those opposing consideration (or neutral), these conflicts were not completely one-sided contests in terms of political access and experience. Because resources were somewhat symmetrical, opponents needed to employ a wide range of strategies to defeat initiators who were not easily co-opted or misled about the reaction of public officials to their concerns. Simply ignoring the grievance or denying that the problem existed did not make the problem disappear.

Opponents

Although the resources of the initiators in the cases presented were impressive, they paled in comparison to those of the agenda deniers who attempted to keep the new issues off the formal or public agenda. The first observation about opponents is that they were powerful actors, especially the economic pressure groups interested in maintaining the status quo. In all cases but two, powerful economic forces were arrayed against the challengers: in the regulatory cases, the accounting and securities industries, the pharmaceutical and medical industries, and the Catholic Church; in the public health cases, the insurance and medical industries and local developers. These groups are not accustomed to losing political battles without a fight.

Second, these opponents had powerful political allies. In the four cases involving regulation, the regulating agency (the SEC or the FDA) was actively involved in preventing the grievance from getting on the agenda. In the case involving medical care, conservative politicians, particularly Republicans, were actively involved in threatening the proponents of national health insurance. In the local water case, the most powerful actor was the El Paso Public Service Board, which did not want to provide the colonias with access to city water. Finally, Austria's major political parties and the country's president said that Waldheim's past was not an issue as they sought to maintain the integrity of the presidency.

Third, the power of the opponents was evident in the outcomes of each case. In six of the seven cases, the issue initiators were not successful in getting the issue on the agenda. In a few of the cases, scandals led to more intensive congressional scrutiny of the grievance (e.g., accounting and securities regulation), but the opponents' strategies soon removed the issue from the attention of decision makers. In only one case—FDA consideration of RU 486—were the opponents unsuccessful. However, in this case, the election of a sympathetic, pro-choice, Democratic president was a crucial factor in gaining agenda access. Had Bill Clinton not been elected in 1992, the fate of the French abortion pill would certainly have been different.

MOST FREQUENTLY USED OPPOSITION STRATEGIES

How do opponents respond to initiators' grievances? The answer to this question, we hypothesized in chapters 1 and 2, depends on how opponents perceive the initiators' resources and legitimacy. In the cases presented here, both initiators and opponents were somewhat experienced actors who had considerable, but not equal, resources. The cases showed that low-cost denial strategies were not used very much, and when they were, they failed to deter initiators. Similarly, the cases documented relatively few cases in which high-cost strategies were employed. Middle-cost strategies were the most commonly used. At the same time, the results suggest that whereas governmental opponents are most likely to use symbolic placation, which makes some effort to recognize the legitimacy of the grievance and address it, affected groups attack the initiators and/or their issue more directly to oppose placing the issue on the agenda.

Government officials (elected and administrative) and potentially affected groups are the two main opponents that initiators face. Each has somewhat different resources and concerns and, therefore, is likely to operate independently and behave differently toward initiators.[2] Government officials have greater technical resources and more personnel. In addition, they tend to be conflict avoiders, often act cautiously, and are reluctant to commit scarce resources in new ways when faced with a new grievance. Experienced in dealing with problems at a detailed, technical level, bureaucrats are careful not to use strong, evocative language (Edelman 1964). Legislators also have several options in terms of actions that can be taken to avoid consideration of an issue. Although they do not speak in bureaucratic jargon, they generally have no need to antagonize the initiators with strong language, unless the issue is of central importance to them. After all, they may look for support and votes from these same groups on other issues in the future. In contrast, affected groups act under fewer constraints, allowing them to act swiftly and forcefully when they face the likelihood of material and/or symbolic losses. Affected groups are likely to attack either the initiating group or the substantive issue it raises.

Although appearing inconsistent at one level, this strategy can present a devastating combination that is hard for initiators to defeat. Government officials who act as agenda deniers often offer to deal with the issue initiator in a somewhat cooperative, compromising way and often oppose the initiating group's demands because of limited government resources. They focus on medium-cost symbolic placating strategies, having no reason to go out of their way to provoke initiating groups. At the same time, affected groups often perceive a threat from initiators and find little reason to cooperate with those whom they feel are trying to take something material or symbolic away from them, so they turn to medium-cost attack strategies.

Attack Strategies: Group Versus Issue

Many groups whose issues are on the formal agenda vigorously oppose new-comers that are seeking to replace them, viewing any person or group that wishes to shift the balance of resources with fear and hostility. In opposing political neo-phytes, the more extreme strategies are employed (high cost or low cost). How-ever, when initiators have political experience and considerable resources, the cases showed that medium-cost attack strategies are those most likely to produce effective results.

If an initiating group will not be defeated by nonrecognition tactics, an op-ponent is likely to adopt an attack strategy. In chapter 1, we hypothesized that the perceived legitimacy of the initiator is crucial in determining at this point whether an opponent attacks the initiating group or its issue position. When the public holds a grievance group in high esteem, it is best for an opponent to attack its substantive position. When the initiator is unknown or held in low esteem, an attack on the group is most likely. Two of the cases provided partial exceptions to this rule, suggesting that if a conflict is intense, the opponent may attack both the group and its issue position. The battle over RU 486 paralleled previous fights over abortion, which has been a major issue in U.S. politics for over two decades. The feelings on both sides ran high, and it is not surprising that Jackman reported both group and issue attacks. The second exception was the issue of Kurt Wald-heim's past and his candidacy for the Austrian presidency. Again, this was a highly emotional issue, invoking Germany's treatment of Jews during World War II, the complicity of the Austrian population, and deep memories that evoked strong feelings, which led opponents to use both group- and issue-based attacks in this case.[3]

Groups with High Legitimacy. When facing a grievance group with a positive image, opponents are more likely to avoid attacking it and go after its issue posi-tion directly, often by invoking symbols that place the proposed policy in a nega-tive context. This generally means raising potential threats or fears of what might happen if the proposed policy is adopted. A first step, however, can emphasize what opponents see as procedural or logical flaws in a proposal. One of the most common themes in the cases was opponents' claim that the problem identified by initiators was not a public problem at all but one that the private sector should solve. We saw this in both Hackey's study of national health insurance and Lopez and Reich's analysis of colonia water access. A similar procedural point is to ar-gue that the issue is beyond the jurisdiction of the government group asked to act, an argument used by the El Paso Service Board to justify its inaction in the water access case, and by accountants opposing government regulation. A related opposition tactic is to dispute the information the initiators present, as Waldheim did with his detractors, offering a larger context in which to evaluate the specific grievance being raised. A more pernicious situation occurs when opponents provide only partial information or misinformation, as opponents of national health care did when they claimed that it would restrict patients' choice of doctors.

Most common, however, are symbolic attack strategies that variously associate the current policy with positive outcomes and the proposed new policy with negative ones that raise threats and fears. There are two common arguments (1) the proposed policy will be costly and might take away something that people already have; and (2) the proposed policy will select particular individuals for undeserved treatment. The first emphasizes cost, and the second is about (un)fairness.

When associating negative symbols with initiators' issues and positive symbols with their own positions, opponents try to link policies with symbols that resonate with large numbers of people. In contemporary U.S. politics, three domains seem to be most widely used. The first is attachment to the national political system and invokes general concepts such as patriotism, Americanism, participation, elections, and other central elements of U.S. democracy. These evoke strong emotions from people, even though their specific meaning is highly ambiguous. At the same time, many Americans have a love-hate arrangement with their government, and there are images that produce a negative response as well, such as concentrated power, centralized authority, and large unwieldy bureaucratic organizations. A second domain links political action (or inaction) to the economic system and economic well-being. People often respond to political issues in terms of their implications for economic growth, low prices through competition, safety and efficiency in providing products and services, and a commitment to the future through progress. On the negative side, policies that are presented as limiting these values and threatening prosperity are rendered problematic. A third area involves individualism and citizen rights and expresses a commitment to health, fairness, a safe environment, a safe workplace, advancement through hard work, and a basic set of individual guarantees called "rights" that provide protection from undue governmental pressure. As with national-level symbols, these concerns can be expressed in terms of negative symbols as well. Any policy that is portrayed as threatening good health (disease), life (death), a clean environment (dirty air), hard work (laziness or cheating), or a right (discrimination) can evoke concern on the part of a major segment of the populace.

The cases studies offered a number of examples of symbolic issue attack. A good example was the one of national health insurance, where the proponents were groups with high legitimacy: Democratic or liberal politicians, academics, labor unions, and other occupational groups. As a consequence, the key to keeping the issue off the agenda was linking the issue with unpopular symbols. As Hackey's chapter showed, the symbolic linkages were effectively made by the opponents. At a number of times, health insurance proposals were called "un-American" and "socialized medicine." In addition, national health insurance was linked to the symbol of "big government" and an out-of-control bureaucracy, which threatened many Americans and made them worry about getting proper health care and going to the doctors of their choice.

In response to the charge that it was not vigorous in regulating the securities market, Hall and Jones reported that the SEC effectively associated proposed additional regulation with negative symbols of big government and bureaucracy while offering the positive image of a self-regulating financial system. Similarly, negative images of government regulation were used to counter claims that the federal government, as opposed to the states, should regulate accounting practices.

Symbols associated with economic well-being and protection of the individual also appeared in the cases. In the conflict over bST, Plein reported that proponents of the hormone emphasized basic economic values: for the farmer, their appeal stressed increased efficiency of dairy farming; for the consumer, the emphasis was on product safety. For everyone, there was the commitment to technology and future progress. In the RU 486 case, Jackman showed that the opponents challenged the pill with negative, threatening symbols by calling it a "death pill" and linked it to negative environmental symbols by calling the drug "a human pesticide" that would bring about "chemical warfare against unborn babies." In addition, as in other pro-life campaigns, opponents portrayed the pill as an attack on the fetus—stressing the fetus's resemblance to a living person. Finally, opponents argued that RU 486 kills not only babies but women as well. Sometimes, opponents expressed their opposition with positive symbols, such as those associated with the environment. For example, in the bST conflict, one of the strongest arguments of the pro-bST forces was to link the growth hormone to forces of nature ("it is natural"), thereby undercutting fears of technological manipulation. Finally, in terms of individual rights, Hackey demonstrated that in the conflict over national health insurance, opponents emphasized how a government plan would lead to a denial of basic individual political rights, eroding individual and personal responsibility and leaving basic choices affecting one's fate to faceless bureaucrats.

Groups with Low Legitimacy. When the initiators are not well known or have low legitimacy, issue attacks are secondary to direct attacks on the initiators that link them to negative images and cast doubt on the issue they are proposing and the worthiness of claimants seeking government benefits. This was most clearly seen in the conflict over access to water in El Paso, where Lopez and Reich argued that although a range of strategies was used to deny colonias water access, the most powerful emphasized the immigrants as a threat to the lifestyle of Americans. In settings like this one, where immigration is an explosive issue, efforts to portray relatively unknown people as illegals, ignorant, free-riders, and aliens resonate with many people. Although factually inaccurate, many see immigrants as parasites taking advantage of a system, as they did in the case of the colonia residents.

In the bST conflict, Plein showed how the pro-bST forces raised questions about the character of the opponents, mocking them as modern-day Luddites for their apparently blind opposition to technology. Similarly, in the RU 486 conflict, opponents of the pill attacked proponents for threatening basic values—life, health, a safe environment—and accused them of being "baby killers" and "destroyers of human life."

Sometimes, attacks on a group emphasize a "we-they" dynamic and involve the creation of a symbolic enemy, or an attack on an existing one, to build in-group support. One way that this is done is by emphasizing how people who are obviously different hold the same position as one's opponents or even endorse their actions. In U.S. politics, for example, conservatives regularly called the positions of mainstream liberal groups "socialist" and from time to time would point out how a position (e.g., on nuclear testing) was the same as that of the Soviet government. Liberals engaged in the same behavior too. For example, an ad that was made for Johnson's 1964 presidential campaign but was never used showed hooded Ku Klux Klan marchers and quoted the former Klan head's favorable comments about Barry Goldwater.

A variation on this form of symbolic attack emphasizes the role of outsiders who do not share a group's values or background characteristics and whose presence in a conflict threatens society. "Outside agitators" are easy to blame, as are people who look different or hold different beliefs from the local majority. This was seen in the use of anti-Semitic stereotypes to rally Austrian support for Kurt Waldheim's candidacy. Rather than dealing directly with the issue of his World War II conduct, he attacked the World Jewish Congress, accusing it of organizing a personal vendetta against him and inappropriately interfering with domestic political processes.

Symbolic Placating Strategies

Attacking an issue position or its proponents signals an unwillingness to recognize the validity of a grievance. We argued that this response is most likely to come from potentially negatively affected groups. We hypothesized, and the cases revealed, a second possible response from opponents that seeks to defuse the demands of issue initiators by symbolically placating proponents. Here, there is some acceptance of the reasonableness of the grievance, accompanied by an unwillingness to address it in the way proponents prefer, which might be due to unavailable resources or disagreement about the best action to take. Symbolic placation, we suggest, is more likely to come from governmental opponents than from affected groups themselves, although we recognize that this is not always the case. For example, during the 1993–1994 health care debate, both medical and insurance organizations opposing the Clinton health care plan offered a number of alternatives, some of which were best seen as symbolic ploys to placate proponents of more vigorous government action.

Symbolic placation emphasizes the common interests of initiators and opponents rather than their adversarial positions. It draws attention to what the different parties can agree on, while offering palliatives to the grievance group. The ambiguity of symbolic strategies' meaning makes them particularly important to understand. In some cases, the symbolic placating proposals come from opponents who genuinely accept the legitimacy of the grievance being raised but believe that the initiators' solution is the wrong one. They hope that by doing something, even if it is symbolic, it will draw attention to the problem and be a step toward developing a better policy. In other cases, opponents support both the initiators' analysis and the solution but believe that there are no resources (or political will) to adopt the program being sought. Finally, there are cases in which neither the grievance nor the proposed solution is a priority for officials, but, for a variety of reasons, they cannot simply do nothing.

Symbolic placation provides what Edelman (1964) called symbolic reassurance, primarily to the unorganized, whereas tangible benefits continue to go to the organized and powerful. For example, Edelman's analysis emphasized how regulatory agencies reassured the public that government was protecting its interests while they allowed the supposedly regulated industry to pursue private gain. Although they appear to resemble real solutions to a problem, symbolic strategies are best understood as attempts to delay, obfuscate, or avoid coming to terms with the core of a grievance. There were a number of examples of their use in the case studies, such as Hall and Jones's analysis of the SEC, which was clearly consistent with Edelman's theory.

One interesting thing about symbolic placating strategies is that they often produce at least partial approval from initiators, although they may want more or faster action. Why is it that initiators don't just denounce symbolic steps such as showcasing or the creation of a commission and cry "the emperor has no clothes" from the highest rooftops? Three different reasons seem plausible. First, especially in situations in which initiators are relatively weak, these symbolic steps often convey initial legitimation of the grievance by those actors who, until that point, had simply denied its existence. Second, symbolic placation can offer recognition to initiators, offering them a place at the table and meeting some of the identity concerns that motivate them. Third, although symbolic strategies run the risk of reassuring the public that something meaningful is being done to address a grievance, they also can draw attention to a problem and give initiators additional time to build alliances and gain resources. For these reasons, initiators may not reject symbolic placation out of hand.

There were a number of examples of symbolic placation strategies in the cases. Particularly prominent and worthy of comment were showcasing and creating commissions.

Showcasing. One of the most effective and widespread strategies for defusing initiators' demands is to give the appearance that the problem is being addressed. In showcasing, this is done by focusing on one small part of the problem. The deliberate narrowing of focus can buy time for opponents as well as potential supporters, who are not convinced that initiators have identified the right solution. As a result, both initiators and opponents sometimes agree on showcasing, although their reasons for doing so may be quite different.

In the case studies, showcasing was most commonly used to thwart initiators' demands and less frequently as a pilot experiment on which a larger new policy could be built. For example, in the conflict over SEC regulation of the securities industry, Hall and Jones reported that when criticism of SEC inactivity increased in the late 1960s and early 1970s, the regulatory agency responded by increasing the number of reporting releases, which emphasized disclosure and filing requirements. Although this activity did not deal with the main concerns of the critics, it gave the impression that the SEC was an activist agency pursuing solutions to problems in the financial marketplace. In the conflict over access to water in El Paso, Lopez and Reich argued that the El Paso Public Service Board rescinded its "no water outside the city" policy in 1991 to satisfy local initiators. Changing this policy after many years gave the impression that the board was listening to colonia complaints. However, the old policy, although not publicly sanctioned, continued to exist de facto, and the board did not help colonias gain any real access to water. In the conflict over health care, it was the opponents of national health insurance, not the government, who took symbolic action as private insurers and health providers expanded the scope and range of their coverage since the 1950s and then used this as evidence that the private sector could solve the health care problem in the United States.

Creating a Commission to Study a Problem. Creating a committee or commission to study a problem and make recommendations is a second widely used symbolic strategy that publicly accepts the reasonableness of an initiator's grievance while it avoids immediate action. In some cases, this is because a government agency (or other group) is genuinely puzzled about the best action to undertake. In other situations, it is simply an effort to publicly communicate concern while trying to avoid doing anything substantive. The delay that occurs while a commission acquires and digests key information often defuses support for the initiators' concerns and can ensure that an issue will be moved to the back burner. Sometimes, however, the work of a committee broadens the base of political support and legitimates initiators' concerns to new groups. As with showcasing, there are times when both initiators and opponents agree to create a commission, even if they disagree about what the eventual outcome should be.[4]

The case studies reported a number of instances in which creating a commission was used. In the late 1970s, the SEC was heavily criticized in Congress for its failure to deal strongly with the Boesky insider trading scandal. Hall and Jones pointed out that in response, the agency conducted a series of studies that examined possible legal options. However, in the end, when the furor had died down, the SEC did not push for additional legislation. Similarly, when Kurt Waldheim was besieged by groups questioning his conduct as a German officer during World War II, Bendix reported that he promised to create a committee of historians to investigate the claims. However, he postponed convening it for a year, thereby undercutting the claim that they would examine the charges seriously. In the conflict over the regulation of accounting practices, Mahon and McGowan noted that professional accounting organizations themselves established commissions over the years to study possible problems. Each came back with some recommendations, but not surprisingly, none included governmental regulation. A variation on this strategy was found in the bST case, where Plein reported that instead of convening a commission to study the issue, the FDA assembled distinguished scientists at public conferences to report previous research findings that bST was safe. This research over several years legitimized the FDA's initially favorable response to the hormone six years earlier.

LEAST FREQUENTLY USED OPPOSITION STRATEGIES

Out of the seven case studies, low-cost strategies were discussed in only three of them.[5] The most frequently used low-cost strategy was denial that a problem existed. In the case of access to clean water, Lopez and Reich showed that the El Paso developers argued that it was a nonproblem because there were alternative water sources for the colonias. However, this case also reflected the greatest resource disparity between the initiators and their opponents, a situation in which the opposition can get away with denial as a tactic to raise the cost to initiators and to avoid dealing with the grievance. However, even in this particular case, it was ultimately unsuccessful, and the opponents were later forced to use other tactics.

Denial was utilized in two instances when the initiators were more politically experienced and had access to some key decision makers. The opponents of national health insurance denied that there was a problem needing governmental action. Their basic argument was that U.S. health care remains strong, is the best in the world, and is the envy of other societies. So why fix what isn't broken? When there is widespread public support for an existing policy, this strategy can be successful. With many people fearful that a government program would restrict their choice of doctors and cut benefits, problem denial was successful. Denial was also used when questions were raised about Waldheim's past when he was running for the Austrian presidency. He and his supporters claimed that they had already addressed the issue, so it was no longer a concern. Given the fervent views of his opponents, that strategy was not successful for very long, and Waldheim had to provide more details, although he continued to maintain popular support in Austria.

High-cost strategies were the least used of any category.[6] Only in the case involving the introduction of RU 486, where opponents raised the prospect of economic boycotts against the pill's European producers and threatened the use of violence against these same companies, the clinics, and the doctors participating in clinical trials, were they present. Because of the strong commitment to and prior use of violence and harassment against abortion clinics associated with the more militant wing of the pro-life movement, the threat had an aura of credibility. However, the election of a president who was sympathetic to consideration and approval of the abortion pill changed the political landscape dramatically, and this tactic failed to keep the issue off the agenda. It did, however, make the issue more complicated for the proponents and led the European firms to hand over U.S. patent rights to the Population Council.

High-cost strategies are not often used, for a variety of reasons. For one thing, threats, including those of violence, are most likely against newcomers in the political arena and low legitimacy groups. When groups are well known and respected, threats against them can create a backlash against an opponent. In addition, in the cases presented in this volume, established political actors who had developed some personal relationships with one another were involved on both sides of most of the disputes. In such situations, any dispute is part of a larger political dialogue over different problems areas that are contested over time. When patterns of conflict produce predictability and continuing relations, using militant tactics with officials and groups with whom one must deal in the future is often counterproductive. For the most part, because the cases did not involve groups bursting onto the scene with a dramatically new issue or involve high-visibility electoral struggles, the use of high-cost tactics was relatively rare.

We offer the hypothesis that the cases reflect the range of issues and tactics that occupy most politicians and bureaucrats in agenda disputes—commonly used verbal attacks and symbolic redefinitions of issues that occur between issue initiators and opponents and are reflected in the key issues of our time: public health, the economy, and ethnic identity. If one examines the political scene today, it does not consist of actors using high-cost strategies, at least in agenda disputes. Where is the government currently using violence and threats of violence to put down issue initiators? Opponents of new issues are more sophisticated today. If this were a book dealing with U.S. history throughout the twentieth century, we would surely have pieces on labor violence, race relations, and antiwar protests. However, our cases were much more recent, except for the study of health care reform in the 1940s.

At other periods, new groups were more likely to be met with violence or threats of its use, but this is far less common today. For one thing, the political repercussions would be too great. The media, public-interest lawyers, and other constituencies would protest its use. In today's political scene, everyone is trying to put the best face on an issue, and this is incompatible with the use of violence. Our cases capture the politics of the time, which is consistent with the use of medium- and low-cost strategies. They are not as dramatic as the use of violence, but they capture important aspects of political interaction. Another possible reason for the relative absence of direct intimidation, which Scott (1985) proposes in a very different context, is that relatively weak groups (which is what most issue initiators are) are reluctant to or cannot provoke stronger opponents (such as government) and often back off before serious intimidation is used.

From this perspective, the politics of contemporary agenda denial is primarily about the nuts and bolts of alternative issue definition—government agencies and interest groups in a battle over political and cultural definitions of what is at stake—rather than violence and threats of violence. Although threats and violence have drama and shock value, in reality, their occurrence in agenda disputes is infrequent. At present, U.S. politics is more about bargaining over issue consideration, the drafting of laws and regulations among interest groups, governmental agendas, and issue groups and the media; the dramatic situations in which the government (or other parties) uses overt threats and violence are relatively few and far between.

CONCLUSION: THE POWER OF COMPETING CULTURAL DEFINITIONS

Our analysis of the cases presented in this volume has emphasized the importance of symbolic and cultural processes—identity politics—in agenda conflicts in general and agenda denial in particular. Each side mobilizes available resources to persuade key decision makers and the public that a particular grievance should or should not be seriously considered for governmental action. There is no doubt that the tangible resources of each side make a significant difference in how such disputes are played out and in determining their ultimate outcome.

Issue initiators are often resource poorer than their opponents, and they face the task of persuading governments to act when there is already a predisposition to do nothing. Yet the cases examined in this book suggest that it is not just the opponents' greater material resources that accounts for their success in defeating initiatives. They are also more experienced (and perhaps more skilled) at symbolic politics. Opponents proved to be quite effective in isolating initiators, in portraying their grievances in negative terms, and in casting doubts about the motives and abilities of the initiators themselves.

From our perspective, the interactions among opponents and their responses to the other side's prior actions shape the process and outcome of agenda conflicts. In contrast, an exclusive emphasis on the contending parties' resources and strategies at the outset of a dispute fails to capture important ways in which new players are drawn into the conflict, how changing definitions of what is at stake alter a conflict's course, and how outcomes are often different from what either side saw—or foresaw—at the outset. Our attention to the dynamics of agenda conflicts leads us to the uses of cultural, rather than tangible, resources to explain how new participants become active and the definition of what is at stake changes.

The key to identity politics here and more generally is the use of symbols that connect an issue to wider cultural concerns. Symbols link a specific grievance or issue position to a more general orientation that groups and individuals already hold. Symbols distill the wider meaning of an issue as people interpret a developing conflict. Through both words and actions, opposing parties in an agenda conflict offer competing interpretations of why an issue is important and how it connects to other areas of people's lives. Symbols are important when they link a policy to something that people particularly value or dislike. Effective political symbols are not just things that people say but are also found in the actions that one side or another takes to dramatize its position. Many political actions are symbolic in nature, and the studies in this book offered a number of examples of symbolic actions undertaken to give the impression that decision makers were responding to a grievance. Often the specific actions are secondary to convincing others that a problem is being addressed. In agenda denial, opponents are frequently successful in invoking negative symbols that threaten something people value: doctor-patient relationships, patriotism, physical health, or economic prosperity.

Agenda conflicts can be understood on two levels. First, agenda conflicts are about whether government will or will not seriously consider a particular grievance issue that initiators bring to it. Second, agenda conflicts are about competing interpretations of political problems, but behind them lie competing worldviews involving how people ought to lead their lives, how society ought to act, what should or should not be done by government, how we should treat the environment, and who threatens people's security. How issue initiators and opponents associate specific issues with these more general worldviews in agenda disputes is our particular concern. From this perspective, initiators must demonstrate that although the specific grievance they raise is new, acting on it is consistent with many long-standing values; opponents emphasize new issues as a threat to core elements of widely held worldviews. In the end, agenda denial occurs not just because of the complicated mechanics of the policy process or the lack of governmental resources, but often because a proposed action challenges existing worldviews and identities in unacceptable ways that opponents demonstrate effectively.

NOTES

1. The fact that these cases have been around for some time and have generated a good deal of conflict over time may tell us as much about what scholars choose to study as it does about the characteristics of the actors. Defining the universe of agenda conflicts and then distinguishing between issues that fail to gain agenda status because of serious efforts

on the part of opponents as opposed to a lack of interest or even commitment on the part of proponents is a methodological issue we recognize but ignore in this volume.

2. We recognize that there are many cases in which government officials come from the affected groups or do their bidding inside government. Here, however, we want to emphasize ways in which the two structural positions are associated with somewhat different behaviors.

3. We emphasize issue versus group attacks as a choice for conceptual purposes but recognize that in most actual conflicts, both occur, in part because opponents are rarely centrally directed. Some may attack the issue, others the group. Here we are concerned with what seems to be the opponents' major emphasis.

4. Although officials may create a commission with an eye to simply getting attention away from a problem, the people who serve on it may sincerely want to see significant actions taken, even if those who appointed them do not. Sometimes, commissions take on a life of their own and make recommendations that attract widespread attention and that officials subsequently have a hard time ignoring.

5. We suspect that at one time or another they are used in most agenda conflicts. However, in conflicts such as the ones studied here, which have considerable history or involve actors with considerable resources on both sides, they are not likely to be effective. Hence their use is apparently relatively uncommon, at least at the stages of conflict on which the authors reported.

6. Threats of electoral opposition and rewards for support have characterized the health care debate in the United States for many years. In addition, in the other conflicts studied here, we are confident that various threats have been used. From the point of view of the authors' presentations, however, such threats were not critical in explaining agenda denial in most of their cases.

REFERENCES

Edelman, M. 1964. *The symbolic uses of politics.* Champaign and Urbana: University of Illinois Press.

Ginsberg, F. D. 1990. *Contested lives: The abortion debate in an American community.* Berkeley and Los Angeles: University of California Press.

Ross, M. H. 1993. *The culture of conflict: Interpretations and interests in comparative perspective.* New Haven, CT, and London: Yale University Press.

Scott, J. C. 1985. *Weapons of the weak: Everyday forms of peasant resistance.* New Haven, CT: Yale University Press.

Contributors

JOHN BENDIX is a political scientist who did his graduate work at Indiana University and has taught at Lewis and Clark College, Bryn Mawr College, Haverford College, and the University of Pennsylvania. His research interests include European politics, social movements, and gender and politics.

ROGER W. COBB is a professor of political science at Brown University. He coedited *The Politics of Problem Definition: Shaping the Policy Agenda* (1994). His interests include agenda setting, problem definition, issue containment, and the policy implications of elderly driving patterns.

ROBERT B. HACKEY is an assistant professor of political science at the University of Massachusetts–Dartmouth. His articles on state and federal health care policy have appeared in the *Journal of Health Politics, Policy and Law,* the *Journal of Trauma, Medical Care Review, Polity,* and *Spectrum: The Journal of State Government.* Prior to joining the faculty at UMass–Dartmouth, Hackey worked as the program manager for trauma system development at the Rhode Island Department of Health. His book *The Politics of State Hospital Regulation* will be published in 1997 by Georgetown University Press.

BILLY R. HALL Jr. received his Ph.D. from Texas A & M in 1995. He currently works in community television in Dallas.

JENNIFER L. JACKMAN holds a Ph.D. in social policy from the Heller School at Brandeis University. Based in Arlington, Virginia, she is director of policy and research for the Feminist Majority Foundation and coordinator of the foundation's Campaign for RU-486 and Contreceptive Research.

BRYAN D. JONES is a professor of political science at the University of Washington. His recent books include *Reconceiving Decision Making in Democratic*

Politics (1994) and *Agendas and Instability in American Politics* (1993), the latter coauthored with Frank Baumgartner.

CYNTHIA M. LOPEZ is a doctoral candidate at the Harvard School of Public Health, Department of Population and International Health. Her thesis examined adverse health outcomes associated with exposure to water contaminants in the colonias of the Rio Grande and Rio Bravo floodplains in El Paso County and Juarez Valley. She has worked as consultant to the Union for Concerned Scientists and the River Watch Network investigating environmental injustice in disadvantaged communities.

JOHN F. MAHON is a professor of management policy in Boston University's School of Management, former chair of the Social Issues in Management Division of the Academy of Management, and former president and cofounder of the International Association for Business and Society. He is the author or coauthor of over sixty articles. His interests are corporate political strategies and corporate responses to regulation.

RICHARD A. McGOWAN is a professor of economics and statistics at the Wallace E. Carroll School of Management at Boston College. He has studied the response of the tobacco and gambling industries to regulation and changing public opinion. He is recognized as an expert in research in tobacco and lotteries and has served on national commissions and state-level committees that deal with these topics.

L. CHRISTOPHER PLEIN is assistant professor of public administration at West Virginia University. His research interests focus on agenda setting and issue definition, science and technology policy, and comparative policy and administration. His work, as author or coauthor, has been published in various edited books and in such journals as *Comparative Politics, Policy Studies Journal,* and *Science, Technology, & Human Values.*

MICHAEL R. REICH is professor of international health policy at the Harvard School of Public Health. His publications include *Toxic Politics: Responses to Chemical Disasters* (1991), which was named best book of the year by the Policy Studies Organization, and, with David Cooper, *PolicyMaker: Computer-Assisted Political Analysis* (1996), a Windows-based software program.

MARC HOWARD ROSS is the William R. Kenan Jr. professor of political science at Bryn Mawr College. He is particularly interested in political conflict and conflict management and has written *The Culture of Conflict: Interpretations and Interests in Comparative Perspective* (1993), *The Management of Conflict: Interpretations and Interests in Comparative Perspective* (1993), and articles on ethnic conflict.

Index